DOING

Faithjustice

DOING
Faithjustice

An Introduction to
Catholic Social Thought

REVISED EDITION

FRED KAMMER, S.J.

Paulist Press
New York/Mahwah, N.J.

Book design by Nighthawk Design
Cover design by Lynn Else

Library of Congress Cataloging-in-Publication Data

Kammer, Fred, 1945-
    Doing faithjustice : an introduction to Catholic social thought / Fred Kammer. – Rev. ed.
        p. cm.
    Includes bibliographical references (p.   ) and index.
    ISBN 0-8091-4227-9
    1. Sociology, Christian (Catholic). 2. Catholic Church—Doctrines. I. Title.
    BX1753. K34 2004
    261.8′088′22—dc21

                                                                    2003014004

Published by Paulist Press
997 Macarthur Boulevard
Mahwah, New Jersey 07430

www.paulistpress.com

Printed and bound in the
United States of America

CONTENTS

*To Ignacio Ellacuría Amando López, Juan Ramón Moreno,
Ignacio Martín-Baró, Joaquín López y López, Segundo
Montes, all of the Society of Jesus, and Júlia Elba Ramos and
Celina Maricet Ramos*

martyrs for Faithjustice in El Salvador, 16 November 1989

INTRODUCTION

I write this book for those who struggle to make this a better, safer world for all of us and for generations to come. I write for those who yearn for justice and dream of peace and who are willing to take steps to transform those yearnings and dreams into reality. I write for those who feed the hungry, visit prisons and hospitals, counsel the afflicted, march on picket lines or on Washington, and do the nitty-gritty of mass mailings, telephone trees, legislative newsletters, alternative investments, and whatever else creates more responsive institutions in our world. I write this book especially for those who pursue peace and justice out of a deep sense of faith and who want to better connect the everydayness of the struggle to those deep currents running within themselves, to the scriptures, and to the history of the believing Judaeo-Christian community.

Many generous people are working to reach out to the poor in our neighborhoods or overseas, to change attitudes and actions, and to reshape the structures of our society. I think, for instance, of friends in legal services for the poor and in Catholic Charities; of churchpeople across America struggling with emergency aid ministries, food pantries, or legislative networks; of those of various faiths collaborating to staff ecumenical shelters for the homeless or running large food kitchens; and of those in full-time service to the poor and needy as lay and religious professionals or volunteers.

This exhausting and frustrating work is often motivated by an innate sense of what is right and wrong in our communities coupled with heroic good will, without benefit of the rich prophetic tradition that stretches back to the first pages of the Bible. This tradition is the rightful heritage of those working on the front lines of charity, justice, and peace. It can give birth to deeper insight, courage, and commitment.

I also write this book to help Catholics and others who are puzzled, shocked, and even angered by what appear to be the more aggressive and recurring voices of the American Catholic bishops and the pope regarding political, social, and economic realities. Beginning with the first pastoral letter of Bishop John Carroll of Baltimore in 1792, six lengthy volumes of pastoral letters of the U.S.

1

bishops now have been published. The topics over the past two hundred years span education, social security, economics, refugees, gun control, Vietnam, farm labor, abortion, capital punishment, agriculture, and the world food crisis.[1] This book should help explain where this demonstrably activist episcopal stance originates and how these pastoral letters are an essential expression of our relationship to God and Jesus the Christ.

We now have a heritage of more than one hundred ten years of what is called "modern Catholic social teaching." In that light, I write finally to share with students of all ages and with others in the believing community the Roman Catholic experience of faith intertwined with justice. I intend not just to promote mutual understanding in a pluralistic society, but to contribute in some small way to the revival of a common language of public or civic virtue that might ground a new and much needed political vision for the twenty-first century.

My hope is that this book might help the readers better understand their own theology of service and advocacy, renew their commitment to the poor, flesh out their spirituality for the long haul, and incorporate them more fully into a "community of memory,"[2] which can share a broad and deep theological and spiritual tradition of justice with our wider society. There are abundant good reasons for this, not the least of which is America's current search for its soul and its place in the world in the midst of consumerism, globalization, terrorism, poverty, and economic ups-and-downs.

In the closing pages of the 1985 best-seller *Habits of the Heart*, sociologist Robert Bellah and his coauthors contend that American individualism driven to its logical end leaves "we the people" as "a special interest group," as Ronald Reagan asserted, whose concern for the economy is the only thing that holds us together as a nation. "We have reached a kind of end of the line," they argue, where the citizen is swallowed up in "economic man."[3]

Survival of a free people, Bellah and his colleagues contend, depends upon the common hope of such diverse commentators as James Madison, Alexis de Tocqueville, and Eugene V. Debs, that there be a revival of a public virtue that is able to find political expression. Public virtue, like every other social obligation or tie between individuals, has become increasingly vulnerable in the grip of an "ontological individualism, the idea that the individual is the only firm reality...."[4]

At risk is what Bellah calls our "social ecology," the deep relationships between human persons and their societies wherein the actions taken by individuals and groups have enormous impact on the lives of others:

> ...social ecology is damaged not only by war, genocide, and political repression. It is also damaged by the destruction of the subtle ties that bind human beings to one another, leaving them frightened and alone. It has been evident for some time that unless we begin to repair the damage to our social ecology, we will destroy ourselves long before natural ecological disaster has time to be realized.[5]

We have committed the cardinal sin for the republican founders of our nation, Bellah argues. "We have put our own good, as individuals, as groups, as a nation, ahead of the common good."[6]

Habits proposes that the litmus test for determining the health of our society, rooted in both our biblical and republican traditions, is how we deal with wealth and poverty. As this book indicates, the United States is in danger of failing that test and betraying its heritage, despite the immense efforts of so many good people. The disparities between rich and poor Americans become worse each year. Our infant mortality rate rivals that of third-world nations. And, despite the rush of some in developing countries and the emerging European nations to emulate us, the American Dream of freedom and a decent life eludes tens of millions of our own citizens of all ages, races, genders, and nationalities.

In 1986, a year after the publication of Bellah's book, the U.S. Catholic bishops concluded a five-year process of widespread dialogue and debate by publishing their second major pastoral letter of the decade. *Economic Justice for All: Catholic Social Teaching and the U.S. Economy* spoke to the heart of the American economic system, challenging its assumptions and calling for significant and systemic changes. As did Bellah and his colleagues, the pastoral letter questioned seriously how we as a nation are confronting wealth and poverty. The letter provoked responses from U.S. Catholics and others ranging from puzzlement, shock, and anger to thoughtful criticism, agreement, and pleasure. Most unfortunately of all, it was greeted by many with complete indifference.

The general public was simply unaware of the long history of Catholic social teaching that the bishops reiterated in the pastoral and applied to the contemporary United States and world economic scene. Conservative commentators, whether Catholic or not, responded with resistance, anger, or disdain. In part, *Economic Justice*

for All ran directly counter to the Reagan administration's brutal neglect of services for the poor in this country.[7] The pastoral letter further offended the conservative Republican hierarchy's aggressive
opposition to advocacy for, and empowerment of, the poor[8] which the
bishops endorsed and actually support financially.[9] Also at risk for
the bishops' detractors is our dominant individualistic ethic that
translates, in the economic field, into laissez-faire economics and a
consumerist lifestyle.

Other negative reactions to the pastoral on economic justice
were fed by a variety of ideological and theological positions that
sharply divide the world of socio-economic-political realities from the
world of religion and church. A superficial reading of American
church-state separation, an increasingly privatized sphere for religion
as lived out by contemporary churchgoers, including Catholics, an
age-old dualism between the world of the flesh and that of the Spirit,
and a post-sixties distrust of authoritative statements, all conspired to
promote either polite dismissal of the pastoral letter or an aggressive
reaction of, "What do the bishops know about economics?"

The Catholic bishops were not alone in challenging society's
obsession with individualism and its segregation of religious concerns
from economics, business, and politics. In contrast to a dominant culture and many subgroups for whom the language of economics and
the language of faith mix like oil and water, a number of major
churches or denominations engaged in an intense dialogue during the
eighties about the interface of economics and faith.[10] That dialogue
has continued and sometimes boiled over during the post-Reagan
administrations of George "Points of Light" Bush, Bill "End Welfare as
We Know It" Clinton, and George W. "Compassionate Conservatism"
Bush. Under each administration and an increasingly conservative-
driven Congress, religious leadership has often found itself standing in
strong opposition to budget, tax, and welfare plans that promised
more hard times for low-income and vulnerable families.

The struggle of various religious teachers to articulate the connection between faith and economic justice has given rise to a variety
of terms and forms of expression: economic justice for all, Christian
faith and economic justice, faith and justice, the faith that does justice,[11] and justice as the acid test of preaching the gospel.[12] The
essence of all these efforts is captured in the striking usage of my
Jesuit friend Bill Watters, pastor of St. Ignatius Church in downtown
Baltimore. "Faithjustice," Bill says, driving home the intimate connection of justice and faith in the Judaeo-Christian tradition by using
a single word.

Faithjustice. The single word forged of the two concepts under-cuts those who would elevate one concept over the other, render one instrumental to the other, separate the two, or otherwise downplay the importance of one, usually justice. As we will see, however, this unitary understanding is actually as old as the Hebrew prophets, was inti-mately familiar to Jesus of Nazareth, and is critically important to understanding the gospel in today's world. Using a single word, in fact, may even help us better grasp the sense of Hebrew words like *mishpat* or *sedaqah*, both of which actually reflect a rich range of meaning but are often translated simply by "righteousness" or "justice."

Sometimes old insights get lost in the midst of new ways of liv-ing and have to be rediscovered and even renamed to grab hold of them again. *Faithjustice* is just such an effort: to claim for contempo-rary Christians an ancient tradition without which the seas of mod-ern social, economic, and political concerns would be harsh sailing or even utterly abandoned to the scientists, economists, and secularists, however well meaning they may be. The hope is, ultimately, to pro-mote *homo serviens* in contrast to the contemporary dominance in American life and myth of *homo consumens* and *homo militaris*. This realistic hope is rooted in coming to know and share the experiences of contemporary people of *faithjustice* in cities and towns across this nation. Their lives defy the individualism and isolation of our society, and their actions challenge society's assumptions about who and what is important in life.

America's prescient visitor Alexis de Tocqueville and others are credited with helping to give currency to the word *individualism* even as they analyzed and criticized it in our society in the nineteenth cen-tury. De Tocqueville wrote:

> Individualism is a calm and considered feeling which dis-poses each citizen to isolate himself from the mass of his fellows and withdraw into the circle of family and friends; with this little society formed to his taste, he gladly leaves the greater society to look after itself.[13]

In a modest contrast, I offer this definition in hope of promot-ing new civic and religious virtue:

> *Faithjustice* is a passionate virtue that disposes citizens to become involved in the greater and lesser societies around themselves in order to create communities where human dignity is protected and enhanced, the gifts of creation are

shared for the greatest good of all, and the poor are
treated with respect and a special love.

To understand its meaning, chapters 1 and 2 will explore the
biblical grounding for this virtue, chapter 3 will provide an overview
of its historical development in the Catholic Christian community,
and chapters 4 and 5 will explore its contemporary meaning. The
conclusion will describe a framework for living faithjustice in our
time.

Whether the faithjustice word survives, the reality of the virtue
described is present in the tangible commitments of people who care.
"People who care" are what lawyers call the "best evidence" of the
truth that I am trying to describe here and that the nation desperately
needs. Faithjustice, we might say, is a habit of the believing heart.

In writing this book, my thinking has been intentionally
informed by my personal biography and geography as a North
American, a Catholic, a southerner, a lawyer, a priest, and as a Jesuit.
Vignettes of life lived in the United States, the South, and the
Catholic Church of the fifties, sixties, seventies, eighties, and nineties
root each chapter's theories in concrete times and places. They also
may explain the chapters' acute angles and departures, and they
might excuse the inevitable, because very personal, shortsightedness.

As a southerner and an American, it is no accident that race and
racism are an important theme in my life, as they remain for my
region and the entire country. I also address the challenge of human
poverty and injustice in the context of the country where my own
work has been, the pragmatic, pluralistic, and yet idealistic United
States. As a Catholic whose advocacy for justice has been both outside
and within Church structures and institutions, I have tried to stretch
between the two worlds, recognizing the great goodness of people
working in both and the capacities for destructiveness in both political and ecclesiastical realms. As a Jesuit, I am indelibly marked by the
vision and strategies of Ignatius of Loyola mediated through a myriad of tutors and friends, with whom I have argued about the contemporary meaning and mission of the Society of Jesus. My
references to Jesuits can be taken and appropriated by readers as a
combination of family and church, since "the Society," as Jesuits call
it, blends both for me.

For those familiar with the 1991 edition of this book, this new
version includes: new material on the jubilee tradition in chapter 1
and on Jesus as peasant and healer and jubilee in chapter 2; integra-
tion of the material on *Centesimus Annus* and other social teaching

documents from the nineties into chapter 3; updated economic and
social data and analysis in chapters 4 and 5, along with social teaching documents; and questions for reflection and discussion at the
close of each of the five core chapters. These questions are provided
at the suggestion of teachers and adult study group leaders who have
been using this book for the past decade.

My thanks begin with the Society: to the New Orleans Province,
the Woodstock Theological Center at Georgetown University, and the
Woodstock Jesuit Community for critical input and the five months
free initially to devote just to this book. Instrumental to my work on
its first edition were support and encouragement from family and
friends, hardware from Tim, Kit, and Katherine, and software from
the board at Catholic Community Services in Baton Rouge. My special thanks to Leon Hooper, S.J., of Woodstock and Jim Martin of
Atlanta for review of parts of the manuscript, and to Dick Sparks,
C.S.P., and Paulist Press for editorial suggestions and encouragement
in the task of revision. Six special friends later did a review and edit-
ing of the complete manuscript, the incredible loving gift of which I
came to savor in the rereading: Jonathan Montaldo, Phil Land, S.J.,
John Kavanaugh, S.J., Kate Haser, and Ed and Marybelle Hardin. Ten
years later, in revising this new edition, I am again indebted to my
Jesuit Province for time away, to the Board of Catholic Charities USA
for a new computer with which to write, to many friends for suggestions for improvements, and to Joe Scott, C.S.P., for the editorial
guidance and support.

Finally, for thirty years of experimentation, feedback, and
shared experiences in developing faithjustice, I thank my brother
Jesuits; the women and men of the Jesuit Volunteer Corps: South; the
members of the National Board of Jesuit Social Ministries; and sisters
and brothers at the Atlanta Legal Aid Society, in parish social ministry in Louisiana, at the Sangre de Cristo Center in New Mexico, at
Catholic Community Services of Baton Rouge, and in Catholic
Charities agencies across the United States. They and a number of
other friends and coworkers, especially in Georgia and Louisiana, live
out daily what I have written about here.

Fred Kammer, S.J.
August 8, 2003

CHAPTER ONE

Ebla and the Cycle of Baal

The monarch was expected to defend the widowed, the orphaned, and the poor from all exploitation and injustice. According to documents unearthed at Ugarit, failure to protect the poor could cost a king his throne.

Howard LaFay
National Geographic

The bus grew strangely quiet as we passed through a small South Mississippi town. In a conspiratorial hush, a voice behind me whispered to his companion, "This is where the lynching was." I was a young teenager riding back across the Deep South to New Orleans for the beginning of school, having left most of my family back in Florida on vacation. I was shocked by the harsh reality so near me there in the hot summer; it cast a dark shadow over the near-idyllic memories of family intimacy and fun on the beach. The relative quiet of the fifties was giving way to the turbulent beginnings of the sixties when civil rights sit-ins, marches, and violence would turn our well-ordered world and my young self-awareness upside down.

❖ ❖ ❖

Growing up Catholic in New Orleans was not exactly Southern in the traditional sense. True, I had painted large confederate flags on the walls of my bedroom. I fancied myself a Civil War buff. (My younger brother's generation would cover my flags over with late sixties rock posters.) My family lived in neighborhoods that were racially segregated, although the history and demographics of New Orleans put Black and White neighborhoods in closer proximity than in most other large cities of the South or North. My contemporaries and I had no Black friends or peers, although we often roller-skated on the same streets as Black youth and walked past one another on the way

9

to our separate schools. A series of Black maids had cared for my brothers, sister, and me since our youngest years, prepared our family meals, and also were second mothers to us. My parents invested them with full authority in their absence; and, in our own way, we had deep affection for them.

Being Catholic, however, put a different slant on things. Our family had Irish, French, Italian, Scotch-Irish, and German lines. We knew about the Klan: that we, along with the Jews, were part of their three Ks of hatred. Though our Catholic schools had been as segregated as the public system in the forties and fifties, articulate voices of reason and compassion in the Catholic community were threatening the social status quo, which we young Southerners had imbibed with the air and water.

My awakening conscience was confronted first by a string of young Jesuit teachers in high school who questioned the assumptions that underlay a separate-but-equal mythology. They challenged us to reach beyond the prejudices of our families and society to a civil and gospel equality. The response of some of my fellow students was often hostile, as parental truths crashed against teacher truths. Archbishop Joseph Francis Rummel also had stunned the church and city when he took a strong public stand against segregation in the fifties and later excommunicated prominent segregationist leaders—the ultimate Catholic sanction. He in turn received some seventy death threats in an atmosphere that smelled to him of schism at times.[1]

❖ ❖ ❖

When the city buses were integrated, many of us confronted our first agonizing break with a tradition that would have us stand rather than take vacant seats next to Blacks or get to our feet if a Black person sat next to us. Of course, notorious bus incidents were covered by TV and newspapers. But on most ordinary buses of New Orleans's enviable city transit system, many young students like me took part in an unpublicized drama of social change. Its scenes were marked by angry words and stage whispers, human courtesy and individual heroism, bigotry and openness. On our better days, we learned to offer our seats to Black women tired from a long day of work, just as we had been taught to do for White women. The so-called New South was being born in our impressionable minds, whether we liked it or not.

❖ ❖ ❖

One particular night in high school stands out for me in terms of the growing crisis. I had come downstairs to the living room to kiss my father goodnight before going to bed. He asked me about school, and I made the

*"mistake" of telling him about an article we had been discussing in class enti-
tled, "The Immorality of Segregation."²* For several hours that night my father
tried to educate his second son in the realities of the South as he had grown
up in it, and to teach me the rational underpinnings of segregation as it had
been passed on to him. It was a mixture of fact, myth, reason, tradition, prej-
udice, Bible, experience, ignorance, and feeling. The scene must have been
repeated in tens of thousands of homes across the nation each year.

It was a failed lesson, however, because of the typical doubts young
teenagers have about their parents' views, the strong counter-education we
were receiving in school, and the innate fallacies and injustices of segregation
itself. Perhaps, too, my father's position had been undermined years before by
his own and my mother's moderation of their inherited social views, their
wider sense of love and justice in which we were nurtured, and the very prohibition of words like "nigger" in our home. You got your mouth washed out
with soap for that one!

❖ ❖ ❖

On Easter night 1963, I told my parents that I wanted to join the
Jesuits after high school graduation that summer and study for the priesthood. My father told me, "Your mother always wanted one of you boys to do
something like that!" The only other vocational guidance he had given us
growing up was that we could be anything we wanted, "except lawyers." He
and his father were both lawyers, and he thought there were too many lawyers
in New Orleans.

❖ ❖ ❖

In December 1973, I left Atlanta after my first years of legal services'
practice to study theology in Chicago. As a going-away present, a friend gave
me a book by Ivan Allen Jr., entitled Mayor: Notes on the Sixties. As
mayor, Allen had presided over the progressive transformation of Atlanta
during the turbulent sixties. Atlanta's changes stood in contrast for me with
the tradition-bound conservatism of New Orleans, which had preferred to be
a queen of the Old South rather than a molder of the New.

By my late twenties, I had taught catechism to rural, poor Black youth
as a Jesuit novice, written an unpublished book on the racial and economic
politics of the War on Poverty in South Louisiana while in college, moder-
ated a Black Catholic youth group and done volunteer work in a Black public high school during philosophy studies in Mobile, and represented
hundreds of Black clients in Atlanta. When I took up Allen's book, then, I

*read with a sense of vividness and poignancy about his experience with cross-
ing the color line in Atlanta in 1947 to promote the Community Chest Drive.
Allen had sought the advice of his father about an invitation to speak at the
kickoff of the drive in the Negro community, to which the elder Allen
responded:*

> *"Ivan, let me have a very honest discussion with you," he said in
> his office the day I went to see him. "My generation has com-
> pletely failed in every way to enlighten or solve the major issue
> which our section of the country has: the racial issue. We haven't
> confronted ourselves with it. There is great prejudice, great trial
> and tribulation over the whole thing. We've kept the nigger not
> in a second-class but in a third or fourth-class position, and as a
> result we've impoverished him and we've impoverished this sec-
> tion of the country. And the Southeast will never amount to any-
> thing until it brings its level of citizenship up. The very idea:
> here we are advocating human decency and freedom all over the
> world, and we find ourselves with dirty skirts at home. It's time
> for some major changes.* Your generation is going to be con-
> fronted with it, and it will be the greatest agony that any
> generation ever went through."[3]

*By the time I read these lines, many American cities had been burned
in the wake of Dr. Martin Luther King Jr.'s assassination; the Kerner
Commission Report had described two Americas, one White and prospering,
the other Black and languishing; and the Vietnam War and the impeached
Nixon presidency seemed to have distracted us from the tragic realities of race
and poverty at home.*

*That made the advice from Ivan Allen Sr., thirty years earlier, all the
more prophetic and painful. What he said confirmed the truth of what I had
seen and felt as events had swirled around me since grammar school. It also
promised that our future pain would be all the more searing the longer we
deferred the question of racial injustice in America.*

❖ ❖ ❖

*In the four coldest winters of my life, studying theology in Chicago in
the mid-seventies, one lesson came over dinner from a guest in my Jesuit community. A member of our Old Testament faculty, she told us of the discovery
of the ancient city-state of Ebla in Syria. Ebla, in turn, became a symbol for
me of the depth and breadth of the ancient responsibility of the human community and its leaders for the poor. This same responsibility was woven*

throughout the Hebrew scriptures and enfleshed in the prophets whom we studied in class.

That awareness later grew ever more tragic and frustrating in the eighties as the nation's leader and spokesman assured us that the "truly needy" were cared for. President Reagan anesthetized us to the growing numbers and worsening plight of the poor, homeless, sick, disabled, and suffering in our midst while orchestrating the greatest rich-get-richer scam up to that point in the nation's history. The prophets seemed dead.

❖ ❖ ❖

During the time in Chicago in which I discovered Ebla, I began in-depth study of The Spiritual Exercises of St. Ignatius of Loyola, *the founder of the Jesuits. The Exercises as a written document is a handbook for directors of individual retreatants turning their lives over to God or deepening their faith journeys. I had made the full thirty-day Ignatian retreat ten years earlier as a Jesuit novice, and for eight days each year thereafter. Only in theology studies, however, did I apprentice in directing others in the Exercises under supervision of a skilled director.*

In the course of my training, I spent two weeks in a seminar under the tutelage of two Sisters of the Cenacle, a religious congregation whose primary ministry is the promotion of the Ignatian retreat. At their retreat center on the South Side of Chicago, Sisters Catherine Roberts and Barbara Ehrler presented deep and nuanced insights into Ignatius's handbook. They interwove much experience with the best of contemporary theology and spirituality. One such insight translated into simple modern terms the medieval language of Ignatius about the crucial temptation of good people. Ignatius had spoken of this powerful strategy and dynamic of evil in terms of riches, leading to honors, leading to pride.

I had meditated on this traditional formulation in many retreats over the years. It took on a new power for me when the sisters translated it into three simple human attitudes: "This is mine" (riches) leads to "Look at me" (honors) and then to "I am" (pride). The first temptation of good and upright people, they explained, is to become owners, forgetting that all accomplishments, virtues, qualities, possessions, reputation, and even hard work are gifts from the Lord. We invest our own value, we center ourselves, in what we have or have done. Then, however subtly, we show it to those around us as if to say, "Look at me." Forgetting the giver of gifts and basking in the admiration and envy of those around us, we turn ourselves into mini-versions of the one whom the scriptures call "I AM," the real center of creation.

A few years earlier, my own Jesuit retreat director had zeroed in on the same point with this simple image, "Fred, there is a hook in every gift." If you hold on too tightly, he explained, you are hooked by it, no longer free but owned, enslaved.

In late September 1975 a group of Italian archaeologists working on the Tell Mardikh dig in Northwestern Syria discovered the largest and perhaps most significant third-millennium library to date. The library confirmed and helped to explain their 1968 discovery of a previously unknown city-state named Ebla. The city-state of Ebla spanned a period from 3000 B.C. until its final destruction by invading Hittites in 1600 B.C. At its height in the mid-third millennium (c. 2300 B.C.), the city proper had about 30,000 inhabitants and it dominated an area populated by 250,000 to 300,000 persons.

Archaeologists who unearthed the library school or archive in 1975 discovered there more than sixteen thousand preserved clay tablets that had baked hard when the city-state was sacked and burned by Akkadians in 2250 B.C. Included were tablets translating Ugaritic and other languages into Eblaite so the discoverers had a relatively easy route into the language of Ebla. There they found that some scriptural references thought to be apocryphal, poetic, or merely imaginary were in fact realities in the ancient Mediterranean world. In time the Ebla find may contribute most significantly to our understanding of the Hebrew scriptures.[4]

The most significant revelation for my purposes from the initial Ebla discoveries was summarized in an article in the December 1978 *National Geographic* entitled, "Splendor of an Unknown Empire":

> All roads lead to Ebla throughout much of the Middle East, long before Rome held sway. Once there, those roads went directly to the steps of the royal palace. Ebla erected no walls around its palace, only around the city itself. Eblaites believed their leaders should be accessible and accountable. A king ascended the throne not strictly through lineage but by election, and was *responsible for the welfare of widows, the orphaned, and the poor. If derelict, a king could be ousted by a group of elders.*[5]

The author comments:

> Wandering through the royal quarters, I reflected on one singularly attractive obligation of kingship in the Middle East. The monarch was expected to defend the widowed, the orphaned, and the poor from all exploitation and

injustice. According to documents unearthed at Ugarit,
failure to protect the poor could cost a king his throne.[6]

This observation provides a glimpse of one aspect of the culture of
the region in which the Hebrews lived and in which their scriptures
would develop. More than simply a regional note, however, it suggests
a more universal understanding of public obligations having deep
roots in the self-understanding of at least some ancient peoples. As
either regional or universal, however, it can also serve to enhance our
understanding of the Israelites' own attitude toward property, power,
and the poor in the midst of their communities.

Triple Revelations from Genesis

When we turn to the first pages of the Hebrew scriptures, we discover
there the two creation stories that open the book of Genesis, each
flowing from a different oral tradition among the Hebrews. The first
and historically later version, beginning with verse 1:1, is the familiar
seven-day creation story, fashioning order from primordial chaos. On
the first day God said, "Let there be light," and so forth, until on the
seventh day "God rested."

What is important in these creation narratives is not the science—or mythology—that was the currency of the day, but the underlying theology or faith assertions that the authors intend to convey,
namely, what they wanted their readers to believe. In the seven-day
creation story, the events of most days end with the same key theological affirmation: "God saw that it was good." It is fundamental to
what is now called creation spirituality[7] and to both Jewish and
Christian revelation that what God saw was good. The very subjects
of creation—the earth, stars, plants, animals, and, ultimately,
humankind—are essentially, by their nature, good.

This goodness proclamation may seem self-evident to some people. Many of our cultural messages and even our religious attitudes,
however, are diametrically opposed to the Genesis view that God
looked upon the completed creation and found it "very good" (Gen
1:31). This opposition can be found in Gnostic and other philosophical traditions dominated by a body/spirit dualism or religious traditions that disdain feelings and emotions. Contemporary American
society's persistent quest for new means and measures of self-esteem
betrays its profound doubt in even the fundamental worth of human

persons; and too much economic development occurs with rank disregard for the basic value of the natural universe around us.

The second and older Genesis story begins in the next verse (Gen 2:4) after the seven-day version. In this story, instead of the progression from light and darkness to water and land, then to fish, birds, animals, and so forth, the storytellers open with Adam's placement in the garden. "The Lord God took the man and put him in the garden of Eden to till it and keep it" (Gen 2:15). God then creates the animals for Adam, and Adam names the animals. In the scriptures the naming event was a sign of power or dominion over the one named; it is also a sign of relationship, of the bond that humans have with nonhuman creatures.[8] This same theme appears in the first creation story as well when the man and woman are instructed by the Lord to subdue and "have dominion" (Gen 1:28) over the earth.

This reveals the second critical faith affirmation of the Genesis narratives: The dominion that humankind is to have over this creation. Not only is creation good, but also we as humans are gifted by the Creator with responsibility for and dominion over the earth around us, over all creation. It is important at this point to distinguish dominion from domination or exploitation. Theologian John T. Pawlikowski explains:

> There is absolutely no basis in this Genesis notion for unbridled economic exploitation of natural resources which has often occurred under modern industrial and agricultural capitalism. A careful reading of the Genesis accounts of human creation clearly gives great encouragement to those ecologists who emphasize that the earth has been left in humanity's hands as a sacred trust. Human dominion over the rest of creation is not to be one of exploitation or simple dominance. Rather, it is to be a caring rule over creation modeled on God's ultimate dominion.[9]

To have dominion is to be like the Lord (*Dominus* in Latin) who first poured out life into creation, to be procreative and cocreative. We then recognize and act from an awareness that we are intimately related to the earth in a mutually nurturing and life-giving communion.

This sense of dominion of creation extends far beyond what we normally associate with the natural environment (e.g., earth, air, and water). Pope John Paul II understands the biblical mandate and responsibility to have a double object: It is applicable to what we can call the "creation given" of the natural world; and it includes the "creation enhanced" that refers to all that we've done with creation since we as working people, *homo faber*, began cultivation of the land.[10] Buildings, science, technology, societies, institutions, schools, laws, games, rules, customs, music, languages, and books—all these components of reality have come to be from the purposeful goodness and providence of God through the instrumentality of human hands, labor, and cocreativity. They now come under the scope of human responsibility for dominion.

Ultimately, the Genesis texts are saying, we have been given all that is good, and we have care and responsibility for it. Goodness and dominion are the first two critical faith assertions in the creation stories. But with them comes a caveat: We are not owners! We are tenants and caretakers of the earth in a sense deeply rooted in the scriptural understanding that this is God's earth, created good by God. That insight profoundly affects our use of the earth and our respectful and even reverent care for the earth and for creation's giftedness.

> Creation is a gift; women and men are to be faithful stewards in caring for the earth. They can justly consider that by their labor they are unfolding the Creator's work.[11]

So compelling is this sense of responsibility and so destructive are attitudes of domination and ownership in the world today, even toward nature, that religious commentators have reclaimed the concept of stewardship. While "dominion" is essentially accurate, using the word "stewardship" provides the appropriate nuance to the biblical faith insight. In a legal term, we are "trustees" of the earth, charged with its care for our own generation and generations to come who are meant to be its continuing beneficiaries.

A third and related insight of the early scriptures is captured in the single phrase, "I will be your God and you shall be my people" (Lev 26:12), an almost short-hand summary of the intimate bondedness between Yahweh and the Hebrew people that is expressed through the covenant of Sinai. There, in the dramatic climax of the Exodus event and journey, the divine liberator, who had acted as the "next of kin"[12] in freeing the enslaved Israelites from Egypt, freely bonded them to one another and to Yahweh as one family.

> Rather, in divine providence it was the momentous achievement of Moses to perceive Yahweh as desiring to

form one family with His people, as intervening in history
to maintain their freedom for His service and thus reveal-
ing the bonds of fraternal justice and fidelity to the
oppressed as primal expressions of His Will for all time.
The God of Moses was Yahweh, a God of radical justice,
not caprice, a generous and loyal kinsman to those who
truly love Him (Exod 20:6) and an ever present redeemer
in times of oppression.[13]

Thus, the inspiration of Moses to intrinsically connect the nature of
the Lord Yahweh and the demands of social justice was "radical" in
the sense of the Latin *radix* (root, foundational). The Israelites then
were constituted a covenant community in which the Lord Yahweh
really dwelled, first in the tent of a nomad and then in the fortress-
sanctuaries and towns of the people as they settled the Promised
Land.

   This religious insight of the Hebrew scriptures is a far cry from
the "Jesus and me" spirituality that some Christians have adopted as
their individualized version of the Judaeo-Christian heritage. On the
contrary, the scriptures maintain strongly that our spiritual heritage
is innately communal from the very first days that a nomad God
made common cause with a chosen people. In radical contrast to the
dominant ethic of American individualism, the scriptures portray
human existence as communal in nature and "that an adequate definition of an individual requires some reference also to community."[14]
A woman religious who had worked in South Africa shared a similar
Zulu insight: *umuntu ngununtu ngabantu* ("a person is a person by
means of—because of—other people").

   Three key concepts, then, are at play here, each fleshing out the
meaning of our creation in the "image and likeness" of God. At the
heart of each is a revelation of God, a sharing of some aspect of God's
own truth and life, which in turn reveals to us a corresponding aspect
of our own truth. First, in the dynamic of creating, the Creator shares
the very fact of divine existence and goodness—God's own goodness.
In so doing, we are created "very good" in our own being and becoming. Secondly, God shares divine dominion over the creation, and, in
that very instant, endows us as cocreators, stewards of the earth with
a dominion of responsible and reverent care for the world. Thirdly,
God reveals divine kinship with us by freely choosing to dwell with
the human community. We are thus constituted as a community of
sisters and brothers to one another, one interdependent family with
the Lord Yahweh. At a glance:

GOD'S TRIPLE REVELATION	OUR TRIPLE TRUTH
1. Sharing God's goodness.	1. Creation/human goodness.
2. Sharing God's dominion.	2. Stewardship
3. Dwelling in the community.	3. Interdependence.

There are important implications for our everyday lives. One is the dignity of our work in the factory, office, home, or community, since it is through this work that we fulfill our invitation to stewardship. We become more like God in our efforts at enhancing the creation.[15]

These Genesis revelations also teach an attitude of reverence for ourselves, our work, our human community, and the earth, providing a foundation for the self-esteem that seems so elusive to current generations. This reverence grounds a pro-life, pro-ecology, pro-community stance that eschews racism, sexism, classism, nationalism, and any other attitudes that demean and violate whole groups of the human community created in God's image or nature itself.

Jubilee

Goodness, stewardship, and community also interplay to form a critical consensus around the sharing of the earth's goods by all the members of the community. The not-familiar-enough Hebrew concepts that epitomize these values are the year of the Lord, the sabbatical year, and the jubilee year. Leviticus 25 explains, first, about the sabbatical and jubilee years:

> The LORD spoke to Moses on Mount Sinai saying, Speak to the people of Israel and say to them: When you enter the land that I am giving you, the land shall observe a sabbath for the Lord. Six years you shall sow your field, and six years you shall prune your vineyard, and gather in their yield; but in the seventh year there shall be a sabbath of complete rest for the land, a sabbath for the LORD: you shall not sow your field or prune your vineyard....
>
> And you shall hallow the fiftieth year and you shall proclaim liberty throughout the land to all its inhabitants. It shall be a jubilee for you: you shall return, every one of you, to your property and every one of you to your family. (Lev 25:1–4, 10)

Then the sacred text explains how property is never to be lost permanently by sale or forfeiture and is to be returned in the jubilee year:

> The land shall not be sold in perpetuity; for the land is mine; with me you are but aliens and tenants. Throughout the land that you hold, you shall provide for the redemption of the land. If anyone of your kin falls into difficulty and sells a piece of property, then the next of kin shall come and redeem what the relative has sold. If the person has no one to redeem it, but then prospers and finds sufficient means to do so, the years since its sale shall be computed and the difference shall be refunded to the person to whom it was sold, and the property shall be returned. (Lev 25:23–28)

And those who are indentured or enslaved because of their poverty, they too are to be freed in the jubilee and returned to their own property:

> If any who are dependent on you become so impoverished that they sell themselves to you, you shall not make them serve as slaves. They shall remain with you as hired or bound laborers. They shall serve with you until the year of the jubilee. Then they and their children with them shall be free from your authority; they shall go back to their own family and return to their ancestral property. (Lev 25:39–41)

In the seventh or sabbatical year, land was to be uncultivated, slaves freed, and debts relieved.

The jubilee year, or grand sabbatical, took its name from the trumpet that sounded to inaugurate the celebration.[16] In the tradition it was to be every forty-ninth or fiftieth year. In that year the people were to be restored to their full sense of community and right order: a community of faith and fidelity, sharing the goods of the earth, with God dwelling in their midst. As Pope John Paul II explains:

> What was true for the sabbatical year was also true for the jubilee year, which fell every 50 years. In the jubilee year, however, the customs of the sabbatical year were broadened and celebrated with even greater solemnity....One of the most significant consequences of the jubilee year was the general "emancipation" of all the dwellers on the land in need of being freed.[17]

This took place by restoring all community members, no matter what their standing or position, to a full share of the community's goods. Property was to be returned to its original owners; slaves were to be freed; and all members restored to full membership, no matter what past misfortune or failure had occurred. With the restoration of freedom and property came a restored sense of dignity and participation in the community of faith. It also affirmed the integrity of the community itself.

Beneath this custom, of course, lay the faith insight that the land was really Yahweh's, who had made it a gift to the community for its use, in the words of the U.S. bishops, as "stewards charged with working for the good of all in the name of God, the sole owner of creation."[18] All the community members, too, were kin to the Lord, not to be enslaved or rejected from active participation in the Lord's family. This initial understanding of the land and its use did not extend to all those outside the Israelite community, with some notable exceptions. Some later Jewish teachers and the early Christian community, however, would find in the jubilee year a model for every community's obligation of distributive justice.[19] Underlying the practice of an equitable distribution of resources was the

> assumption that genuine need was due either to a breakdown in the equitable distribution of community resources or to the possession of a social identity, such as that of widow or orphan, over which an individual had no control.[20]

Although the jubilee tradition might be considered idyllic or primitive, it was rooted in deeply religious concepts and presented a social ideal for the people.[21]

This same sense of communality with the Lord and the earth, of distributing resources to meet basic human needs, and of resistance to exclusion from community participation persists today. It can be found in both particular cultural or ethnic groups and even in our own Anglo-American legal institutions. The Native Americans among us retain a sensitivity to common ownership that often runs against the dominant private property ethic of American capitalism and much of our culture. Belief in tribal ownership and resistance to fencing the land, for example, seems close to the caution from Leviticus that, "The land shall not be sold in perpetuity..." (25:23). Native American customs also may suggest at a deeper level the close bondedness with Mother Earth that is transparent in the Genesis sto-

ries and the nurturing of the earth found in the jubilee custom of letting the fields be regenerated in each seventh year.

This compelling sense of the communal destination intended
for the earth's goods is not just the province of ancient or so-called
primitive peoples. A similar biblical sense of human community and
the subordinate role of property rights seem built into the fabric of
contemporary laws as well. "Starting all over"; "restoring a person to
right order"; "no one should be so down that they cannot get up
again"; "beginning again"—these are shorthand, for example, for our
bankruptcy or insolvency laws. A basic premise is woven through the
American legal tradition of bankruptcy and sanctioned by the
Constitution[22] that property rights ultimately are subordinate to
human needs and human dignity. In bankruptcy proceedings, we say
in effect to those insolvents who are so down-and-out that they cannot
get up again, "We cancel your debts; you can begin again." It is a fresh-
start doctrine reminiscent of the jubilee year.

Part of our bankruptcy system involves the related concept of
homestead exemptions. Homestead exemptions are not just the familiar protection of certain income or assets from taxes, although even
that function suggests that people need to preserve some basic minimum for survival, even against the otherwise legitimate needs of the
body politic. The exemptions also insure that, in the event of bankruptcy, the bankrupt person or family is allowed to keep certain min-
imal goods as a kind of "grubstake" to begin again. They are not to
be left standing naked in a barrel.[23]

Even in our modern laws, then, there seems to survive a kind of
jubilee year and its underpinning rationale—that the goods of the
earth are meant for everybody, and that we are one human community. If someone is brought so low that they cannot get up, the community helps them on their feet again and lets them start life over.

The bankruptcy and homestead provisions are related as well to
the amnesty concept in criminal law. Amnesty is a kind of forgiveness
doctrine, recognized by most of us when a governor grants amnesty
to a person accused or convicted of a crime. Similarly, the 1986
Immigration Reform and Control Act granted a kind of amnesty in
its provisions for citizenship application for undocumented persons
who had been living and working in the United States for an extended
period. These concepts all seem rooted in the image of the sovereign
who can forgive debts, injustices, and crimes in the interest of reestablishing the right order of the community, bringing peace to warring
factions, and helping the entire community to have a fresh start.

Most recently, the jubilee concept was strongly urged upon the international community for the jubilee or millennium year 2000 by Pope John Paul II,[24] other religious leaders,[25] social justice advocates, and even popular rock stars. The application here was to the enormous burden of international debt payments borne by many of the world's poorest nations. These countries, like the enslaved debtors of ancient Israel, were unable to pay their debts and simultaneously meet the basic needs of their populations for food, education, social services, and basic health care. Concepts that the scriptures applied to the community of Israel were now urged upon the entire community of nations. In fact, under the impetus of jubilee observances, significant debt relief was agreed to by the creditor nations of the world and is now being slowly implemented for many poor debtor nations.

The Role of the Poor

The poor then play a critical part in this biblical view of the world and its understanding of persons, property, and community. The great prophet Isaiah puts it this way:

> Is such the fast that I choose,
>   a day to humble oneself?
> Is it to bow down the head like a bulrush,
>   and to lie in sackcloth and ashes?
> Will you call this a fast,
>   a day acceptable to the LORD?
> Is not this the fast that I choose:
>   to loose the bonds of injustice,
>   to undo the thongs of the yoke,
> to let the oppressed go free,
> and to break every yoke?
> Is it not to share your bread with the hungry,
>   and bring the homeless poor into your house;
> when you see the naked, to cover them,
>   and not to hide yourself from your own kin?
> Then your light shall break forth like the dawn,
>   and your healing shall spring up quickly;
> your vindicator shall go before you,
>   the glory of the Lord shall be your rear guard.
> Then you shall call, and the LORD will answer;
>   you shall cry for help, and he will say, Here I am.
>   (Isa 58:5–9)

Isaiah was underscoring the central place of the poor in the religious experience of the people, in their lived understanding of creation's goodness and their responsibility for it as a community of
fidelity.

From the time of the Deuteronomic laws, the covenant, and the
earliest prophets, there was special mention of the poor and a special
place for them existed in the community. The Hebrew word for the
poor is the *anawim,* the little ones, originally those "overwhelmed by
want."[26] In the Old Testament, paralleling those to be protected by the
king in Ebla, this group is primarily widows, orphans, and strangers
(refugees, sojourners, migrants, immigrants). They are the poor and
powerless in their society. Their very existence and the harsh conditions of their lives reflected Israel's violation of the social virtues
rooted in its ancient ideals. Their poverty was often the result of
unjust oppression. As such, they comprised:

> Yahweh's poor (anawim)—i.e., of the socially oppressed
> whose redress could only come from Yahweh, and who,
> therefore, became virtually synonymous with the just, the
> faithful remnant with the right to call upon the Lord.[27]

In this special status before Yahweh, the *anawim* embodied Israel's
own history of enslavement in Egypt, when only the Lord could free
them. Like the Hebrews in Egypt, these poor had special protection
from, and special access to, the Lord:

> You shall not wrong or oppress a resident alien, for you
> were aliens in the land of Egypt. You shall not abuse any
> widow or orphan. If you do abuse them, when they cry out
> to me, I will surely heed their cry. (Exod 22:21–23)

Their special status reflected a combination of powerlessness, poverty,
and systemic exclusion from full membership in the community and
the protection it afforded. Yahweh, then, was their protector.

Today, many commentators on the scriptures continue to use
anawim in a developed sense that now explicitly includes four groups:
widows, orphans, strangers, and the poor. This broad group of "the
poor" more often than not described the actual economic condition
of the first three and is sometimes used to include them. The poor
also covered others whose primary status was solely economic
poverty. All four are linked in the interconnection of poverty, powerlessness, and exclusion from the community and in the oppression

they suffer at the hands of the larger community. Believers are charged to see to it that the *anawim* are not without the means to meet their basic needs, nor are they to be excluded from the community or its decision making by their lack of means.

As the scriptures and their faith understanding develop, care for the *anawim* actually became the test of Israel's faithfulness. Rather than the objects of optional charity or pious generosity, the poor became the measure of Israel's fidelity to the Lord Yahweh; and their right treatment lay at the heart of the concept of biblical justice and righteousness. Peruvian theologian Gustavo Gutiérrez puts the matter boldly:

> To know Yahweh, which in Biblical language is equivalent to saying to love Yahweh, is to establish just relationships among men, it is to recognize the rights of the poor. The God of Biblical revelation is known through interhuman justice. When justice does not exist, God is not known; he is absent.[28]

Scripture scholar John R. Donahue, a key resource person for the U.S. Catholic bishops on their 1986 pastoral letter on economic justice, reiterates the point that we are not dealing with just examples or expressions of faith, but its center:

> The core of Israel's faith is equated with the doing of justice....The doing of justice is not the application of religious faith, but its substance. Without it, God remains unknown.[29]

To restate this rather startling connection made by both Gutiérrez and Donahue, *without the doing of justice, God remains unknown!* The boldness of that assertion would surprise many churchgoers.

Why is not caring for the poor—the failure to do justice—actually infidelity to God, a form of atheism? Why is justice at the core of faith for the nation of Isaiah and for contemporary faith communities?

Failing to do justice is partly infidelity because those who forget the poor cease to be dependent on Yahweh for creation and salvation. They erect other gods for themselves. From Genesis came the multiple revelations that this creation is good, a gift from a continually generous God who never forgets us and who will not leave us orphans. Not caring for the poor is a sign of losing this sense of Yahweh's graciousness and compassion and, instead, hoarding the things of the earth over/against other members of the community.

Repeatedly the Israelites invest their sense of value and security in things: their wealth, success, status, power, and treaties. These become gods for them. A favorite scriptural image for this is chariots and horses; in the societies in which these scriptures developed, chariots and horses were an overwhelming war machine. They were the privilege of rulers and the wealthy, who relied for security on these prized instruments of war power rather than the Lord. Yahweh, however, is one at whose rebuke "both rider and horse lay stunned" (Ps 76:6). Of Yahweh, the psalmist says, "His delight is not in the strength of the horse" (Ps 147:10).

Not caring for the poor is infidelity to God, moreover, because people who forget the poor no longer really believe in the divine being whom Yahweh reveals or in their own truth as reflected in the face of the Lord. The "I AM WHO AM" is self-revealed in the scriptures as a God of the people, the community, who dwells in their midst and is passionately concerned for their well-being. Not caring for the poor is a sign that they do not know who God is; they do not understand what John Donahue calls the "web of relationships"[30] which have at their heart the covenanting God. That is why without the doing of justice God remains unknown.

If the poor around us are uncared for in contemporary societies, we too cannot know the one who says, "I will be your God, and you will be my people." This God-of-the-community gave creation to us as goodness to be shared by stewards of the earth, not owners. If we forget the poor, we have forgotten God and the truth of our own radical interconnectedness: to God as life-giver and to one another as sisters and brothers.

The Cycle of Baal

One framework for understanding this better is found in a process I call the cycle of Baal. As a hermeneutic device, the cycle exposes more clearly the connection between the truth of who God is revealed to be in the Hebrew scriptures and our truth reflected in that same revelation. The cycle says something about faith communities and civic communities and also addresses the personal religious experiences of Christians and other people of faith.

Original Blessing

This pattern of understanding revelation begins with a moment contemplating the profound mystery of creation as what Matthew Fox calls original blessing,[31] the original vision of Yahweh melding nature, humankind, and the divine presence. The Genesis faith-understanding comes into play: the goodness and right order existing among the people, a sense of being stewards of creation, and their awareness of themselves as community. They care for the *anawim* in their midst: the widows, the orphans, and the strangers in an agricultural and herding society who basically have nothing. No land, no flocks, no wealth. The scriptures mandate, for example, that farmers not harvest all of the grain out of the field so that the poor widow and orphan can come behind and glean the fields for enough to eat, to keep themselves alive. This example expresses the basic sense of community, of right order, of shared goods. Yahweh is in the midst of this kinship community, and all is well, even prospering.

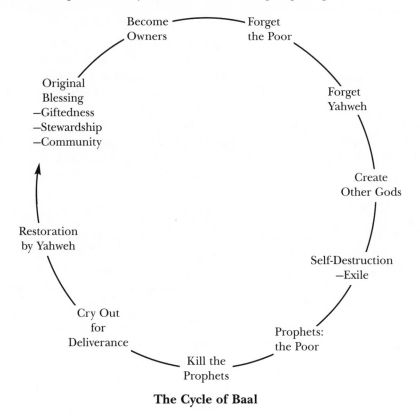

The Cycle of Baal

Become Owners

What evolves in the people, because of the good things they have and their own hard work to develop them (creation given and enhanced), is a sense that they are really owners. Their self-identity is transformed in a radical fashion that says, "This is mine. I have produced this. I am owner." Their importance is invested in what they have, not in their own goodness and divine image that is gift from God. Their pride is localized in their prosperity and accomplishments: the size of their flocks, the number and beauty of their children, the building of the temple, the success of their armies, and even their observance of religious customs.

This is a subtle, but powerfully pervasive, evolution reflecting an inner dynamic of wealth that is so frequently the target of warnings and cautions from religious leaders of many different traditions. Jesus himself tells a parable about just such a person who possesses so much that his greatest concern is holding onto and storing up his wealth:

> The land of a rich man produced abundantly. And he thought to himself, "What should I do, for I have no place to store my crops?" Then he said, "I will do this: I will pull down my barns and build larger ones, and there I will store all my grain and my goods. And I will say to my soul, Soul, you have ample goods laid up for many years; relax, eat, drink, be merry." But God said to him, "You fool! This very night your life is being demanded of you. And the things you have prepared, whose will they be?" So it is with those who store up treasures for themselves but are not rich toward God. (Luke 12:16–21)

This man's harvest success is everyone's dream—to never have to work again! Yet, in this parable told by Jesus, he is punished by God. The innate danger of the wealth is that it becomes dominant, it turns the order of creation on its head and our possessions have dominion over us, and not vice versa.

Forget the Poor

The dominant passion in the life of the person in Jesus' parable—who is already rich—is the amassing of more wealth, not the needs of the community. The wealthy farmer's self-centeredness is unmistakable in the "I" and "my" and "myself" that dominate his thoughts. This sense of "ownership" breeds an organic development: forgetting the *anawim*. The farmer forgets the poor. Instead of leaving the surplus harvest to be gleaned from the fields by those in need in the community, as required by the scriptures, the farmer's dominant concern is building larger barns to contain it.

Forget Yahweh

That forgetting of the *anawim* was the critical sign of a more profound memory loss: forgetting Yahweh. It betrayed the more fundamental atheism of not knowing who God is and not really caring. We forget who and how Yahweh has been revealed, as a passionate lover of a people in the midst of whom stands God's own tent. And we forget the truth of ourselves.

This was not an unexpected turn of events. Yahweh repeatedly had warned the Israelites about the seduction of prosperity and the tendency to forgetfulness that would result. In the following text from Deuteronomy, God describes this process; first there is the giving of good gifts:

> For the LORD your God is bringing you into a good land, a land with flowing streams, with springs and underground waters welling up in valleys and hills, a land of wheat and barley, of vines and fig trees and pomegranates, a land of olive trees and honey, a land where you may eat bread without scarcity, where you will lack nothing.... (Deut 8:7–9)

Then, once their needs are met and they are comfortable, they would forget the Lord:

> When you have eaten your fill and have built fine houses and live in them, and when your herds and flocks have multiplied, and your silver and gold is multiplied, and all that you have is multiplied, then do not exalt yourself, forgetting the LORD your God, who brought you out of the land of Egypt, out of the house of slavery, who led you through the great and terrible wilderness.... (Deut 8:12–15)

Then they would take the credit themselves for what they have received:

> Do not say to yourself, "My power and the might of my own hand have gotten me this wealth." But remember the LORD your God, for it is he who gives you power to get wealth, so that he may confirm his covenant that he swore to your ancestors, as he is doing today. (Deut 8:17–18)

And, finally, they would bring destruction on themselves by their forgetfulness and pride:

> If you do forget the LORD your God and follow other gods to serve and worship them, I solemnly warn you today that you shall surely perish. Like the nations that the LORD is destroying before you, so shall you perish, because you would not obey the voice of the LORD your God. (Deut 8:19–20)

This text from Deuteronomy closes predicting, in the wake of the forgetting of Yahweh, the next turns of the cycle of Baal: the resort to false gods and the resulting destruction of the community of Israel.

Create Other Gods

Humans never seem to really renounce God, but only make their gods more convenient, more like themselves. Complete and formal atheism often is quite unfashionable. The Hebrews—like most societies—had a religious identity, religious leaders, and religious practices and traditions, all the makings of a religious culture. Culturally, then, it was far more natural to reshape God than to be atheists, to create gods who were compatible with their own evolving sense of themselves as owners and property holders, gods whose worship and allegiance would not disturb those status-rights.

The gods to which they so often turned were the fertility gods of Canaan, the foremost of which is "Hadad, the Canaanite fertility god par excellence."[32] Local versions of Hadad, called the Baals, were the lords of each territory. Often their worship occurred in the mountains, the high places. These were gods more to human liking, gods who could be controlled or at least with whom deals could be made. They were not the jealous God Yahweh who stubbornly insisted on an intimate relationship with a chosen people, who wanted hearts, not sacrifices.

No, the Baals were gods satisfied with a few critically timed sacrifices and with cultic prostitution "thought to have the inevitable effect of constraining the divinity in a magical way to give what was desired (i.e., fertility)."[33] Once appeased in this way, these gods not only were to assure fertility, but they certainly were not to interfere with ownership. The Israelites could exercise status-rights without sanction, forget the web of relationships that originally defined their community, and ignore the poor among them.

Self-Destruction

What followed was self-destruction. Scripture tells the story in terms of punishment, of Yahweh letting the Israelites succumb to their enemies, of God raising up some neighboring and greater nation that invades the Promised Land, destroys Jerusalem, demolishes the temple, kills many of the people, sells their children into slavery, takes the rest into exile, and so forth. The story is repeated throughout the scriptures.[34]

A geopolitical analysis might suggest that the Hebrews had the poor fortune of location on the main thoroughfare between the great powers that rose and fell throughout their history—namely, Egypt, Babylon, Assyria, and Rome. Each time major conflict ensued, they seemed to have made poor alliances. Like a chronic gambler at the track, they picked one loser after another with whom to align themselves, and suffered the expected consequences. A theological analysis, as is offered in the prophets, was that they relied on the wisdom of their own schemes and clever treaties, and not on the Lord Yahweh who was their one sure protector. Thus followed destruction.

Prophets: The Poor

Then the prophets came, raised up by the Lord Yahweh. Whether the people were in exile, in slavery, or merely in political and moral disarray, the message of the prophets was the same strong medicine. Their primary theme was not, you have forgotten the rituals of the temple or you have forsaken the scriptures. Their central message was not to accuse the people of worshipping false gods. Seeing into and speaking the truth—which is the business of prophets—their message was, you have forgotten the poor. As Isaiah proclaimed, our God does not want sackcloth and ashes, holydays and sacrifices. Our God wants captives freed, bonds broken, the hungry fed, the naked clothed, and the poor restored to their rightful place in the midst of the community. That was the prophets' message over and over, as we hear from Jeremiah:

> Thus says the LORD of hosts, the God of Israel: Amend your ways and your doings, and let me dwell with you in this place. Do not trust in these deceptive words: "This is the temple of the LORD, the temple of the LORD, the temple of the LORD." For if you truly amend your ways and your doings, if you truly act justly one with another, if you do not oppress the alien, the orphan, and the widow, or shed innocent blood in this place, and if you do not go after other gods to your own hurt, then I will dwell with you in this place, in the land that I gave of old to your ancestors forever and ever. (Jer 7:3–7)

The prophets came into the midst of the Hebrew people and protested that, because the hungry were unfed, the poor homeless, and the orphans uncared for, they had forgotten who their God was. And by forgetting the revealed God, they had lost their identity that was rooted in the truth of God and of this living community, ministering to the needs of the poor.

Kill the Prophets

The message of the prophets was not a popular message. The prophets were people of passion, embodying the pathos and passion of Yahweh the Lord. They were especially critical of the kings and of the monarchy itself as a corruption of the covenant closeness of Yahweh and the Lord's kinship community.[35] None of us likes being reprimanded, least of all kings, especially if it means letting go of our treasures of one kind or another. So most prophets received, not the respect and reverence for one called by God nor the thanks of a truly contrite people, but the usual fate of prophets: banishment or death.

The Lord seemed to have an inexhaustible supply of prophets who continued to rise up from the most unlikely places—reluctant truth-tellers at the bidding of Yahweh. Again and again their message was repeated in the hearing of the people and their rulers: You have forgotten the poor.

Cry Out for Deliverance

Eventually, from the midst of their own suffering and captivity, the Hebrews repented. They cried out for mercy and forgiveness, begging the Lord to again be their liberator and to restore them to their promised land and all that it symbolized to them about their chosenness. The Psalms were filled with their laments to the Lord:

> O God, why do you cast us off forever?
>> Why does your anger smoke against the sheep of your
>>> pasture?
> Remember your congregation, which you acquired long
>> ago,
>> which you redeemed to be the tribe of your heritage.
> Remember Mount Zion, where you came to dwell.
> Direct your steps to the perpetual ruins;
>> the enemy has destroyed everything in the sanctuary.
>> (Ps 74:1–3)

The people cried out to be freed from slavery and exile, brought back to the Promised Land, and restored to right order and the sense of a community of fidelity to Yahweh and to one another.

Restoration

Invariably, Yahweh heard the cries of the people, and restored them to the land and to their intimate community with God and with one another. In reestablishing the covenant community, the temple is rebuilt; the law of the covenant is rediscovered; the songs of their religion are sung again; and Yahweh is celebrated in the midst of the chosen people. The restoration is always painted in brush strokes of beauty and grandeur, joy overflowing:

> For thus says the LORD:
> Sing aloud with gladness for Jacob,
>> and raise shouts for the chief of the nations;
> proclaim, give praise, and say,

"Save, O LORD, your people,
the remnant of Israel."
See, I am going to bring them from the land of the north,
and gather them from the farthest parts of the earth,
among them the blind and the lame,
those with child and those in labor, together;
a great company, they shall return here.
With weeping they shall come,
and with consolations I will lead them back,
I will let them walk by brooks of water,
in a straight path in which they shall not stumble;
for I have become a father to Israel, and Ephraim is my
firstborn.
Hear the word of the LORD, O nations,
and declare it in the coastlands far away;
say, "He who scattered Israel will gather him,
and will keep him as a shepherd a flock."
For the LORD has ransomed Jacob,
and has redeemed him from hands too strong for him.
They shall come and sing aloud on the height of Zion,
and they shall be radiant over the goodness of the Lord,
over the grain, the wine, and the oil,
and over the young of the flock and the herd;
their life shall become like a watered garden,
and they shall never languish again.
Then shall the young women rejoice in the dance,
and the young men and the old shall be merry.
I will turn their mourning into joy,
I will comfort them, and give them gladness for sorrow.
I will give the priests their fill of fatness,
and my people shall be satisfied with my bounty,
says the LORD. (Jer 31:7–14)

The cycle of Baal has come full turn, as the community is restored to the land promised to them by Yahweh. Each time it was a new creation, a new exodus, a new liberation in which Yahweh redeemed the kinship community and reestablished the original blessing.

In liberating and creating anew, Yahweh does justice for the community, all of whom have experienced the status of the *anawim* in their exile and suffering. In the process, the three fundamental insights of their early scriptures were reinforced: the goodness of creation, their stewardship over these gifts, and their identity as community in which God dwelled and all, especially the poor, were cared for. Yahweh's redemptive activity was itself a model of reaching out in love to those in need, a schooling for the restored community in its attitudes of justice toward the *anawim*.

Then, despite their painful exile experience and the bitterness of their own tears, despite the lesson of justice at the gracious hands of Yahweh, they repeat the cycle of Baal all over again. After too short a time, they take what they have for granted, become owners again, forget the poor, and embark on the same journey to faithlessness and destruction. Over and over again. Yet, as Psalm 106 proclaims,

> Many times he delivered them,
>   but they were rebellious in their purposes,
>   and were brought low through their iniquity.
> Nevertheless he regarded their distress
>   when he heard their cry.
> For their sake he remembered his covenant,
>   and showed compassion according to the abundance of
>   his steadfast love.
> He caused them to be pitied
>   by all who held them captive. (Ps 106:43–46)

The cycle of Baal is repeated all across the Hebrew scriptures. As such, it forms a framework for understanding more clearly the poignant history of the chosen people and the truths taught them by Yahweh through the preaching of the prophets and their concrete history of forgetfulness, faithlessness, and self-destruction.

This also can be the fate of nations that forget their own giftedness, that turn their eyes from their inner cities and rural poverty or the destitution of much of the third world, and that close their ears to the prophets who call them back to their traditions of faithfulness and community. That is the message of Pope John Paul II in his retelling to the United States of Jesus' parable of the Rich Man and Lazarus, models for him of the first world sitting in wealth and splendor while the third world lies in agony like a beggar at our door.

This cycle of Baal can enlighten our own individual spiritual journeys as well. When we are doing well, popular and admired, successful at career or family or community leadership or even ministry, we begin being self-congratulatory. We forget about other peoples' needs, ignoring the web of relationships that binds us to the earth and its people. We forget who Yahweh really is and that all we have is a gift from God, to be shared with God's people. We don't want a God whose presence in community and in the poor makes demands on our privacy or our property. We create other gods or we find a god we can handle with a weekly trip to church or other religious practices. Then, to our constant surprise, we bring destruction upon ourselves!

In the midst of our own amazement and chagrin that this could happen to me, someone plays prophet for us. They tell us, "You brought this on yourself." It is the Hollywood and televangelist syndrome; it happens to people who are the daily bread of television and the tabloids and who are widely admired and imitated. Why are we so shocked when they are committed to an institution for alcohol or drug addiction, make shambles of multiple marriages, or commit suicide? "They had it all," we say. "What happened?"

The same thing happens to us all. When we realize the truth of what we have done to ourselves, if we do, we cry out to the Lord. We get back our sense of right order. We are renewed in compassion for those who are less fortunate. We are restored to the community, a community in which God resides and the poor are cared for in dignity.... Then we forget again. The cycle of Baal.

The story is similar for the Israelites as a collective people, for modern groups and nations, and for ourselves as individuals. When we forget the poor, we are forgetting the truth of ourselves as revealed in the light of the truth of God. Whenever we do so, we bring darkness and blindness upon ourselves and, ultimately, destruction.

This radical consideration of the cycle of Baal sets us at the heart of religious faith, because in choosing who our God is we are making ourselves like our God. If we flee to the mountains (or the seashore or the suburbs) and there construct the gods with whom we can make deals, we are invariably making over ourselves in their likeness. Psalm 135 puts it this way:

> The idols of the nations are silver and gold,
>   the work of human hands.
> They have mouths, but they do not speak;
>   they have eyes, but they do not see;
> they have ears, but they do not hear,
>   and there is no breath in their mouths.
> Those who make them
>   and all who trust them
>   shall become like them. (Ps 135:15–18)

The shocking truth of the scriptures is that our everyday decisions determine the basic direction of our entire lives. We can choose to be like the Lord Yahweh, loving first, sharing the good of ourselves in the goods of creation, and standing in the midst of a faith community as passionate lovers and protectors of the poor. Or, we can be like the gods of the mountainsides, neither hearing nor seeing the poor in our midst, and having stone-cold hearts.

The U.S. Catholic bishops summarized this reading of the Hebrew scriptures in *Economic Justice for All:*

> Central to the Biblical presentation of justice is that the justice of a community is measured by its treatment of the powerless of society, most often described as the widow, the orphan, the poor and the stranger (non-Israelite) in the land. The law, the prophets and the wisdom literature of the Old Testament all show deep concern for the proper treatment of such people. What these groups have in common is their vulnerability and lack of power. They are often alone and have no protector or advocate. Therefore, it is God who hears their cries (Pss 109:21; 113:7) and the king who is God's anointed is commanded to have special concern for them.[36]

As we have seen, the duty shared by Ebla's kings and Israel's rulers was also the duty of the entire community of Yahweh.

Scholars tell us, in fact, that there was an evolution in what the Hebrew scriptures prescribe about caring for the *anawim*. Originally, the duty to care for the poor was the responsibility of the entire community. With the rise of the monarchy, this responsibility became a royal task. However, "when the monarchy fails ethically and historically, Yahweh becomes the defender."[37] The Lord God, liberator of the Hebrews from Egypt, will raise up the poor, the scriptures say, because of the failure of the people and their rulers.

Ironically, God will accomplish this by reversing the process we have just noted. First, God will choose a royal defender of the poor; then, through the action of that liberator, God will again commission a new people of a new covenant to take upon themselves the responsibility for justice and the *anawim*. Understanding the revelation of the Hebrew scriptures about the truths of creation and of ourselves as a covenant community, however, is a prerequisite to entering into the further revelation in the Christian scriptures of God's action as savior and molder of a new faith community. Again, as the bishops note,

These perspectives provide the foundation for a biblical vision of economic justice. Every human person is created in the image of God and the denial of dignity to a person is a blot on this image. Creation is a gift to all men and women, not to be appropriated for the benefit of a few; its beauty is an object of joy and reverence. The same God who came to the aid of an oppressed people and formed them into a covenant community continues to hear the cry of the oppressed and to create communities which are to hear God's word. God's love and life are present when people can live in a community of faith and hope. These cardinal points of the faith of Israel also furnish the religious context for understanding the saving action of God in the life and the teaching of Jesus.[38]

The poor, then, are understood from the Hebrew scriptures to stand at the center of the divine revelation: of who God is, what creation is for, how the human community is to live with one another, and what our own truth is. It is here that any understanding of *faithjustice* must begin. Here is the soil in which it is planted, and from here it will grow and mature in the life and teaching of Jesus of Nazareth.

QUESTIONS FOR REFLECTION AND DISCUSSION

1. What are the three central revelations from the early pages of Genesis that lay a foundation for understanding the Church's current emphasis on *faithjustice*?

2. In the Hebrew scriptures, what was the sabbatical year? The jubilee year? How were they related?

3. Who were the *anawim* in Israelite society? Who are the *anawim* in contemporary U.S. society? In global society?

4. The responsibility to care for the *anawim* evolved in three stages in the Hebrew scriptures; what were they?

5. What was the role of the prophet in Israelite society? In today's society?

6. What are examples of the cycle of Baal in literature? In world history? In contemporary society?

7. Jewish rulers and others often relied on chariots and horses for their power; what would be the "chariots and horses" in contemporary nations?

8. The 1996 so-called welfare reform law primarily affected three groups: single parents (mostly women), their children, and undocumented and documented immigrants. Is there any connection with the tradition of the *anawim*?

CHAPTER TWO

A Year of Favor from the Lord

> "...to bring good news to the poor. He has sent me to pro-
> claim release to the captives and recovery of sight to the
> blind, to let the oppressed go free, to proclaim the year of
> the Lord's favor."
>
> Jesus of Nazareth in the Synagogue (Luke 4:18–19)

After Dr. Martin Luther King was assassinated on April 4, 1968, there was a fire set every day for a hundred days in Mobile, Alabama. The racial tension burned as hot as the arson fires, and there were angry demonstrations and threats. At twenty-three, I participated in my first civil rights march in those days as people of all faiths and races tried to demonstrate their continuing concern for Dr. King's agenda and their solidarity in the face of racist violence. On the streets in poor Black communities downtown, however, a group of Sinsinawa Dominican Sisters were most visibly involved and concerned, despite the advice from supportive Black leadership that for their own safety they leave their convent in the ghetto until things cooled down. One of them, Sister Lorraine Rivers, was subsequently honored by the Neighborhood Organized Workers, the local Black leadership group, with its annual justice award.

Many of these crucial events occurred in Mobile during the spring break at Spring Hill College, while most students were away. In my class on contemporary Protestant and Catholic theology, Reverend George Lankford, a Methodist, described those events for returning students. If the modern church had saints, he declared, then surely the sisters working in the Black community were nominees.

❖ ❖ ❖

Half-Irish and half-Japanese, Father Jimmy Yamauchi taught theology to students at Spring Hill College with an energy that brought to life what so often seemed dead and irrelevant even to Jesuit scholastics, as those of us in training were called. "Yama" put flesh on the dry intellectualized bones of the Trinity by recasting the question of Father, Son, and Spirit in terms of action and relationship. "What do they do," he asked, "especially in relation to one another?" Asking more specifically, what is "father-ness," Yama answered that it was a radical "to-the-son-ness" that oriented God completely to the well-being of God's children, sharing life, love, goodness, creativity, and dominion with us. Using Jesus' favorite image for the Creator God, Yama reminded us that God loves us with the parental passion of "Abba" (Daddy, Papa).

❖ ❖ ❖

During my first internship at the Atlanta Legal Aid Society as a summer law clerk, there was also a Presbyterian-minister-turned-attorney on the staff. One day in discussing our mutual interests he told me only half-whimsically, "When I was in the active ministry, I used to call people and beg them to help or to do the right thing. Now, I just call and threaten to sue them!"

❖ ❖ ❖

After law school, during my first tenure as a staff attorney in Atlanta, I used to spend a monthly weekend of rest and reflection at the Trappist Monastery in nearby Conyers, Georgia. There I met Father Thomas Francis, then retreat director at the guest house. In a retreat with Tom during a later summer, I was trying to answer the question of whether to request ordination to the priesthood, which included the perennial Jesuit "hyphenated priest problem," namely, "What does it mean to be a priest-scientist, priest-astronomer, priest-administrator, and, in my case, a priest-lawyer?" Tom then reminded me that in Jesus' story of the Good Samaritan both the priest and the lawyer had passed by the wounded man on the side of the road without stopping to attend to his needs.

The point he made was unmistakable! Neither priest nor lawyer, by itself or in combination, is sufficient. Jesus repeatedly underscores the absolute necessity that we must act out of love in genuine caring for those in need around us. That mandate is more foundational than any career we pursue. Ultimately, too, it can be the unifying principle of whatever we do.

At the Mass of Thanksgiving in New Orleans on the day after my ordination in June 1976, I selected the Good Samaritan text to preach from: I reminded my family and friends of the underlying call to self-sacrificing love, no matter what our journey in life. I also reminded them and myself–using the text of Ivan Allen from Mayor: Notes on the Sixties *quoted in chapter 1–that for us the closest parallel to scriptural relations between Jews and Samaritans was the alienation between Black and White in America.*

❖ ❖ ❖

At a large gathering of Southern Jesuits grappling with the church's call to integrate religious faith and social justice, an old high school teacher of mine reminded the assembly that, "In the words of Robert Penn Warren, 'What is man but his passion.'"[1] His point, he said, was that we had to be passionately concerned about the poor and about building the reign of Christ. Nothing else mattered.

Understanding Jesus in the gospels deepens our insight, and beckons us to enter more deeply, into *faithjustice*. Reading Jesus, however, is not like meeting a hero in a first novel. Instead, the evangelists sketch their Jesus in front of a broad and deep backdrop into which are woven the themes and images in the Hebrew scriptures developed in chapter 1. It is against this tapestry that the first half of this chapter presents major lines of what Jesus says and does, discussing, in turn, healing, three famous speeches, the dominant image of the Reign of God, and Jesus' dual passion for Abba God and God's Reign. This shapes an answer to his own question to the disciples who have walked with him, "Who do you say that I am?"

Understanding Jesus also means sampling the rich reflection of the faith community formed among his disciples, beginning with the first generations who considered themselves heirs of his Spirit. They were charged by him to preach his good news and were known as followers of his way. Contemporary Christians too, baptized in the same Spirit, look to the dynamic power of that Spirit of Jesus to shape their own embodiment of his way. The second half of this chapter addresses the role of the Spirit in their lives and the ways the Spirit empowers them to live a contemporary *faithjustice*.

Before we turn to the pages of the New Testament, however, it may be helpful to take a quick look at some aspects of the social and cultural situation into which Jesus of Nazareth is born. We do this because, as has happened for two thousand years, those who read the scriptures tend to imagine them in their own culture and environment, transposing the people and events into another time and place

and, in the process, losing some of the meaning and integrity of what
they are reading.

Jesus the Peasant

Jesus is presented to us as a carpenter. Our twenty-first century image
of carpenters is filled with pictures of middle-class union members
working in their own shop or on an urban construction site, driving
a truck with their name stenciled on the doors, owning their own
home and boat, and being paid a solid union wage on an hourly basis.
We read the sacred texts as modern people who live in large urban
areas, work in a highly technological society, drive to the supermarket, and who espouse values like democracy, individualism, universal
education, and upward mobility, all of which are recent developments
in human history. As scripture scholar Jerome H. Neyrey explains:

> Jesus lived not in a city, but in a small insignificant village.
> In Mark's gospel, for example, Jesus never enters a city at
> all until he goes up to Jerusalem for Passover. He lived
> exclusively in the peasant villages in the countryside. Jesus
> was an artisan; this meant that his family was landless, and
> so he was a day laborer. This put him near the bottom of
> the social ladder of his day.[2]

As Neyrey further explains, drawing on a growing body of studies
applying the social sciences to the time of the scriptures, Jesus lived
in an agrarian society unlike our industrial and technological one.
His world was highly stratified with a few aristocrats (3 to 5 percent)
at the top, living in the cities and controlling most of the wealth,
largely land. The aristocrats are joined by a small "retainer group"
consisting of scribes, priests, and merchants.

Ninety percent of the people in Jesus' society are located at the
bottom of the social ladder. Few of these people live in the cities;
most are peasant farmers or, worse, day laborers or slaves. "Jesus is
part of that ninety percent." Neyrey further explains the conditions
under which the peasants worked:

> Peasants, moreover, lived narrow, confined lives. They
> were always heavily taxed, and taxes in Jesus' time in
> Galilee could devour fifty percent of the produce. With
> heavy taxation, drought, and the like, peasants basically

lived a subsistence existence, just on the edge of survival. Many of them were being rapidly forced off their land at this time because of debt foreclosure.[3]

When Jesus talks of the forgiveness of debt, then, it will carry major significance among his largely peasant audiences.

Those of us who are U.S. residents have been socialized in a country where the separation of church and state is a tenet of our Constitution and a factor in the communities in which we reside and in our understanding of our own religion. It was not so in Jesus' time, and that is a critical factor in understanding his mission and message. As Neyrey explains, "...'power' and 'religion' were almost totally inter-twined in Jesus' day."[4] Imagine contemporary Iran, he suggests, where religious leaders also function as the political elite. In Jesus' society, the Jerusalem Temple, along with its system and priesthood, were controlled by the high priests and the Sadducees, who were the dom-inant political strata as well. They even collected taxes for the Romans.

Lastly, it is important to remember that Jesus lived in very tur-bulent and violent times. Numerous "bandits" rose up against the local authorities and the grinding tax system. There were also many "prophets" who proclaimed a new deliverance from oppression in Judea. Similarly, many others proclaimed themselves "king" and sought economic reforms in the frightful plight of the peasants. Neyrey concludes that this would shape the perceptions of Jesus by all who heard him or heard of him:

> Jesus was a very "political" figure, in the sense that he would be perceived by peasants and elites alike as having much in common with the host of messianic prophets and peasant kings flourishing at the time. The issue is not that Jesus urged political revolution or any such social pro-gram. Rather, given the pervasive scene of endlessly aris-ing prophets and (bandit) kings in Jesus' time, his words and actions would naturally lead people to think of him in terms of these political currents.[5]

With the vast differences between the views of the rich and the poor, Jesus would be seen in radically different terms. When the peasants acclaim him as a "king," Herod, the Temple, and the Jerusalem elites would view Jesus as a constant social and political threat. This background can help us then better appreciate both the actions of Jesus and the reactions of various people in the gospels.

Jesus the Healer

One of the most significant and continuing actions of Jesus is healing of the sick, possessed, and disabled. In chapter 1 of Mark's Gospel, in a busy day at the beginning of the Galilean ministry, Jesus cures a demoniac, Simon's mother-in-law, and, at sunset, a crowd of the ill and possessed who are brought to the door of the house of Simon and Andrew. When he sends his disciples out on mission, he charges them to cast out demons and to heal the sick: "Then Jesus summoned his twelve disciples and gave them authority over unclean spirits, to cast them out, and to cure every disease and every sickness" (Matt 10:1).

Healing is also an early sign in the Acts of the Apostles of the power of Christ's Spirit active in the person of the apostles after the resurrection and ascension of Jesus into heaven (Acts 3:1–10). In the centuries that followed, healing became an intrinsic part of the church's ministry and continues as such in a vast network of hospitals, nursing homes, and home health services. Why is healing so central to the ministry of Jesus?

In Jesus' society, those who were ill or disabled—often considered to be caused by possession by a demon—were isolated from the community. Leviticus required, for example, that those who were judged to have leprosy were to cry out, "Unclean, unclean" (13:45–46), when approached by others. Like sickness or disability today, people were marginalized by their condition and alienated from the community.

What does Jesus do when he encounters those who have been cut off and marginalized by sickness and disability? First, he steps across the boundaries and social barriers around them. Then, in direct violation of the religious laws, he touches them; Jesus puts his hands on their eyes, ears, tongues, or other affected areas. By that action, Jesus risks being declared unclean himself and ostracized just as they have been.[6] After he touches and heals these people, Jesus often instructs them to return home (Matt 9:6–7; Mark 2:11, 5:19, 8:26; Luke 8:39) or, with lepers, to go and show themselves to the priest (Matt 8:4; Luke 5:14, 17:14) so that they could be declared clean and then allowed to return home (Lev 14:8). He is restoring them, not just to good health, but back to their families and communities, setting relationships right among them. Healing brings the reconciliation that is central to the jubilee tradition and, as Jesus himself claims, a sign that the Reign of God is among them (Luke 11:20).

In contemporary society, sickness and disability continue to isolate people from their families and communities. Some diseases legally require isolation or quarantine, even today. In addition, our struggle over recent decades to effect architectural, mechanical, or social changes on behalf of persons with disabilities is often called "handicapped access," reflecting the fact that, without these changes, such persons were often unable to participate in the life of the community in public buildings, supermarkets, movie theatres, museums, and even places of worship. Healing ministry, then, can be seen today as an expression, not only of God's compassion and healing, but of the covenant with God that requires covenantal relationships among all people.[7]

Three Jesus Proclamations

The Nazareth Speech

From the beginning of his adult ministry, when the public Jesus first appears, the evangelists carefully set the tone for his ministry and proclamation. To use political imagery, his campaign speech in the synagogue in Nazareth underscores themes familiar to his listeners and is designed to attract followers touched and moved by those themes.

In the fourth chapter of Luke, Jesus returns from the baptism at the Jordan, filled with the Holy Spirit and the purification of the desert temptations:

> When he came to Nazareth, where he had been brought up, he went to the synagogue on the sabbath day, as was his custom. He stood up to read, and the scroll of the prophet Isaiah was given to him. He unrolled the scroll and found the place where it was written:
>
> "The Spirit of the Lord is upon me,
>   because he has anointed me
>   to bring good news to the poor.
> He has sent me to proclaim release to the captives
>   and recovery of sight to the blind,
>   to let the oppressed go free,
> to proclaim the year of the Lord's favor."

> And he rolled up the scroll, gave it back to the attendant, and sat down. The eyes of all in the synagogue were fixed on him. Then he began to say to them, "Today this scripture has been fulfilled in your hearing." (Luke 4:16–21)

"The year of the Lord's favor!" This is not new coinage, a hired speechwriter's new frontier or kinder, gentler America. As the U.S. Catholic bishops explain:

> Jesus himself is the proclamation of the Great Jubilee. "Today," He added, "this scripture passage is fulfilled in your hearing" (Luke 4:21). In the fullness of time, it is Jesus who proclaims the good news to the poor. It is Jesus who gives sight to the blind and frees the oppressed. By His words and above all by His actions, Jesus ushered in a "year of the Lord's favor," becoming in His passion and death the ransom for many (Mark 10:45). "The Jubilee, a 'year of the Lord's favor,' characterizes all the activity of Jesus."[8]

This is the long-promised jubilee year. In choosing this highly charged title, Luke's Jesus asserts that he is coming to restore things to right order. Jesus invokes the full imagery of what the Hebrew scriptures promised: freeing slaves, canceling debts, return of property, and restoration as God's kinship community to the land.

Too often, we forget that Jesus himself was a Jew, a child of the Hebrew scriptures. He grew up with these texts; listened to them; and heard the rabbis teach and interpret them. In his presence, his mother and father and the elders discussed and prayed these texts; and people all around him knew and quoted them freely. He was steeped in these scriptures.

Jesus is presented as a man of the synagogue, in the habit of attending, Luke says, rooting Jesus deeply in the tradition. So he understands the scriptures, what they explicitly say and the long and deep history that gives the texts body and sinew. So when Luke's Jesus says, I've come "to bring good news to the poor....to proclaim release to the captives and recovery of sight to the blind, to let the oppressed go free, to proclaim the year of the Lord's favor," this cannot be taken as a casual declaration. This Jesus projects the whole matrix of meanings: the goodness and right order of creation; our own stewardship of this creation; how Yahweh meant us to live together in covenant community, sharing the goods of creation; and the privileged place of the *anawim* at the heart of faithful living.

As a campaign speech, Luke sets a definitive tone for us, one which his listeners recognize in the texts and the themes from Isaiah echoing through them. This Jesus is about the business of rebuilding the community of creation, giftedness, compassion, and *faithjustice*. In fact, Luke tailors the scriptural references to his own purposes, sharpening their impact by stressing their concreteness and universality. Luke rejects elements of Isaiah's text spiritualizing its meaning or narrowing the focus only to Israel.[9] Jesus speaks of the economically, physically, and socially poor, of those imprisoned for their debts, and of the downtrodden longing for a jubilee year.

The Lucan Jesus is positioning himself squarely in the line of the prophets: "Truly I tell you, no prophet is accepted in the prophet's hometown" (Luke 4:24). As in the cycle of Baal, Jesus comes as the prophets do, calling the people to care for the *anawim* as the litmus test of their fidelity to Yahweh and their identity as God's people. People's reactions, strikingly early in the gospels, are like that of their ancestors:

> When they heard this, all in the synagogue were filled with rage. They got up, drove him out of the town, and led him to the brow of the hill on which their town was built, so that they might hurl him off the cliff. But he passed through the midst of them and went on his way. (Luke 4:28–30)

While Jesus eludes them this first time, ultimately he will share the traditional prophet's fate in his Roman execution.

The Mountain Speech

Continuing along his campaign trail, Jesus names the people who are members of his party. The list resonates with scriptural antecedents:

> Blessed are the poor in spirit, for theirs is the kingdom of heaven.
> Blessed are those who mourn, for they will be comforted.
> Blessed are the meek, for they will inherit the earth.
> Blessed are those who hunger and thirst for righteousness, for they will be filled.

> Blessed are the merciful, for they will receive mercy.
> Blessed are the pure in heart, for they will see God.
> Blessed are the peacemakers, for they will be called children of God.
> Blessed are those who are persecuted for righteousness' sake, for theirs is the kingdom of heaven.
> Blessed are you when people revile you and persecute you and utter all kinds of evil against you falsely on my account. Rejoice and be glad, for your reward is great in heaven, for in the same way they persecuted the prophets who were before you. (Matt 5:3–12)[10]

In Matthew, there seem to be at least two distinct groups with whom Jesus identifies his ministry. The first and most obvious group is the *anawim* themselves, represented here by the poor, those who mourn, and the meek. These three reflect the older and probably original beatitudes,[11] and are also found in Luke 6:20b–23. Then Jesus names a second group that we might call, in a more contemporary term, the advocates. These are those who are merciful; those who seek righteousness or justice; those who are peacemakers; and those who are persecuted for the sake of justice. This second group is those who take the side of the poor, those who stand by them over against an oblivious and often hostile society. Jesus himself belongs to both groups.

The Judgment Speech

The cause and party of Jesus are then clearly named. He has come to set right the original vision of Yahweh, and Jesus will be received by the *anawim* and those who stand with them. This is not enough for Jesus, however. Not only is his community of followers to have a special care for the little ones of the scriptures, but also at the end of his public ministry Matthew's Jesus makes clear to them a new and profound identification with the poor. This radical identification Jesus takes upon himself. The scene is the familiar judgment story in Matthew 25, Jesus' last discourse before the passion narrative.

In the judgment parable, the divine Son of Man separates the assembled nations into two groups, likened to sheep and goats. To those on his right the king says:

> Come, you that are blessed by my Father, inherit the kingdom prepared for you from the foundation of the world;

for I was hungry and you gave me food, I was thirsty and you gave me something to drink, I was a stranger and you welcomed me, I was naked and you gave me clothing, I was sick and you took care of me, I was in prison and you visited me.

Those whom Jesus calls "the righteous" then ask:

Lord, when was it that we saw you hungry and gave you food, or thirsty and gave you something to drink? And when was it that we saw you a stranger and welcomed you, or naked and gave you clothing? And when was it that we saw you sick or in prison and visited you?

The judge's answer has echoed down through the ages: "Truly I tell you, just as you did it to one of the least of these who are members of my family, you did it to me."

On the other side of the scene wait those Jesus calls goats, to whom the king then says:

You that are accursed, depart from me into the eternal fire prepared for the devil and his angels; for I was hungry and you gave me no food, I was thirsty and you gave me nothing to drink, I was a stranger and you did not welcome me, naked and you did not give me clothing, sick and in prison and you did not visit me.

These people in turn ask: "Lord, when was it that we saw you hungry or thirsty or a stranger or naked or sick or in prison, and did not take care of you?" The king's answer is equally famous: "Truly I tell you, just as you did not do it to one of the least of these, you did not do it to me." (Matt 25:34–46)

In creating this dramatic scene, Jesus carries on the royal tradition we saw at Ebla and in the scriptures ("the kingdom prepared for you from the foundation of the world"). As the Hebrew kings were charged with responsibility for the *anawim*, now the same theme is repeated in the image of Christ the vindicator at the end of history. Jesus picks up the royal mantle of caring for the little ones and the poor, giving Christ the King a fullness of meaning that easily could escape us in this post-royalty modern world. There also is not just judgment of good and evil here in this scene, but the apocalyptic revelation of what had been hidden, the very presence of Christ in the little ones of history.

As we saw in chapter 1, the community and the kings of Israel failed at their duty to the poor. Yahweh the Lord then became the defender of the poor and the liberator of the oppressed. Jesus then is seen in light of that revelation and the evolving responsibility for the *anawim*, for he incorporates into himself the duty of the people, the kings, and the Lord Yahweh. Embodying within himself the justice of God[12] Jesus then calls his disciples to the same mission.

The Reign of God[13]

As the dominant motif of his preaching, teaching, and actions, Jesus proclaims the Reign of God, which he talks about continuously, as his dream of how the world was meant to be. When Jesus preaches about the Reign of God he is taking his listeners back to the Genesis vision of original blessing, the ancient sense of right order and justice. The reign of God is a symbol loaded for Jesus' listeners with Yahweh's rule, the establishment of *faithjustice,* and the coming of the Messiah who will bring it all to pass.[14] Those who listen to Jesus are thrust deep into the faith awareness of how they were created and called to be with God and the covenant community, into the web of kinship relations which they have with one another and with Yahweh their vindicator and ruler. The poor and oppressed hear this message, laden with jubilee promise, with special sensitivity and renewed hope for its fulfillment in Jesus.

The entire ministry of Jesus the Nazarene is shaped by the three fundamental themes that underlie God's original vision, now the Reign of God that Jesus proclaims. Jesus actually embodies them personally and in many relationships with the people around him. First of all, to a people in poverty Jesus proclaims a ministry of life-in-abundance: He is the vine from which the branches draw sustenance and the bread of life.[15] The first "sign" in John's Gospel is at a wedding banquet, making wine for the guests. Jesus heals the sick, consoles the grieving, and literally gives life to the dead.

His persistent practice of fellowship meals with public sinners, tax collectors, and other outcasts not only rejects society's taboos, but affirms the underlying goodness of all people, created in God's own image. Among the marginalized, Jesus is particularly affirming in his relationships to women. He betrays "no hesitation in engaging in serious conversation with women, even though this was frowned on in the teachings of his people...."[16] He treats women with respect and dignity; women are considered to be his disciples; and the Reign is clearly for women as well as men.[17] The use of parables as Jesus' characteristic teaching mechanism shows that his understanding of fundamental goodness extends beyond human persons to nature itself.[18]

In Jesus, the stewardship theme is equally prominent in both teaching and action. Not only do his parables underscore the proper use and sharing of the goods of creation (e.g., the already rich harvester in Luke 12); but in his encounter with the Rich Young Man Jesus applies that same lesson. As Mark tells the story, found in all the synoptics, a man runs up to Jesus and asks him, "Good Teacher, what must I do to inherit eternal life?" Jesus repeats the core commandments to the young man who declares that he has been faithful to these prescriptions since he was a child.

> Jesus said to him, "Why do you call me good? No one is good but God alone. You know the commandments: 'You shall not murder; You shall not commit adultery; You shall not steal; You shall not bear false witness; You shall not defraud; Honor your father and mother.'" He said to him, "Teacher, I have kept all these since my youth." Jesus, looking at him, loved him and said, "You lack one thing; go, sell what you own, and give the money to the poor, and you will have treasure in heaven; then come, follow me." When he heard this, he was shocked and went away grieving, for he had many possessions. Then Jesus looked around and said to his disciples, "How hard it will be for those who have wealth to enter the kingdom of God!" (Mark 10:17–23)

The point here is not that wealth or goods in themselves are evil; nor does Jesus ask this total sacrifice of every other person of wealth whom he encounters. Rather, Jesus perceives that this young man, to whom he takes an immediate liking, is no longer steward of his gifts. The young man has been hooked by them. Having become both owner and owned, his possessions are now a barrier to his relationship to God and God's people.

Jesus himself is tempted from stewardship to ownership. In the encounter with Satan in the desert that characterizes the forces that would try to move him from his own truth, Jesus is tempted to turn stones into bread, seize power over the kingdoms of the world, and claim divine protection and status for himself. Each temptation is, in a sense, a claim of ownership that would twist the purpose of these very gifts from the service of God and those around Jesus to his own aggrandizement. Jesus refuses these desert temptations. Ultimately, Jesus will affirm his own stewardship, even over his life, in his Gethsemane prayer that "your will be done" and then in his blood.

Finally, Jesus embodies the covenant community theme by his constant reaching out to draw all others into the love of "Abba, my Father." As noted above, Jesus reaches out to women in his own society and to those considered outcasts. More than that, however, Jesus crosses the boundaries between Jews and Samaritans and even extends the ministry of compassion to Gentiles. Those who belong to the band of Jesus will be, not his servants, but sisters and brothers, children of one God. They are to be part of the new covenant in his own blood and in the Spirit.

Most importantly, Jesus reveals a clear personal awareness of the central role of the *anawim* in the covenant community. In addition to frequent teaching about their blessedness and the perils of wealth, Jesus includes them among his own disciples. He constantly goes out of his way to heal the sick, blind, lepers, and others on the margins of society even though their condition was attributed by most people to sinfulness and divine disfavor. Finally, Jesus effects his own dying reconciliation of a criminal executed with him.

Through his proclamations, parables, healing, and other actions, Jesus carries on the royal tradition of Israel. He proclaims his Reign as one of justice, peace, and love; it will be home for the *anawim* and those who stand with them in solidarity. God's Reign is the pearl of great price, the treasure found hidden in the field for which one would sell every other possession and pay any cost (Matt 13:44–46).

When he waxes rhapsodic in the Last Supper discourse on the night before he died, Jesus translates his mission from Reign imagery back into the intimate kinship language of the Sinai covenant which his death and resurrection transforms anew:

> ...that they may all be one. As you, Father, are in me and I
> am in you, may they also be in us, so that the world may
> believe that you have sent me. The glory that you have
> given me I have given them, so that they may be one, as we
> are one, I in them and you in me, that they may become
> completely one, so that the world may know that you have
> sent me and have loved them even as you have loved me.
> (John 17:21–23)

The Creator's vision has become the dream of Jesus, symbolized in the profoundly theological and scriptural language of God's Reign. The dream is rooted in the realities of creation's goodness, human stewardship, and the covenant community of Israel. The web of relationships that bound Yahweh to the chosen people is transformed in the repeated refrain at the Last Supper of the oneness of Jesus, the disciples, Abba, and the Spirit.

Jesus understands this vision of Yahweh and makes it his own in his public ministry, personal encounters, and preaching. Appropriating this vision to himself, Jesus further develops the insight of the Hebrew scriptures that without the doing of justice, God remains unknown. Using the royal judgment scene of Matthew 25, Jesus takes his followers beyond both caring for and standing with the poor. He identifies himself with the *anawim* and blesses those who see him and reach out to him in them.

Those standing before the judgment seat are reported to be surprised by the royal announcement of judgment; they ask, "When did we see you hungry, Lord?" They, both the just and the unjust, knew the commands of justice, the scholars tell us; but they are shocked by Jesus' identification with the poor.[19] In his answer, Jesus the Christ reveals himself now as the center of a new web of relationships between God and us, a new covenant of kinship with the *anawim* as its privileged locus. By responding or not to the least of Jesus' sisters and brothers, those under judgment have responded—or not—to Christ. Without the doing of justice, Christ remains unknown!

It is important to remind ourselves about whom Jesus is speaking: the hungry, the homeless, the naked, and the poor. Against the background of the scriptures' widows, orphans, and strangers, he is literally naming those in his society who are the lowest classes, physically the worst off, and socially the outcasts. Reading these texts in our time and our nation, Jesus is saying that he is to be found in people on welfare, those in the supermarket lines using food stamps, the homeless and ill who accost us on our streets, and those suffering in HIV/AIDS shelters and mental institutions. In this era of mean-spiritedness in politics when some would restore public hangings in county squares, Jesus explicitly identifies himself with those languishing in prisons and on death row.

Those who were proper and religious in his time found this message of Jesus unacceptable as preached. He challenged their assumptions about religious practices and being right with God just as the prophets had done before him. He had to be killed, just as the prophets were.

Life in the Spirit

For those who follow this Jesus in the present century, the unfolding of *faithjustice* parallels the revelation of who God is and how God has been involved in the lives of the faith community across history. Chapter 1 explored the meaning of *faithjustice* against the background of the Creator Yahweh who was intimately involved in the lives of the Hebrew people, who pitched a tent among them, and who could only be found inextricably caught up into their relations with one another. Jesus the Nazarene builds upon and expands that understanding and deepens our grasp of *faithjustice* through his own ministry of compassion for the little ones and commitment to building the Reign of God. The developing revelation of life in the Spirit of Jesus, which continues from Pentecost to the present, adds to and enriches our understanding of how the poor continue to hold the center of our relationship to God. The *anawim* remain the privileged gauge of our faith, and justice maintains its constant challenge to all who claim to follow Jesus.

We often call the Spirit the "sanctifier," the one who makes us holy. The first letter of John invites us to reflect upon that role of the Spirit:

> Beloved, let us love one another, because love is from God; everyone who loves is born of God and knows God. Whoever does not love does not know God, for God is love. God's love was revealed among us in this way: God sent his only Son into the world so that we might live through him. In this is love, not that we loved God but that he loved us and sent his Son to be the atoning sacrifice for our sins. Beloved, since God loved us so much, we also ought to love one another.
>
> We love because he first loved us. Those who say, "I love God," and hate their brothers or sisters, are liars; for those who do not love a brother or sister whom they have seen, cannot love God whom they have not seen. The commandment we have from him is this: those who love God must love their brothers and sisters also. (1 John 4:7–11, 19–21)

Without explicitly naming the Spirit, this text represents one small, yet essential, part of the early Christian community's evolving reflection on who Jesus was and who they were as his followers, baptized in

his Spirit. By discussing the love dynamic at the core of their relationship to God and one another, the text prods us to examine further who we now are as their descendants, heirs of the same Spirit. It
takes us beyond the sense of our own truth developed in reflection
on God's revelation to the Hebrew people and in Jesus.

In each stage of God's self-revelation, there is a correlative revelation of who we are. When God's own goodness, creativity, and love
for the community are revealed, that revelation underscores our own
goodness, creativity, and bondedness to one another and to the earth.
Jesus then says to us that he has come to set right the relationships
among us, restoring the Reign in a year of the Lord. He identifies
himself with the poor in new ways, and tells us that the poor and
those who advocate for them are blessed in every generation.
Building the Reign then remains a priority concern for those yearn-
ing to follow Jesus. In the preceding text from John's first epistle, the
community continues to reflect upon our truth in the light of the
Holy Spirit.

Stepping back to take the long view for a moment, theologians
sometimes speak of salvation history as divided into three phases corresponding to the three-personed revelation of who God is. In other
words, the Age of the Creator[20] corresponds to the revelation of God
living in the midst of the Hebrew people, passionately caring for
them, and continually drawing them back to fidelity by the prophets
and other chosen ones.

Salvation History

Age of the Creator	Jesus	Age of the Spirit

The Age of Jesus comprises that very brief period of the life of
Jesus of Nazareth reflected in the gospels. The New Testament Jesus
is seen through the eyes of faith as God breaking into human history,
proclaiming the year of the Lord, reaching out to the *anawim* of
Yahweh, and profoundly identifying with them. Jesus passionately
prophesies against those who would substitute the oppression of the
law for the living kinship bond of Yahweh and Yahweh's people. Jesus
calls God "Abba" in a new revelation of intimacy with God. Then, in
death and resurrection, Jesus seals this God's love for us in blood and
testifies to "his way" as the definitive model for all of us as children
of God. In presenting that model, Jesus tells us that he is giving us "a
new commandment: love one another." More than the love of neighbor required in the Jewish Covenant, more than loving others as we

would have them love us, Jesus sets a new and higher standard, "Just as I have loved you, you also should love one another" (John 13:34). Then, in a final movement, Father and Son together send the Spirit to the disciples to empower the continuation of the Reign according to the pattern of Christ Jesus.

The Age of the Spirit then spans human history from the powerful and charismatic first day of Pentecost to the end of time as we shall know it, when Jesus will come again as ultimate liberator. This age is about us and the presence and power of God in us. It is about now and this place, about billions of people struggling on one small planet for life and love, and the simple realities of personal journeys, families, work, birth, life, and death. Understanding the Spirit is about our lives.

John's letter proclaims that God is present in the midst of us as a dynamic force rather than a static physical presence. From our point of view, the letter suggests that we will experience this Spirit not so much in one particular person but in a community of persons. God is present especially in the very privileged movement and dynamic of loving. The Johannine reflection upon the Jesus-event here is that God is our loving parent and so we are sisters and brothers to one another. God's Spirit is life-force and bond in the kinship community, the very cement of our bondedness as a loving people. To say that one loves the Lord God, then, without loving the bone and marrow of the sisters and brothers who rub against us all day, for John that is a lie. It is the foolish and self-deceptive illusion of children playing games in the marketplace of life. We cannot say we love the unseen God without a passionate concern for God's people enfleshed in the concrete here and now.

For most of us who grew up Catholic, however, this Holy Spirit has always been somewhat difficult to grasp. Our understanding of the Spirit did not get much beyond the bird imagery that we learned from grammar school religion classes and far too much popular church art. The bird did not seem to have much else to do either. After all, Jesus was the savior, sent by the Father. The Spirit seemed an unnecessary appendage. Being called the Holy Ghost was not much help either to a generation attuned to horror movies and Halloween. Despite the fact that "ghost" was derived from the Germanic word for spirit, the reality was that most children considered this member of the Trinity to be somewhat of a phantom anyway.

In a scaled-down version of Thomistic theology fed to high schoolers before Vatican II, the Spirit was described as the bond of love between the Father and the Son, who was the full image of the

Father's complete self and thus possessed the fullness of Godness. Although it may have looked logical, it seemed to have little to do with real life. Most students memorized a list of gifts of the Spirit and other aspects of the mysterious third person of the Trinity, received years earlier in confirmation. Nevertheless, the Spirit still seemed a distant shadow compared to the Father and Son and even to Mary and the saints.[21] In fact, except for charismatics, most adult Roman Catholics still have about the same use for the Spirit now as we had then.

Only in college, when Father Yamauchi got down to the working end of this Spirit did theology and reality come face to face. Look at Jesus, he said. What does the Spirit do in the life of the Nazarene? Jesus enters onto the public stage after a private early adult life, living and working in Capernaum. His own prayer, reflection, and experience finally coalesce in a sense of public mission and preaching that begins with the Jordan baptism by John. There in that dramatic moment Jesus sees the skies open and "the Spirit of God descending like a dove." Then, the voice from heaven proclaims, "This is my Son, the beloved, with whom I am well pleased" (Matt 3:16–17). It is both divine confirmation of his own sense of mission and the affirming power to carry it out in the ministry on which he then embarks.

From the banks of the Jordan at the beginning of the public life it is the Spirit who energizes, empowers, and enables Jesus in the passion of his life and ministry: Abba God and the restored Reign of God! In this action, the Spirit manifests its creative power, recalling the power that hovered over the waters of Genesis and brought forth order from chaos. It is the same power that brought forth a new creation in Mary's conception of Jesus (Luke 1:35).

The Spirit appears first as this power moving Jesus to take to the road in his public ministry. Jesus claims this Spirit is his motivation and drive in his first reported sermon in Nazareth: "The Spirit of the Lord is upon me...anointed me...to bring good news to the poor..." (Luke 4:18). The Spirit is crucial then to the first phase of Jesus' public life, the Galilee mission of preaching, teaching, and healing concentrated mostly in the towns and villages of his native region.

Later, the Jordan experience of the favor of God seems to occur again for Jesus standing in the cloud on the mountain of transfiguration, although this time the Spirit is not visible in dove form. "[F]rom the cloud a voice said, 'This is my Son, the beloved; with him I am well pleased; listen to him'" (Matt 17:5). This event occurs immediately after Jesus tells the disciples for the first time that he must go to Jerusalem to confront the leadership, to be tortured, and to die. This begins the second and shorter phase of Jesus' public life, the Jerusalem mission, in which Jesus turns his face to Jerusalem.

This experience itself manifests a second action of the Spirit in the life of Jesus and others, a confirming and refining of his mission. Any original expectation that Jesus and the disciples may have had of widespread acceptance of his preaching of the Reign has now faded. Instead of the conversion of the Jews, Jesus has experienced increasing opposition of the religious and social leadership symbolized in the constant parade of scribes, elders, and Pharisees sent from Jerusalem to oppose him. He thus becomes even more the prophet and, as prophets before, proceeds to Jerusalem to confront those who have perverted the covenant relationships.

This determination is the work of the Spirit of Yahweh the vindicator, the prophetic Spirit of Isaiah, Jeremiah, Micah, and all the prophets of the covenant. This Spirit is passion, strength, and wisdom. This Spirit provides the endurance that faces adversity, suffers persecution, and remains faithful to the end. This is a missioning Spirit that breaks through locked doors and failed hearts on Pentecost and recommissions the followers of Jesus to cast aside fears and shattered illusions of greatness and to put on a boldness that seems beyond them. That boldness is the work of a Spirit that Jesus called the Advocate, "The Advocate, the holy spirit, whom the Father will send in my name, will teach you everything, and remind you of all that I have said to you" (John 14:26).

For those who stand in the shoes of Jesus as *alter Christus,* another Christ, the Spirit is the same power for us to love the Lord God and to preach God's Reign. Filled with this Spirit at baptism and confirmation, we experience both the creative power of the Spirit making us new people and its confirming, refining, and recommissioning action. The Spirit makes the healing good news possible in our mouths, like the Jesus of Galilee. It also is the Spirit of the Jesus of Jerusalem, however, who sharpens our tongues for prophetic challenges to those who forget what the Reign of God is meant to be. It makes us advocates for those for whom the good news comes.

Understanding Ourselves as "We"

This kind of analysis puts twentieth-century Christians smack in the middle of a relational faith understanding of who we are flowing out of the gradual unfolding of who the Trinity is. Against a culture that defines self as I and me and mine, of radical individualism, Christian truth offers a radically relational understanding of the self. We understand who we are only in and through our relations to one another, especially in light of the knowledge of ourselves flowing out of knowing Trinity.

Look more closely at Jesus' practice of calling God "Abba, Father." In a more metaphysical sense that transcends gender, a relational understanding asks, what does it mean to be parent and to talk of God in these terms? What does it mean to be defined primarily in terms of relatedness? What is father-ness or mother-ness? The answer is to-the-child-ness. It is the total orientation to the well-being of the child. To go back to the creation story, we are reminded of the fullness of the original blessing where God, imaged now as a loving parent, gives us not only the earth for our happiness, but pours out divine goodness and power upon us and into us. God then sets us free to live as responsible co-creators, much as good parents must let go of their children and empower them to adult responsibility. God loves us with the passion of Abba, Jesus says.

What then is it to be a child, and to speak of Jesus in terms of son-ness? It means to-the-parent-ness, a radical orientation of the self to the will of the parent. Look at Jesus of Nazareth. How is Jesus portrayed in the gospels? What is said over and over again in as many ways and situations as possible? *I have come to do the Father's will.* If, as Robert Penn Warren declares, a person is his or her passions, then Jesus defines himself as to-the-father. "For whoever does the will of my Father in heaven is my brother and sister and mother" (Matt 12:50). "For whatever the Father does, the son does likewise" (John 5:19). "All things have been handed over to me by my Father" (Luke 10:22). "If you knew me, you would know my Father also" (John 8:19). "The Father and I are one" (John 10:30). "Have I been with you all this time, Philip, and you still do not know me? Whoever has seen me has seen the Father" (John 14:9). "I have called you friends, because I have made known to you everything that I have heard from my Father" (John 15:15). Finally, he will pray in the garden in those intense dramatic moments before the final confrontations with his enemies: "Abba, Father, for you all things are possible; remove this cup from me; yet, not what I want, but what you want" (Mark 14:36). Over and over again, when Jesus says he must be about his Father's business, he is trying to get through to his listeners his driving purpose and passion in life. He is a son per se, a child concerned only for its parent's desires.

Whereas "Father" was used for God only fifteen times in the Old Testament, "my Father" is used by Jesus twenty-seven times in

John, sixteen times in Matthew, and four times in Luke. For Jesus, "Abba" was an intimate word and its usage was meant to transform Israel's relationship to the Lord:

> Jesus in his own time needed to release the name of God from the remoteness to which it had been relegated. He revealed again a God who is *Emmanuel,* "God with us" (Mt 1:23). He was not denying his Jewish heritage when he gave the new name, *Abba,* to God. The whole Old Testament realisation of God's concern to save his people which was contained in the name, *Yahweh,* was subsumed under the name, *Abba,* and made accessible in a new way. Hallowing the name did not mean for Jesus, keeping it locked up, sacred, untouchable, never to be pronounced. We must surely take seriously Jesus' stance towards the untouchables of his society: the lepers, sinners, prostitutes, tax collectors. It was to them that he entrusted the name, *Abba,* as we have seen, and allowed it to be used by them, presumably running the risk of having it bandied about in the not too polite society in which he mixed. It was from out of this society that *Abba* found its way into the early church.[22]

God, whose name had become unpronounceable for observant Hebrews, became God the intimate parent, actually possessing the qualities and features of both loving mother and father. While we are challenged today not to masculinize God in ways that reinforce sexist thought and actual discrimination, our generation also is desperately in need of the intimacy of God who still can be *Abba* for us.[23]

Driven by his love for Abba God—being Son—Jesus moves in passionate action. The gospels portray him as almost obsessed, not for some abstract meditation on things eternal, but for the reality-transformation that he calls "the Reign of God." It is Jesus' obsession, a driving passion for what Abba God wants. Jesus understands God's Will by taking his listeners back to the first chapter of Genesis: to the goodness and giftedness of the earth; to stewardship of creation; to a creation-sharing community in which God dwells; and to personal and community responsibility for the little ones. The beauty and challenge of the original blessing is all there in his first public preaching:

> The Spirit of the Lord is upon me,
>   because he has anointed me
>   to bring glad tidings to the poor.

> He has sent me to proclaim release to the captives
>   and recovery of sight to the blind,
>   to let the oppressed go free,
>   to proclaim the year of the Lord's favor. (Luke 4:18–19)

Where does this all come from, this passion and preaching? The Spirit is upon me, Jesus says. The Spirit leads Jesus in his twofold mission: Abba and the Reign of God. The Spirit bonds Jesus to Yahweh and, in the same dynamic movement, to Yahweh's children, his sisters and brothers. And those who would pretend to separate these two loves are trying to tear apart the purpose and uniting dynamic of God's Spirit. The second command—loving your neighbor as yourself—is like the first, Jesus says. "On these two commandments hang all the law and the prophets" (Matt 22:40). Separating them is a lie, John's first epistle says (1 John 4:20). This is why it is not faith and justice, faith doing justice, faith-based justice, or faith with justice; it is faithjustice.

Now we understand. We other Christs are called to the same twofold passion of Jesus: Abba and the Reign of God. The pathos[24] of God, which inflamed the prophets and became the driving passion of Jesus of Nazareth, now seizes us. To be so possessed by the Spirit of God, however, is no common thing in these days of computers, technocrats, and poll-driven candidacies. In the dedication to the 1989 book *His Eminence and Hizzoner*, Edward Koch, then mayor of New York City, wrote the following:

> I dedicate this book to the City of New York and its people, whom I fiercely love. I conveyed that same thought in an epitaph I composed in 1987 after recovering from a stroke. It said: "He was fiercely proud of his Jewish faith; he fiercely defended the city of New York; and he fiercely loved the people of the city of New York." Bishop Edmond Egan, then of the Archdiocese, paid me a great compliment when he told me he loved my epitaph "because there are so few people who are fierce about anything."[25]

Sadly, too few people are "fierce about anything." In the face of that indifference, we now are called to stand in the place of Jesus across the Age of the Spirit, in fidelity to God and in service to our sisters and brothers, with a special passion for the *anawim*.

We can do this because the same Spirit that empowered and enabled Jesus in his mission is given to us, enabling us now in our mission, our truth. Even Jesus' prayer—"thy will be done" and "thy kingdom come"—becomes our own prayer, embodying both his passion for Abba God and his commitment to restoring the original vision of creation in the Reign of God.

> Our Father in heaven,
>> hallowed be your name.
>> Your kingdom come.
>> Your will be done,
>>> on earth as it is in heaven.
>> Give us this day our daily bread.
>> And forgive us our debts,
>>> as we also have forgiven our debtors.
>> And do not bring us to the time of trial,
>>> but rescue us from the evil one. (Matt 6:9–13)

The Spirit of God empowers and enables our fidelity and service, a fierce passion for the *anawim* and for justice because it has its source in and flows from the hearts of Abba God and Jesus. The Spirit creates *faithjustice* anew in the chaos of our time just as the Spirit of God hovered over the waters of Genesis, generated the new creation born in the assent of the young woman Mary of Nazareth, and boldly recreated the disciples of Jesus in the power of Pentecost.

Come, Holy Spirit, come!

QUESTIONS FOR REFLECTION AND DISCUSSION

1. What do the social conditions of Jesus' time have to tell us about the content and reception of his mission and message?

2. What is the "year of the Lord's favor" in Luke 4?

3. What is the social and theological significance of healing in the ministry of Jesus?

4. How does the Reign of God in the preaching of Jesus of Nazareth relate to the three central revelations from Genesis discussed in chapter 1?

5. Why does the Church continue a healing ministry in its hospitals, nursing homes, and other health services?

6. How do the revelations of God through Jesus of Nazareth and the Spirit of Pentecost fill out our understanding of ourselves as Christians and our responsibility for faithjustice?

7. Often people say that they do not hear this tradition preached in their parishes. Is this true in your experience? Why? Why not? What could you do to insure that this tradition is part of your parish life?

CHAPTER THREE

The Roots of Faithjustice

> The joys and the hopes, the griefs and the anxieties of the
> people of this age, especially those who are poor or in any
> way afflicted, these too are the joys and hopes, the griefs
> and anxieties of the followers of Christ.
>
> The Second Vatican Council (1965)

*In Dallas in 1961 at the Summer School of Catholic Action, a week-long reli-
gious program for high school students, Father Louis J. Twomey, S.J., taught
three courses: on racism, labor relations, and anti-communism. I attended all
three, in each being introduced into the body of Catholic social teaching that
was all too unknown to most Catholics. Those three courses represented three
axes around which revolved Lou's prophetic work for social justice in New
Orleans and across the world between 1947, when he established the Institute
of Human Relations at Loyola University, and his death in 1969.*

*Listening to Lou was a powerful experience, and often provoked the
kind of reactions described by his friend novelist Walker Percy, who was with
Lou in 1964 at a state campus appearance in South Louisiana:*

> *He stood up and gazed around at the assembled students and fac-
> ulty and said in his big hoarse orator's voice something like:
> "Why don't I see a single black face here?" Shocked silence.
> Outraged silence. Murmurings. Stirrings. Chair scrapings.
> Students rose angrily to defend, justify. After all it was only
> 1964 and that was a long time ago.*[1]

*I look back now and realize Lou was instrumental not only in providing me with
insights and information, but also in exposing me to a model of priest different
from the pastors of the parishes of my youth or the teachers in my high school.*

*In one respect, Lou was only one of more than a dozen prominent
"labor priests" across the United States who embodied the Catholic Church's*

effort to address the problems of workers and to keep the working class closely aligned to the Church while also keeping it free of supposed communist inroads. In another way, Lou was bigger than New Orleans and bigger than life. His Christ's Blueprint for the South, *a newsletter begun in 1948, introduced generations of Jesuits to the Church's social teaching. It reached far outside the Society of Jesus and across the world, inspiring Brother Andrew of Calcutta to found his community of Indian brothers to work among the poor. Lou's collected correspondence numbers 40,000 letters among which would be a few brief ones of my own as I wrote to request articles available from his regular "For the Asking" list.*

Before he died, Lou finally was honored for his work by presidents, judges, union and civic leaders, and even the Jesuit Superior General Pedro Arrupe. Arrupe asked Lou to help in drafting his 1967 letter "On the Interracial Apostolate" to Jesuits worldwide. Lou also was criticized as a "communist," "agitator," "carpetbagger," "nigger-lover," "rabid integrationist," "fellow traveler," and so forth by representatives of management interests, anti-communists, racists, prominent Catholics, and even some fellow Jesuits. One notable critic was well-known Catholic columnist William Buckley. Buckley had dismissed the right of Pope John XXIII to teach on social concerns as well as the substance of his 1961 encyclical letter Mater et Magistra *with the quip "Mater, si; Magistra, no." Because Lou rose to the pope's defense and criticized Buckley's position as "incredible and peevish," "flippancy," and "unworthy of high quality journalism," Buckley attacked Lou at length in an article in a national Catholic magazine in 1962 and in an address at Notre Dame University.*

❖ ❖ ❖

The joke when I arrived in Chicago for theology studies was that there were three ways to tell a run-down neighborhood: a police precinct station; a currency exchange; and "Marge's slum bus tour" at the opening of the school year. Sister Marjorie Tuite, O.P., was coordinator of the social formation program at the Jesuit School of Theology. In that capacity she brought a long history of personal commitment to racial and social justice into the education of Jesuit and other divinity students. Marge was a towering figure who encouraged, cajoled, nurtured, angered, and inspired students, irritated some faculty, and persisted in the task of trying to raise the level of consciousness of social realities and the depth of commitment to social justice in the entire academic community. Over monthly hamburgers at The Eagle in Hyde Park, Marge shared with me the frustrations of the task of doing social justice and laughed her great laugh at herself and life's vagaries.

❖ ❖ ❖

Around 1980, a young layman working with Jesuits as a member of the Jesuit Volunteer Corps attended a national meeting of Jesuits in social ministry. After our prolonged discussions of what was and was not being done by Jesuits in matters of peace and social justice and reflecting on the too frequent incongruity between our words and our deeds, he said, "In the area of social justice, Jesuits have great...(pause)...documents." Some years later, I was reminded of his comment in reading the following section of the U.S. Catholic bishops' 1986 pastoral letter Economic Justice for All:

> All the moral principles that govern the just operation of any economic endeavor apply to the church and its agencies and institutions; indeed the church should be exemplary....*We would be insincere were we to deny a need for renewal in the economic life of the church itself and for renewed zeal on the part of the church in examining its role in the larger context of reinforcing in U.S. society and culture those values that support economic justice.*[2]

Our pragmatic society rightfully demands that credibility hinge on actions, not words.

If the faith of the Judaeo-Christian scriptures is the ground in which is planted a contemporary faithjustice, then its roots are the faith experience, service and advocacy, and reflection upon social realities of the believing Christian community since apostolic times. That faith reflection took particular forms in the patristic and medieval periods, and, for Catholics at least, has been brought to its fullest bloom in the past 110 years in a comprehensive and continuing movement named modern Catholic social teaching. It is also called "our best kept secret."[3]

Understanding the basic contours of this body of thought and perceiving its developing trends is the purpose of this rather lengthy chapter. It combines a necessarily brief historical overview of our Christian social heritage with tight, concise treatments of the key pieces of the modern Catholic tradition. This approach balances the desire to introduce readers to these elements of Catholic social thought with the realistic expectation that many will never have the opportunity to study the full texts and their contexts and critics. Some basic understanding of two thousand years of development is essential, however, to fashioning a contemporary stance of faithjustice, which will be the focus of chapters 4 and 5.

Our secret is, first, that the Catholic Church has developed a substantial body of teaching on social, economic, political, and cultural matters. Secondly, our secret includes what that body of teaching contains.[4] The most recent widespread evidence for the existence of this great Catholic secret was the reaction of surprise, shock, disappointment, and even resistance of many American Catholics to the U.S. bishops' major pastoral letters on peace (1983) and economic justice (1986). For these Catholics, their bishops had gone beyond the pale, delving into matters not only un-American but outside authentic Catholic tradition. As a cursory reading of these letters would have shown, the bishops were carefully grounding their public positions in scripture, tradition, and this body of modern Catholic social teaching.

Modern Catholic social teaching, composed primarily of papal and conciliar documents, is unknown to most Catholic audiences for a number of reasons. The Washington-based Center of Concern[5] offers four:

1. The documents usually seem to be rather abstract, dry in content, and not very attractive to read.

2. The topics frequently are quite challenging, dealing as they do with controversial social issues, and therefore they may disturb readers and make them uncomfortable.

3. A "papal encyclical" is, at least in many people's minds, almost immediately associated with *On Human Life* (*Humanae Vitae*, 1968) and all the debates, disputes, and dissent over the Church's position on birth control.

4. In general, authoritative statements—whether from Church or government—have less attraction today than acts of authentic witness.[6]

To the center's reasons, I would add three of my own that reflect the evolution of American Catholicism.

First, most of us growing up Catholic in America in the period of the development of modern Catholic social thought were engaged in another more major social concern: becoming as American as possible and absorbing the civic faith of the nation. The dominant socioeconomic theme of our immigrant and post-immigrant upbringing in homes, schools, and parishes was to become productive, upstanding citizens above any criticism from our predominantly Protestant neighbors. The Catholic faithful had weathered three waves of anti-Catholic bigotry in the nineteenth century,[7] seen anti-Catholicism again rear its ugly head against Governor Al Smith's presidential candidacy, and finally succeeded in mainstreaming by the time of the election of Catholic President John Fitzgerald Kennedy.

This American Catholic success was not achieved without major efforts at good citizenship, controversies within the Catholic community about whether it was possible to be both American and Catholic, extraordinary hard work, and a high premium on educational excellence in the largely immigrant community. We also mingled great quantities of Catholic blood with other Americans in the Civil, Mexican, and World Wars, matching our patriotism to any who may have challenged our right to be here. Our movement in large numbers into the economic middle class and the professions by the mid-twentieth century was a sure sign that we had made it at last. In aggressively pursuing the business of becoming American, we were in many ways too busy to be aware of developing Catholic social thought.

Second, in the process of becoming Americans in a hostile environment, we also labored to construct a formidable Catholic culture whose parishes, schools of all levels, hospitals, nursing homes, and charitable agencies were a model private system, not only in America but also across the world. Not only did we erect fortress Catholicism, as it is sometimes called, through an admirable array of institutions; but we also reached out across the world, sending thousands of missionaries and millions of dollars to spread the faith to the unbaptized of Asia, Africa, and Latin America. In working hard to satisfy our Catholic agenda, as we were taught it, we were oblivious to Catholic social teaching.

Third, in the course of our successful journey to the middle of America, the majority of Catholics bought the American myth wholesale. For example, as early as 138 years ago,

> The president of the St. Vincent de Paul Society in 1865 assured the international organization in Paris that the American Catholic poor were poor only temporarily. Where there is health, temperance, and industry, there can be no poverty in the United States.[8]

By the middle of the twentieth century, the view that over time all industrious Americans would arrive at the relative security of the middle class was as dominant among Catholics as among other Americans. To the extent that the documents comprising the body of modern Catholic social teaching call into question assumptions underlying liberal capitalism and American free enterprise, as they do, those documents threaten to resurrect the American–Catholic tension resolved *de facto* by millions of mainstreamed Catholics. The documents remain unknown in part, then, because for too many of us the accusation of being un-American is far more stinging than that of being un-Christian or un-Catholic.

Charity and Action

It would be erroneous, however, to equate the ignorance of Catholic social teaching on the part of American Catholics with inaction on the social front. On the contrary, especially in the arena of charitable endeavors, the American community has been extremely active from the early stages of the Catholic Church in the United States.

In 1789, when John Carroll was elected the first bishop in the United States, there were no Catholic charitable institutions as such. The first institution in the territory that is now the United States had been started in New Orleans in 1727 by eleven Ursuline sisters from France. Begun first as a school, it opened an orphanage two years later to care for orphans who survived a massacre of French settlers by Natchez Indians.[9] Subsequently, the sisters began a hospital and a "house of refuge for women of questionable character."[10]

The first Catholic charitable institution in the original states was St. Joseph Academy that comprised a day school for poor children, a boarding school, and an orphanage in Emmitsburg, Maryland. It was founded by Sister Elizabeth Seton, the first American-born saint. Mother Seton established her community in 1809 and, by her death in 1821, her Sisters of Charity included twenty communities operating schools, orphanages, and many other charitable institutions.

Children were the focus of many of the earliest institutional efforts of the Catholic community, largely led by women religious:

> The haven for most Catholic dependent or neglected children was the orphan asylum. Of the seventy-seven private asylums founded for children by 1850, twenty-one were

> Catholic, usually staffed by the Sisters of Charity....Faced
> with staggering numbers, dioceses and congregations gen-
> erally built large congregate institutions.[11]

These facilities often provided safety-net homes for "half-orphans" whose families were temporarily unable or unwilling to care for their children. They provided a way for the Catholic community to care for its own and to preserve faith and culture as waves and waves of immigrants flooded New York, Boston, Baltimore, and Midwestern cities.[12]

At the center of church life and operating as an effective social agency was the Catholic parish. "Parishes offered training in English, citizenship classes, referrals for jobs, emergency assistance, and social opportunities, as well as religious instruction and devotions."[13] In addition, benevolent societies grew up in the immigrant communities, partly to protect the Catholics from secret societies such as the Masons and partly to ameliorate poverty and harsh economic times by such means as sickness and death benefits.[14]

In 1845, the Vincent de Paul Society was established in St. Louis through the leadership of Father John Timon, a Vincentian, and Judge Bryan Mullanphy. This was twelve years after the founding of the charitable organization by Frederick Ozanam in France. Twelve years later, the first confraternity of the Ladies of Charity was also established in St. Louis "to offer its own help to the poor through home visits and personal service, as well as material assistance."[15] In addition, the U.S. bishops meeting in the Second Council of Baltimore in 1866 recommended the establishment of Catholic industrial schools and protectories for youth to keep them out of reformatories hostile to Catholicism.

Other charitable efforts in the nineteenth century included: the founding of the Christ Child Society in 1887 to provide the service of laywomen to needy children; the establishment of foundling homes, which were a new type of orphanage, and shelters for pregnant women; and the development of Catholic homes for the aged. The first such home was the Lafon Asylum of the Holy Family, founded in 1842 in New Orleans by the Sisters of the Holy Family, to care for aged Black women. Twelve such homes for the aged had been established by the Little Sisters of the Poor by 1872.

By the turn of the twentieth century, 827 voluntary charitable institutions under Catholic auspices provided long-term care to the aged, the infirm, and dependent children. The U.S. bishops summarized the work of the religious congregations who carried the brunt of these efforts in their 1999 pastoral letter *In All Things Charity*:

Ten years later, in 1910, 445 Catholic orphanages and
institutions were caring for 88,860 dependent children. By
1919, the Sisters of Charity and the Daughters of Charity
operated sixty-two maternity hospitals, infant homes, and
orphanages, and cared for 10,653 infants and children.
Sisters of the Good Shepherd cared for 7,036 delinquent
and neglected girls in fifty-eight institutions. Sisters in
more than forty other congregations cared for another
41,000 infants and children. Religious priests and brothers
cared for 4,900 in their protectories, industrial schools,
and orphanages.[16]

This large institutional base also provided the opportunity for
Catholics to wade into the public debates over desertion, divorce,
alcohol, illegitimacy, and birth control in the early part of the twentieth century,[17] a tradition that continues to the present time.

During the twentieth century many such institutions became
part of formally organized diocesan Catholic Charities agencies.

There were five diocesan Catholic Charities agencies prior
to World War I. By 1931 there were 30 with 28 branches.
In 1985, there were 160 with 410 branch offices, as well as
175 residential and support service facilities offering specialized services for youth, the disabled, and the elderly.
While orphanages virtually disappeared during this
period because of reductions in parental mortality, especially maternal, and increased emphasis on adoption and
foster care, diocesan agencies and specialized child caring
institutions grew.[18]

Catholic Charities agencies now provide a wide range of human
and social services funded by a variety of church, private, and public
funds. According to its 2000 annual survey, member agencies of
Catholic Charities USA served 9.5 million individuals, providing
emergency shelter and permanent housing, food assistance, counseling, child care, adoption services, refugee resettlement, and a wealth
of other professional and volunteer resources.[19] These charities agencies constitute the largest private human service network in the
United States.

Catholic health care ministries evolved during this country's history as well, including such developments as hospitals, nursing
homes, urban and rural clinics, and home health services. The

Catholic Health Association (CHA) was founded in 1915 to respond to the widespread call for hospital standardization in the early part of the twentieth century. Its first president was Reverend Charles B. Moulinier, S.J., "Within five years, CHA had established itself as an effective national organization, with state and provincial conferences, an expanded executive board, and an official monthly journal."[20] CHA includes as members 592 hospitals, 272 long-term care facilities, 58 health systems, and 264 religious institutes. This represents extraordinary growth and development from the early eighteenth-century hospital begun in New Orleans by the Ursuline sisters. As with social services and schools, Catholic health care is the largest privately sponsored network in the country.

In an area that we might term social action or social change, the American Catholic experience is much more recent and limited. A primary concern of the Church, of course, focused on the labor movement, with major disputes among the hierarchy and grassroots Catholics about what position the Church should take on various strikes, lockouts, and, in the earliest days, on whether unions themselves should be condemned.[21] After resolution of the official Catholic position in favor of unions in the papal encyclical *Rerum Novarum* in 1891, the twentieth-century American Church promoted training of labor leaders and rank-and-file members and better labor-management relations through institutes of industrial relations and labor schools, often based in Catholic universities. These are associated more popularly with the labor priests who became highly visible especially in the forties, fifties, and sixties.

Catholic universities also provided a home for the development of social work as a profession and the field of sociology. Loyola University of Chicago began the first Catholic social work school in 1912, followed by Fordham University in 1916. The National Catholic School of Social Service was begun in 1920 by the National Conference of Catholic Women and later joined to the school of social work at Catholic University after World War II.[22] Social work schools offered knowledge and skills gained from the work of charitable organizations. "The developing science of sociology provided insights into social forces that contributed to poverty and affected people's ability to function successfully...."[23] The National Conference of Catholic Charities, as early as its 1912 meeting, also stressed the importance of preventing poverty, rather than just relieving its effects.

In rural America, Edwin Vincent O'Hara, a priest of the St. Louis archdiocese (later bishop of Kansas City, Missouri), founded the National Catholic Rural Life Conference (NCRLC) in 1923. In its almost eighty years, NCRLC has undertaken rural Catholic education, organized cooperatives and credit unions, and advocated land justice and stewardship. In its *Manifesto on Rural Life* in 1939, NCRLC underscored the social obligation attaching to private property ownership and promoted a concept of ownership as stewardship exercised on behalf of the common good.[24]

Catholic efforts at social action have included the small but influential radical Catholicism of the Catholic Worker movement, begun by Peter Maurin and Dorothy Day in 1933. The Worker's threefold program encompasses the promotion of gospel radicalism through the publication of *The Catholic Worker* and roundtable discussions; houses of hospitality to feed, cloth, and house the poor and homeless; and advocacy of farming communes "where scholars and workers would work and study together on the land in self-sufficient and independent communities."[25]

The sixties saw a highly visible Catholic peace movement arise, associated in the popular imagination with Fathers Daniel and Philip Berrigan. Their antecedents, while few and varied, included a Catholic Association for International Peace, founded in the 1920s by Monsignor John A. Ryan[26] and others and espousing the just-war theory, and the Catholic Worker movement, which opposed World War II and became "the best-known supporter of pacifism in the Catholic community."[27] Names like Gordon Zahn, Eileen Egan, and James W. Douglass, as well as the Berrigans, are associated with Catholic opposition to the Vietnam War and the continuation of the nuclear arms race.

In the sixties and seventies, a small but influential body of Catholic activists became involved in grassroots community organizing among low-income communities, usually in large urban centers. Their experience of empowerment among poor and middle-class neighborhoods and Vatican II's emphasis on the concerns of the poor helped to prime the founding by the U.S. Catholic bishops of the Catholic Campaign for Human Development in 1970.[28] The Campaign now funds over ten million dollars of community organizing and economic development projects across the United States, made possible by the generosity of U.S. Catholics in an annual collection usually taken up around Thanksgiving in U.S. dioceses.

These small efforts at developing a body of Catholic social thought and action addressed to questions of land use, poverty, or peace, however, represent only small tributaries in the flow of Catholic theology and philosophy, often running against the main current. Going back several centuries, Catholic social thought from 1634 to 1829 has been described as "conformist"[29] and in the nineteenth century it was decidedly "conservative, cautious, and individually oriented."[30] Although significant efforts were made to expand Catholic charitable and social outreach and institutions and official Catholic leadership recognized the need to support labor unions, Catholics entered the twentieth century strongly on the side of the American way of liberal capitalism, individualism, and unfettered free enterprise.

In 1919, the U.S. bishops endorsed a program of social justice and moderate social reform—a forerunner of many New Deal programs—and it became "a platform for the mainstream of American Catholic social thought in the twentieth century."[31] Even so, that agenda of social reform was based primarily on recourse to human reason and not on papal social teaching. Moreover, even that tradition of social thought was as unknown to most twentieth-century American Catholics as was papal or Vatican social teaching.

A New Opportunity?

Despite past Catholic obliviousness to our own tradition, there is now a modest renewed interest in Catholic social teaching in America. In part it has been stimulated by the increasing visibility of statements on peace and economic justice and a variety of other topics by the American bishops over the last twenty years. At their meeting in November 2001, for example, the bishops issued significant public statements on the September 11, 2001, terrorist attacks and the subsequent war in Afghanistan, solidarity with Africa, a pastoral plan for pro-life activities, and on the Asian and Pacific peoples within the U.S. Catholic Church and society.[32]

Even more compelling may be the nature of the acute social, economic, political, ecological, and cultural problems that we face in the United States and across the world. Problems of poverty, hunger, pollution, armaments, war, and racism now confront us with a new immediacy through the media and with a severity never before experienced. Moreover, the deeper we look into these problems and their causes, the more complexity we discover. Now, too, world events are further complicated by rapid and stunning changes sweeping Eastern Europe, Asia, and the former Soviet Union, the cultural and economic force of globalization, widespread terrorism, and serious threats to our global environment.

Because of the immediacy, severity, and complexity of these problems, we find both our national community, the Catholic community, the ecumenical community, and the international community torn apart in the search for just and peaceful solutions. In this context,

> More and more people are rediscovering—or discovering for the first time—the rich heritage of the Church's social teachings. We are responding with enthusiasm and sometimes with astonishment: "I didn't know there were so many good things in the encyclicals!"[33]

The possibility of improved insight into both the problems we face and reasonable solutions, all as part of understanding the demands of contemporary faithjustice, prompts the overview of modern Catholic social teaching that the second part of this chapter contains.

Excellent introductory and comprehensive resources have been published in recent years and are available for in-depth analyses of various documents and underlying themes and trends in the modern tradition.[34] This chapter simply introduces the century-old tradition, traces the major steps in its development, highlights one or two key ideas at each developmental stage, and concludes with sections on important trends and ongoing challenges. Before doing so, however, it is necessary to take a longer introductory view across Christian history.

The Older Tradition

From the earliest apostolic times, the Christian community engaged in both social action and social reflection. Paul urges generous almsgiving in the special collection for the Christians in Jerusalem. Deacons are appointed to make sure that widows and orphans are cared for—that justice is done—in the distribution of the community's goods. Slaveholders are summoned to a new relationship with their slaves. Jews and Gentiles are melded, not without misunderstanding and pain, into one community.

Teachings of the Church leaders in the early postapostolic centuries underscored the biblical tradition that "the goods of the earth were created by God for the benefit of every person without exception and that all have special duties toward those in need."[35] Strong warnings about the dangers of wealth and the punishment for failing to give alms can be found, for example, in the writings of Cyprian, St.

John Chrysostom, Origen, St. Augustine, and St. Clement of Alexandria.[36] St. Basil writes in his *Homily on Avarice:*

> So you are not a miser, nor do you rob, yet you treat as your own what you have received in trust for others! Do we not say that the man who steals the coat of another is a thief? And what other name does he deserve who, being able to clothe the naked, yet refuses? The bread you keep belongs to the hungry; the clothes you store away belong to the naked; the shoes that moulder in your closets belong to those that have none; the money you have buried belongs to the needy. Therefore, you have wronged all those to whom you could have given and did not.[37]

This was a typically bold and blunt statement from the Church leaders of this early period.

Theologians, bishops, and preachers urged the Christian community to be as compassionate as their God was, reiterating that creation was for all humanity. They also accepted and developed the identification of Christ with the poor and the requisite Christian duty to the poor: "Because he is a poor man, feed him; because Christ is then fed, feed him" (St. John Chrysostom).[38] Finally, they saw that the distinction between classes and the failure to share the goods of the community assaulted the unity of the one body of Christ, "their understanding of the Church as a community of love and of sharing."[39]

The monasteries of the Middle Ages were not only centers of prayer, scholarship, and education, but "they contributed greatly to the cultural and economic life of the towns and cities that sprang up around them."[40] Religious congregations and individual charismatic leaders promoted the development of a number of helping institutions—hospitals, hospices for pilgrims, orphanages, shelters for unwed mothers—that laid the foundation for the modern "large network of hospitals, orphanages and schools, to serve the poor and society at large."[41] In doing so, the church community was filling in the inadequacies and lacunae existing in the organization of medieval society and later nation-states.[42]

At the same time, the medieval monasteries, universities, and religious congregations developed the body of philosophical and theological thought that married Christian values with the philosophical traditions of Greek, Latin, Jewish, and Arab worlds. Scholastic thinkers of the stature of St. Thomas Aquinas developed the underlying concepts of both personal and social justice that laid the foundations for modern Catholic social teaching. For example, the following adage was universally accepted in the Middle Ages: "He who takes what is necessary does not commit theft, but takes possession of what is his own." As Rene Laurentin explains, the medieval Church until the sixteenth century commonly taught that "the common purpose for all goods is prior to appropriation. The right of private property is a secondary human right, destined to facilitate the proper use of goods."[43]

Out of that philosophical tradition, the U.S. bishops note the development of three dimensions of basic justice that state "the *minimum* levels of mutual care and respect that all persons owe to each other in an imperfect world":

> *Commutative justice calls for fundamental fairness in all agreements and exchanges between individuals or private social groups.* It demands respect for the equal dignity of all persons in economic transactions, contracts or promises....
>
> *Distributive justice requires that the allocation of income, wealth and power in society be evaluated in light of its effects on persons whose basic material needs are unmet.* The Second Vatican Council stated: "The right to have a share of earthly goods sufficient for oneself and one's family belongs to everyone. The fathers and doctors of the church held this view, teaching that we are obliged to come to the relief of the poor and to do so not merely out of our superfluous goods." Minimum material resources are an absolute necessity for human life....
>
> Justice also has implications for the way the larger social, economic and political institutions of society are organized. *Social justice implies that persons have an obligation to be active and productive participants in the life of society and that society has a duty to enable them to participate in this way.* This form of justice can also be called "contributive," for it stresses the duty of all who are able to help create the goods, services and other non-material or spiritual values necessary for the welfare of the whole community.[44]

Even these three dimensions of basic justice, the bishops note, fall short of the goal of biblical justice—*faithjustice*—that portrays a society "marked by the fullness of love, compassion, holiness and peace."[45] These aspects of justice, however, are foundational to that society.

Modern Catholic Social Teaching

A 1988 Vatican document calls Catholic social teaching a "rich heritage" that "must be preserved with fidelity and developed by responding gradually to the new emerging needs of human co-existence."[46] The Vatican distinguishes a social doctrine (a favorite phrase of Pope John Paul II), which stresses the theoretical aspect, and social teaching, which stresses the historical and practical aspect. The document concedes, however, that "both stand for the same reality."

Under the heading of this theoretical dimension, the Vatican lists organic and systematic reflection, universal criteria that can be accepted by all, and permanent ethical principles. The historical dimension is that in which the use of these ethical principles is framed in a real view of society and its problems at a particular point in time. Finally, the practical dimension proposes the effective application of these ethical principles, based on the interpretation of historical conditions, to concrete circumstances.[47]

Rather than a static body of immutable truths that the older term *doctrine* has suggested to some,[48] the Vatican concedes that there is at the heart of Catholic social doctrine "the organic and systematic development of the church's moral reflection on the new and complex social problems."[49] Its sources are the scriptures, the teaching of the ancient and great theologians of the Church, and the magisterium; and

> Its foundation and primary object are the dignity of the
> human person with its inalienable rights, which form the
> nucleus of the "truth about man."[50]

The tasks imposed upon the Church by this social teaching are three-fold: announcing the truth about human dignity and rights; denouncing unjust situations in society; and contributing to positive changes in society and real human progress.[51]

Rather than easy answers to difficult problems, the Center of Concern suggests that the contribution of Catholic social teaching is:

> a *social wisdom* based on:
> —biblical insights
> —the tradition of the early writers of the Church
> —scholastic philosophy

—theological reflection
—and the contemporary experience of the People of God
   struggling to live our faith in justice.[52]

The development of this body of thought is a "dynamic inductive-deductive process" that utilizes a three-step approach well known to Catholics steeped in the social tradition: see, judge, and act. The Vatican document summarizes this same three-step process:

> Seeing is perception and study of real problems and their causes, the analysis of which, however, belongs to the human and social sciences.
>
> Judging is interpretation of that same reality in the light of the sources of social doctrine which determine the judgment pronounced with regard to social phenomena and their ethical implications. In this intermediate phase is found the function proper to the magisterium of the church which consists precisely in interpreting reality from the viewpoint of faith and offering "what it has of its own: a global view about man and humanity." Obviously in seeing and judging reality, the church is not and cannot be neutral because she cannot help but adapt to the scale of values enunciated in the Gospel. If, hypothetically speaking, she were to conform to other scales of values, her teaching would not be what it in fact is, but would be reduced to a biased philosophy or ideology.
>
> Action is aimed at implementing these choices. It requires a real conversion, that inner transformation which is availability, openness and transparency to the purifying light of God.[53]

The process of see, judge, and act then leads to concrete choices in the socioeconomic arena that have their foundation in the faithful tradition of the believing community.

The key building blocks in modern Catholic social teaching are the encyclical or teaching letters of the popes and the conciliar documents of the Second Vatican Council and synods of bishops, all of which missionary and theologian Donal Dorr calls "Vatican social teaching."[54] Although some perhaps rightfully have complained of the identification of Church with hierarchy,[55] the *de facto* situation is described by moral theologian Charles Curran:

...the role of the universal and authoritative Catholic teaching put primary emphasis, especially as the twentieth century progressed, on the official papal teaching as found in the encyclicals and addresses of the popes, so that little or no mention was made of a specifically American Catholic contribution. Especially after the 1931 encyclical of Pius XI entitled *Quadragesimo Anno*, the books and textbooks which did appear on social ethics tended to be commentaries on the official papal documents.[56]

This should come as no surprise in a church operating principally out of a dominant hierarchical institution model since well before Vatican Council I (1869–70).

What must be underscored, however, is that the modern papal encyclicals had antecedents in the intellectual ferment of Catholic and other intellectuals and theologians and in the social and political action of concerned Catholics.

In addition, the writings of social centers like the Koningswinter group of Munchen-Gladbach and the celebrated Social Weeks of France helped develop the body of Catholic Social thought. The work of countless individuals like Dorothy Day and Peter Maurin, Jacques Maritain, Barbara Ward, John Courtney Murray, and Dom Helder Camara, as well as the important contributions of other Christians, of the other world faiths and of concerned secularists need to be acknowledged.[57]

Not only did the teaching arise from the church community, but it also took flesh in the lives of numerous Catholics, especially symbolized in the "labor priests" of the mid-twentieth century.

Take the period of the 1930's, 40's, and 50's. The social ministry was defined rather concretely in the life of the labor priest. There were the labor priests and they represented, if you will, the truth that there was a social teaching.[58]

These priests, like Lou Twomey of New Orleans, often were solitary and unpopular prophetic voices preaching its content. In the sixties and seventies, many women religious like Marge Tuite and Patricia Caraher came to represent the voice of the social tradition in this country through their commitment to confront racism and poverty.

The late nineteenth and early twentieth century also saw the development of the Social Gospel movement in American Protestantism as its response to the challenge of modern industrial society. Unlike some of Catholic social teaching, the Social Gospel came, not from the theologian's study, "but from the practical experience of Protestant ministers working in urban situations and realizing that the individualistic piety and preaching for which they had been trained was of little help in dealing with the urban poor."[59] Like Catholic social teaching, however, it too fashioned a theology that addressed the social structures and institutions that gave rise to conditions of poverty and human misery.

The Social Gospel included a renewed sense of the Reign of God in the prophetic tradition, an awareness of social and public sins, social solidarity, which was a concept of redemption of society from various social sins, and a communitarian understanding of the role of the Holy Spirit, inspiration, and prophecy. Although the movement itself is generally considered to have ended with the 1920s, some commentators argue that it has persisted in American Christianity, most notably in the civil rights movement of the sixties and seventies.[60]

The key documents of modern Catholic social teaching might be described in terms of classics, moderns, and contemporaries. The two great classics were the encyclical letters of 1891 and 1931 by Popes Leo XIII and Pius XI, beginning in the heat of the industrial revolution and setting the initial framework of the discussion. The two moderns are the letters of Pope John XXIII that immediately preceded the Second Vatican Council and influenced its work. The council itself marks the highwater of the movement, beginning a thirty-five year wave of contemporary thought and reflection.

Fourteen primary documents (and several others) are discussed in the section that follows. Most are encyclicals, taking their Latin names from the first words of the Latin texts. While by no means uniform, the older documents are usually referred to by their Latin titles. For the documents since Vatican II, the English and Latin titles are both used by various commentators, although the common English titles may not be translations of the Latin. Two documents from the U.S. bishops are included, the two major pastoral letters of the eighties on peace and economic justice. In both content and process of consultation and deliberation, they represent the most significant contributions of the Church in the United States to the development of modern Catholic social teaching.

In the presentations that follow, an initial "setting" section provides some notes on the shaping of document itself or the larger international or U.S. context in which it appeared. This is especially appropriate if, as Philip Land argues, "...each encyclical has been a specific project addressed to a specific problem."[61] There follows a "content" section designed only to give a brief overview of the document. The "key ideas" section, however, provides an introduction to what might be called the building blocks of modern Catholic social teaching, ideas that are developed in a particular document but seem to persist in the overall tradition, even with varied teachers. These key ideas particularly help shape the contemporary debate about how this faith community contemplates social reality and its own role in the world.[62]

RERUM NOVARUM, 1891
On the Condition of Labor
—Pope Leo XIII

Setting: A new situation was created in nineteenth-century Europe and America following upon the Industrial Revolution. Liberalism, capitalism, and socialism competed for intellectual and political allegiance. Some European Catholic leaders were discussing the problems of the economic system and the increasingly harsh plight of industrial workers. One such key group was the Fribourg Union, founded in 1884 and headed by the future Cardinal Mermillod, who had been a consultant for Pope Leo XIII in the formation of a Vatican-supported economic study group in 1881. The group developed an influential body of social thought[63] as well as a commitment to pursue social legislation.

Unions were also developing in a tense and conflict-filled industrial arena. In the United States, a majority of bishops supported the Knights of Labor and narrowly averted a papal condemnation of the Knights in the late 1880s based on a series of issues revolving around membership by workers of all faiths and no faith.[64]

Summary: Pope Leo XIII examined the misery and poverty of workers and their families in industrialized countries [paragraph 5], noting the destitution of the many and the concentration of wealth in the hands of the few, promoting greed and worker exploitation [6]. Rejecting socialism's class warfare and its denial of property rights, Leo affirmed private possession and the common purpose of property [14], distinguishing just ownership from just use [35]. He also taught the obligation of employers to pay a living wage [63], workers' rights to organize [69–72], and collaboration for social change rather than class struggle.

The Church has a right to speak out on social issues, Leo wrote; and it can both educate citizens to act justly and promote social reconciliation [24–5]. The state in turn must intervene whenever the common good or a particular class suffers or is threatened and no other remedy is available. It, however, should do only what is absolutely needed [53]. The state should protect property rights for "the largest possible number" [65], rights of association and religion, and have special concern for the poor, so workers can be housed, clothed, and live without hardship [51].

KEY IDEAS

Moral Outrage. With the opening pronouncement that "the poor must be speedily and fittingly cared for, since the great majority of them live undeservedly in miserable and wretched conditions" [5], Pope Leo set the Church firmly in the midst of the burning social question of his day. He denounced "a devouring usury" and the concentration of economic power "so that a very few rich and exceedingly rich men have laid a yoke almost of slavery on the unnumbered masses of non-owning workers" [6]. In so doing, Leo laid a solid foundation on which later social teachings could be built that was more than just the encyclical's content; "perhaps even more important was the character of the document as a cry of protest against the exploitation of poor workers."[65]

The pope's intervention was a formal and solemn rejection of a dominant economic tenet of the day, "that labour is a commodity to be bought at market prices determined by the law of supply and demand rather than by the human needs of the worker."[66] It was a stinging protest against the economic status quo, and its effect over time was to move social issues to the center of the mission of the Church and to encourage those already so committed.[67]

Workers' Rights and Duties. Pope Leo built upon the foundational concept of human dignity and the related belief that work is not just a commodity to be bought and sold. From these he developed specific rights belonging to workers: freedom to receive and spend wages as they see fit [9]; to integrity of family life, including provision of necessities to children [19–20]; a wage sufficient to support a worker who is "thrifty and upright" and, by implication, his or her family [63]. The concept of a family wage will be clarified and grow across the 110-year tradition, but its roots are clearly here in Pope Leo's writing.

Leo upheld rights to reasonable hours, rest periods, health safeguards, and working conditions, and special provisions for women and children, including minimum age requirements [59, 60, and 64]; freedom to attend to religious obligations [31]; no work on Sundays or holydays [58]; and the right to form workers' associations [69–72]. These rights also will be expanded and developed by succeeding teachers of the tradition. Workers also were bound to work well and conscientiously, not to injure the property or person of employers, to refrain from violence or rioting, and to be thrifty and prudent [30 and 65].

QUADRAGESIMO ANNO, 1931
On Reconstructing the Social Order
—Pope Pius XI

Setting: It was forty years since *Rerum Novarum,* and Pius XI began the pattern of issuing major documents on its anniversaries.[68] The world was in the grip of the Great Depression, raising concerns about the viability of the Western economic system after a period of apparent success. There were large masses of unemployed workers across Europe and America. Many people were acutely aware of the increasing concentration of enormous wealth and political power in the hands of the very few, creating doubts about the promise of free enterprise to give more people an opportunity to become entrepreneurs[69] and fueling increasing class struggles.

A nascent corporatist-fascist economic model in Portugal and Italy seemed to offer an alternative to both liberal capitalism and communism or socialism.[70] Through Jesuit Superior General Wlodimir Ledochowski, Pius secretly secured the services of a forty-year-old German Jesuit theologian, Father Oswald von Nell-Breuning, to draft his encyclical.[71]

Summary: Pius first reviewed the impact of *Rerum Novarum.* Reiterating the Church's right and duty to speak out on social matters, he upheld private property against collectivism, but stressed its social responsibility. He affirmed the state's duty to insure that private property contributes to the common good.

Pius rejected the unjust claims of capital and labor, and advocated a principle of just distribution to all classes in keeping with the norms of the common good. He proposed just wages as a family wage, a share in profits, and a share in ownership as responses to the continuing plight of nonowning urban workers "whose groans cry to God" and the "huge army of rural wage workers, pushed to the lowest level of existence and deprived of all hope of ever acquiring 'some property in land.'" [59]

Rejecting socialism and "economic dictatorship which has recently displaced free competition" [88], Pius urged a reordering of society according to justice and charity. He promoted a blend of the corporatism discussed for fifty years by reformers together the ancient guilds, where class cooperation based on vocational groups would replace competition.

KEY IDEA

Subsidiarity. Pope Pius XI introduced a critically important Catholic social teaching concept, one that has remained current to today.[72] In his discussion of the social order, he stated the principle:

> As history abundantly proves, it is true that on account of changed conditions many things which were done by small associations in former times cannot be done now save by large associations. Still, that most weighty principle, which cannot be set aside or changed, remains fixed and unshaken in social philosophy: *Just as it is gravely wrong to take from individuals what they can accomplish by their own initiative and industry and give it to the community, so also it is an injustice and at the same time a grave evil and disturbance of right order to assign to a greater and higher association what lesser and subordinate organizations can do.* For every social activity ought of its very nature to furnish help to the members of the body social, and never destroy and absorb them [79, emphasis supplied].

In the next paragraph, Pius specifically applied subsidiarity to the authority of the state and thus interpretations have generally focused on the political sector. Instead of being for or against "big government," Catholic social theory has stressed through subsidiarity that larger political entities should not absorb the effective functions of smaller and more local ones. This was in part a reaction against the centralizing tendencies of socialism. At the same time, if smaller and more localized entities were not able to cope adequately with a problem or need, then larger entities—the state—have a responsibility to act. Circumstances then determine the appropriateness of "big" or "small" government.

The U.S. bishops later related subsidiarity to "institutional pluralism." It provides space, they say, "for freedom, initiative and creativity on the part of many social agents."[73] Subsidiarity insists that all parties work in ways that build up society, and that each one does so in ways expressive of their distinctive capacities. This underscores the importance of families; neighborhood groups; small businesses; professional associations; community organizations; and local, state, and national government. It also underscores the importance of international organizations to respond to needs and concerns of international scope.

Ultimately, the principle of subsidiarity is rooted in human dignity, in the sense that we are most human and responsive to our humanity in making decisions and solving problems as close to those affected by them as possible. Subsidiarity also implies something about small is beautiful, environments where persons matter, and participative decision making.[74]

Pius XII

Pope Pius XII wrote no major social encyclical, but did continue the development of Catholic social thought in various addresses and writings. Most notable among these were nineteen Christmas messages on sociopolitical questions. I would like to highlight two here. In 1944 Pius called democracy "the form of government most in keeping with natural law."[75] Its implication was a duty of participation on the part of citizens which the pope described:

> When people call for a democracy and better democracy, that demand can have no other meaning than that citizens shall be increasingly placed in a position to hold their own opinions, to voice them, and to make them effective in promoting the general welfare. Further, it is not a matter of indifference whether one undertakes to hold and voice opinions and make them effective in promoting public good. It is the proper task of a person conscious of his own responsibility.[76]

As a bridge from the classics, *Rerum Novarum* and *Quadragesimo Anno*, to the modern encyclicals of Pope John XXIII, a second important contribution was in drawing out and clarifying the concept of private property and its social purposes. As Leo and Pius XI had done, Pius XII insisted on the right and importance of private ownership of property. "But, in contrast to Leo XIII, he did not hesitate to give the first priority to the general right of all people to the use of the goods of the earth."[77]

For Pius, the right of an individual to a particular item of private property is a means for carrying out, and subordinate to, the general right of all people to use property.

> Undoubtedly the natural order, deriving from God, demands also private property....But all this remains subordinated to the natural scope of material goods and cannot emancipate itself from the first and fundamental right which concedes their use to all men; but it should rather serve to make possible the actuation of this right in conformity with its scope.[78]

In this way, Pius XII brought the private property concept in Catholic social teaching into clearer focus, although further development followed in the ensuing decades.

MATER ET MAGISTRA, 1961
Christianity and Social Progress
—Pope John XXIII

Setting: On the seventieth anniversary of *Rerum Novarum*, the reality of the third world had come to consciousness, including both the imbalance between rich and poor nations and the harsh conditions of workers in what might be considered pre-industrial societies. After World War II, Western industrialized nations had seen a rise in economic well-being and the development of the welfare state as "humanized versions of capitalism."[79] Economics were now seen in the context of world markets from which the Western nations had become increasingly wealthy in part due to the extravagant use of the energy and raw materials of the poorer nations.

In 1959, Pope John XXIII had summoned the Second Vatican Council to begin in 1962, the first such gathering in almost a century. American Catholics had come of age with the election of John F. Kennedy as the first Catholic president, and Kennedy structured a new national response to the third world in the formation of the Peace Corps.

Summary: Pope John reviewed the social teaching of *Rerum Novarum, Quadragesimo Anno,* and the private property position of Pius XII. He described new economic, social, and political circumstances necessitating his encyclical. He confirmed previous papal teaching on both private initiative and state intervention, the demands of justice in the workplace, including a share in ownership, and new demands created by the international context of the economy. He stressed the importance of small-and-moderate-size enterprises and the social function of private property.

Pope John then called for new forms of agricultural aid, support, and practices. Acknowledging the threat to peace from economic imbalances, he urged culturally respectful, generous, private and governmental emergency and developmental aid to countries in need. He discouraged inappropriate population control; and he promoted international cooperation based upon a recognition of increasing interdependence and the demands of justice and morality. The pope concluded stressing human dignity and a recommitment to the principles of Catholic social teaching.

KEY IDEAS

The Response to Socialization. Pope John unleashed a church shock wave beginning with this sentence:

> One of the principal characteristics of our time is the multiplication of social relationships, that is, a daily more complex interdependence of citizens, introducing into their lives and activities many and varied forms of association, recognized for the most part in private and even in public law [59].

While "socialization" did not appear either in the official Latin text or the above English version, it replaced the awkward "multiplication of social relationships" in the original unofficial Italian working text.

By socialization, Pope John described a feature of modern society whereby people's lives were more and more caught up and shaped by large private and public institutions, whether unions, governments, laws, school systems, or companies. While some erroneously accused John of endorsing socialism, he saw two things happening: numerous services, advantages, and the satisfaction of personal rights [61]; and a restrictive multiplication of rules and laws governing various relationships [62]. Rather than reject socialization in favor of rugged individualism,[80] John called for government to balance individual and group freedoms with the state's regulatory and promotional activity [66].

State Intervention. Pope John effected a major attitude change toward government action concerning economic realities. In a context of optimistic acceptance of the Western economic system with its promises of development, John did not call for radical restructuring. Instead, he confirms private property rights, as had his predecessors. But John sees that individual property holders could not be relied on to effectuate their property's common purposes. In fact, some invoked the Church's support of private property to bolster their opposition to social justice.

"To a great degree, *Mater et Magistra* transfers responsibility for that decision to the state, in a development that has great significance for the Catholic approach to private property."[81] Pope John put state action on a par with private initiative to accomplish the social responsibility of property. He wrote that, without such government action, a commonwealth would suffer "incurable disorders" and "exploitation of the weak by the unscrupulous strong" [58]. In this, John not only minimized prior suspicion of state control and state initiatives in Catholic social teaching, but also put the Church squarely on the side of social reforms within and between nations.[82] This prompted strong conservative reactions.

PACEM IN TERRIS, 1963
Peace on Earth
—Pope John XXIII

Setting: Two years after *Mater et Magistra* and during the first session of the Vatican Council, John XXIII issued this second major social encyclical. The world was fraught with the tensions of the cold war after two world wars and the Korean conflict. The Berlin wall had been erected; and the Cuban missile crisis was resolved the preceding year with some papal help.[83] The Vietnam War was in the first critical stages of U.S. involvement. In the United States, family and community bomb shelters and school civil defense drills were part of the accepted atmosphere in which U.S. residents, like many others, feared a nuclear holocaust.

Outgoing President Dwight D. Eisenhower had provided a largely unheeded warning of the growing political and economic power of the "military-industrial complex" as defense budgets spiraled upward. A multibillion arms trade included much of the third world.

Summary: This first encyclical to "all people of good will" declared that peace will come only "if the order set down by God be dutifully observed" [1]. In a human rights manifesto,[84] Pope John used reason and natural law to set out rights and duties of persons, public authorities, and the world community. He included economic, political and religious rights, immigration rights, and the mutual responsibilities of citizens.

John noted improvements in the status and expectations of workers, increased participation of women, colonialism's decline, and rejection of racial discrimination which "can in no way be justified..." [44]. He discussed civil authority and the common good, including civil disobedience, responsibility to the poor, and protection of rights.

The pope set forth elements essential to relations between states, including: elimination of racism, self-development, obligations to provide aid, and rights of refugees. He deplored the "enormous stocks of armaments" [109], the fears they create, and their negative impact on economic resources; and he demanded that the arms race cease. Stressing international interdependence, John saw the need for a worldwide authority for the universal common good; he also supported the United Nations. Pope John died a few months after this letter.

KEY IDEAS

Economic Rights. Pope John introduced the concept of economic rights, drawn from a logical analysis of human dignity. He included the opportunity to work and to do so without coercion, a just wage for the worker and family to live dignified lives, and private property, even a share of productive goods [18–22]. The individual rights enumerated here had been asserted before, but not as based upon natural law common to all people.

John's related treatment of the right to life [11] specifically included adequate food, clothing, shelter, rest, medical care, necessary social services, and, in the case of sickness, inability to work, widowhood, or unemployment, some form of "security."

This economic rights concept was carried forward by Pope John Paul II in his 1981 encyclical *On Human Work* and by the U.S. bishops in their 1986 pastoral *Economic Justice for All* [80]. It was also contained in the United Nations' 1948 Universal Declaration of Human Rights. It implied, as John indicated, duties of the state, not just to promote economic well-being, but to engage in positive steps such as providing essential services and insurance systems to guarantee these rights [63–65]. This too prompted strong conservative reaction.[85]

Economics and Armaments. Pope John noted "with deep sorrow" [109] arms stockpiling in the developed countries, including the enormous consumption of economic and intellectual resources in the arms race. That diversion of resources denied developing countries the collaboration which they needed for progress. This point then became a persistent theme in Catholic social teaching, which reinforced the Church's repeated cry for a cessation of the arms race in the interest of both peace and progress.

In *Mater et Magistra,* John observed that developing nations too were directly involved in devoting large sums of money to accruing armaments [69]. The arms race was draining off scientific, technical, and economic resources [198], and it was diverting even our human energies from important works to destruction [204].

Earlier, Pope Pius XII, speaking from the midst of World War II, had made the related, but inverted, connection. Aware of the economic factors that had contributed to that war, Pius insisted that there could not be a real postwar peace without widespread economic reconstruction.[86] The connection between peace and justice runs both ways: The arms race threatens economic justice; economic injustice threatens peace.

GAUDIUM ET SPES, 1965
The Church in the Modern World
—Vatican II

Setting: The document originated in a call from Cardinals Suenens, Montini, and Lercaro at the close of the first session of the council for the Church to look outward and to address the world's needs. The Church was awakening to its international character as Asian, African, and Latin American bishops joined the first-world majority and brought the concerns of a worldwide faith community. The radical economic imbalances and threats to peace and humanity itself— the "joys and hopes, griefs and anxieties"—which had prompted Pope John's two encyclicals, were very much on the minds of the authors. They shared John's concerns.

The document was widely debated and drew its content from the participants themselves rather than preparatory committees. Considered to be the most characteristic and important document of the council, it was inspired by John XXIII, called for by Cardinal Montini (Paul VI), and partly written by Archbishop Karol Wojtyla who became John Paul II. It was promulgated on the last working day of the council.

Summary: In this most authoritative document in Catholic social teaching, part one developed teaching on human dignity, social relations, essential social needs, and the role of the Church in the world. Part two focused on "problems of special urgency": marriage and family life, including overpopulation, responsible parenthood, respect for life, and family stability; cultural diversity and development; and socioeconomic life. It discussed fundamental imbalances between rich and poor, the requirements of justice, a sufficient share of earthly goods for all, the duties of public authorities, and the common good.

The final section of the Pastoral Constitution stressed the crisis of modern weaponry, and that peace could only be built on the basis of respect, harmony, justice, and love. It legitimated both nonviolence and conscientious objection, and rejected blind obedience to commands, wars of subjugation, and acts of war directed toward population centers. The council condemned the arms race as a human trap and devastation for the poor. They closed calling for elimination of injustices, increased international cooperation, integral development, and ecumenical cooperation.

KEY IDEAS

Church and World. Although the document on the Church in the modern world has important things to say on a variety of issues touching peace and justice, its major accomplishment was both singular and complex. It first created a new stance: "It was the first time that a document of the solemn magisterium of the church spoke so amply about the directly temporal aspects of Christian life."[87] In doing so it moved the social agenda to center stage; it made social gospel not an off-brand, but an essential part, of the good news of Jesus to which all Christians were committed. Rejecting the privatization of the gospel that nurtures political apathy, "Vatican II recognized that the Church shares responsibility for secular as well as religious history."[88] It was a new Church self-understanding!

Gaudium et Spes created a stance of both responsibility and service. "Christians cannot yearn for anything more ardently than to serve the people of the modern world ever more generously and effectively" [93]. The document put the Church squarely at the service of humanity.[89] Catholicism broke out of the sanctuary, chancery, and parish to stand squarely in the heart of the polis; and in so doing it brought the griefs and anxieties of humanity into the heart of the Church and its mission. Subsequently, as we will see, synods and popes would draw out its implications for the nature of evangelization, a broadened Christology, and the "Christian virtue" of solidarity.

The council members also committed the Catholic community to dialogue not only with other Christians and people of faith but also with the world itself [92], a mutual process already enfleshed in the three-year development of the document itself, in its address to "the whole of humanity," and in its charge to the Church to listen and learn from others. The authors called upon the Church to step beyond dialogue to collaboration with others in transforming the world.

This ecclesiological foundation did more than bring the social concern of the preconciliar popes to the center of the Church. In the process they seeded the Church's own gradual transformation, planted its own freedom from enslaving ties to the powerful and privileged, and cultivated a widespread and passionate commitment to the poor. That concern prophesied a new harvest of martyrs in the following decades whose blood would be spilled for Christ found especially in the *anawim* of Asia, Africa, and Central and South America.[90]

POPULORUM PROGRESSIO, 1967
The Development of Peoples
—Pope Paul VI

Setting: Sixteen months after Vatican II, Pope Paul wrote the first encyclical devoted to the theme of development as part of his task of implementing the council. He noted the "worldwide dimensions of social conflict" as the social question had shifted from a focus on rich and poor individuals to rich and poor nations. Russia and the United States competed to expand their sphere of influence, including markets and military bases, in newly independent nations. A long economic boom existed in the capitalist world, including substantial foreign investment.

U.S. President Johnson declared a War on Poverty and the Great Society, including Medicare and Medicaid. Johnson escalated the U.S. commitment to over 400,000 troops in Vietnam. Fourteen thousand troops sent to the Dominican Republic in 1965 were withdrawn by 1966. The civil rights movement was in full swing, but riots in Newark and Detroit marred the hot summer in 1967.

Summary: Facing the global situation of stark imbalances between rich and poor nations, Pope Paul analyzed three primary causes: the legacy of colonialism, a neo-colonial situation of international economic domination and national political and economic domination, and the imbalance of power among nations.[91] He sketched out a vision of genuine and integral development and its requirements. He reiterated the status of private property rights within a larger social duty and recommended expropriation by governments of unused or poorly used estates or those that brought hardship to peoples or countries [24].

Paul challenged the injustice of so-called free trade and insisted upon trade restrictions, a strong role for international and multilateral organizations, economic planning and development aid, and a support system for poorer nations. He urged immediate action to build a just economic order, not on the principles of liberalistic capitalism, but upon solidarity between rich and poor, dialogue, universal charity, retention of the competitive market, and structural changes. The pope ended noting that "development is the new name for peace" [76] and exhorted Catholics, Christians, and all people of good will to urgent action.

KEY IDEAS

Development. Addressing a world that divided nations into developed and underdeveloped, Pope Paul put forward a broad, complex, and demanding concept of development. First, he protested that development was not just economic. Rather, it must be integral in two senses: the whole person and every person. As such, development engaged the individual person in the task of self-fulfillment, a personal responsibility. Paul spoke therefore of the importance of "the deep thought and reflection of wise men in search of a new humanism..." [20]. To achieve that authentic development we must move "from less human conditions to those which are more human": from material deprivation of life's essentials, the moral deficiencies of selfishness, and oppressive social structures to the possession of necessities, knowledge, culture, respect for the dignity of others, cooperation, a desire for peace, and supreme and spiritual values [21].

Paul stressed development "at the service of humanity" [34], including not just a share in the earth's goods, industrialization, and productive work, but also literacy, family life, and legitimate pluralism. He underscored the importance of development's respect for culture, including the arts, intellectual life, and religion.

Development and Peace. The second part of Paul's vision was that, "The complete development of the individual must be joined with that of the human race and must be accomplished by mutual effort" [43]. He recognized a new "moral fact,"[92] namely the interdependence that connected every person to the problems of unequal distribution of the means of subsistence originally intended for everybody to use and enjoy. He called it a "duty of solidarity" that rested on both individuals and nations [48], creating for advanced nations a very serious obligation to help the peoples of developing nations.

This obligation included sharing of superfluous wealth, creation of a worldwide common fund, an end to the "scandalous and intolerable crime" of the arms race [53], debt relief, trade equity, the elimination of nationalism and racism, and multilateral and international collaboration and unity. "World unity, ever more effective, should allow all peoples to become the artisans of their destiny" [65]. Not to do so, thus maintaining excessive economic, social, and cultural inequalities among nations, arouses tensions, conflicts, and endangers peace, which can only be built upon justice achieved by constant daily effort [76].

OCTOGESIMA ADVENIENS, 1971
A Call to Action
—Pope Paul VI

Setting: This was an apostolic letter from Pope Paul VI to Cardinal Maurice Roy, president of the Pontifical Commission on Justice and Peace, on the eightieth anniversary of *Rerum Novarum*.[93] The Western world was moving into a post-industrial society with new problems. The United Nation's first development decade (1960s) had come to an end with the rich-poor gap widening. Cardinal Roy had written to the United Nations in 1970 of "the international community's growing disenchantment with purely economic development," partly the result of grossly unequal market strength. He called for political and social action.[94]

Most importantly, 130 Latin American bishops met at Medellin in Columbia in a 1968 assembly opened by Paul VI. In "a singular prophetic moment in which the Church in Latin America began to identify itself with the poor,"[95] the bishops committed the Latin American Church to a dynamic new pastoral course linking evangelization and justice.

Summary: Pope Paul began by noting that local churches must fashion their own concrete responses to the urgent needs for social, political, and economic changes. He named new social problems touching upon urbanization, youth, women's equality, union rights, the marginal new poor, discrimination, immigration, unemployment, the media, and environmental exploitation.

Leery of the economic focus of development, yet not completely persuaded of Medellin's call for liberation,[96] Paul nevertheless moved the center of discussion of social justice from economics to politics [46]. He stressed aspirations for equality and participation, the duty to take part, and education on rights and social duties. Paul affirmed political activity to change trade, debt, and monetary policy and to control multinational corporations and the media. However, he warned against the ideologies of socialism, Marxism, liberalism, and "progress" in terms of "merely quantitative economic growth" [41]. He also cautioned against the escape from responsible action into newly popular utopias.

Finally, Paul called all Christians individually and through their organizations to reflect on their social, economic, and political situations, apply gospel principles, and take responsibility for appropriate political action.

KEY IDEAS

Between Ideology and Utopia. Pope Paul advocates political action as "primarily an activity, not an ideology" [25]. Paul criticizes "the possible ambiguity of every social ideology" [27] offering "a final and sufficient explanation of everything...a new idol...its totalitarian and coercive character" [28]. In this context, he discusses socialism, Marxism, and liberalism. On the other side, Paul warns against an anti-ideology appeal to utopias, "often a convenient excuse for those who wish to escape from concrete tasks in order to take refuge in an imaginary world" [37]. What then is the Christian to do, especially when the Church does not offer a "3rd way" between capitalism and collectivism?[97]

Paul's answer seems to be grounded in two related themes: the role of the local church, analyzing and judging its situation, which may lead to a pluralism of action responses; and an inductive approach focused on concrete sociopolitical realities, not deduced from ideology. The individual Christian and local church then must "see, judge, and act," discerning "the degree of commitment possible" to a particular movement or political solution, while safeguarding larger values [31]. The Reign of God is both "already" and "not yet," he is saying.

Political, not Partisan. The above approach to the Church's "political" activity might be tested, for example, on the distinction between such actions as clear Vatican pronouncements on political issues contrasted with the prohibition of priests from political office. A 1989 Vatican document speaks of "two concepts of politics and political commitment."[98] The first concerns action for human dignity, social justice, and the common good in sociopolitical realities. This is distinguished by the Vatican from: "Political commitment, on the other hand, in the sense of concrete decisions to be made, programs to be drawn up, campaigns to be conducted, peoples' representation to be managed, power to be exercised...."[99]

This latter concept of political activity might be distinguished more helpfully as the "partisan" political activity usually associated with political parties and public office. Our entire faith tradition requires the Church to be political, eschewing the divorce between faith and daily life, "one of the gravest errors of our time."[100] The domain of the publicly partisan, however, arguably might be reserved to the laity as part of an apostolic strategy[101] to preserve for the clergy "their freedom in the evangelization of the political reality."[102] It might also keep the Church free of too close and "official" a connection to any party and party ideology.[103]

JUSTITIA IN MUNDO, 1971
Justice in the World
—Synod of Bishops, Rome

Setting: Near the end of 1971, a second synod of bishops gathered in Rome as part of the ongoing mechanism set up by Vatican II for continuing collegial episcopal reflection. Again the influence of the consciousness of being a worldwide Church was carried to the synod by the attendance of a substantial number of native bishops of Asia, Africa, and Latin America. They also brought the strong thrust toward social justice, liberation, and a commitment to the poor from the Medellin conference of 1968, which was in the process of implementation. This message of Medellin became part of an active dialogue with other bishops in attendance, as well as Vatican officials and members of the Pontifical Commission on Justice and Peace established by Paul VI in 1967. Like the council, the synod included lay and other consultants.

The U.S. bishops entered the seventies with concerns reflected in their pastoral letters: the Vietnam War, increasing abortions, and welfare reform. In 1970, they launched the Campaign for Human Development to address poverty and powerlessness.[104]

Summary: "Scrutinizing the signs of the times," the synod saw serious injustices, oppression by unjust systems, and an inner awareness stirring people to liberation and responsibility for their destiny. Action for justice is a "constitutive dimension of the preaching of the gospel," the bishops declared. Facing new and ancient divisions, the arms race, the concentration of wealth and power, and the exaggerated resource demands of richer nations, they reaffirmed the right to development. Naming the "voiceless victims of injustice" [20], including migrants, refugees, the persecuted, political prisoners, the old, orphans, and the sick, they pressed for increased dialogue and reaffirmed an active Church role.

The bishops confirmed that Christian love of neighbor and justice were one, essential to gospel credibility [35]. The Church must respect the rights of its members and have a credible lifestyle as well. Education for justice was stressed. They called for: cooperation between rich and poor churches and ecumenical collaboration; support for specific United Nations initiatives on human rights, disarmament, aid, and development; and for rich nations to reduce consumption, increase their multilateral fund contributions, and include poor nations in international decision making.

KEY IDEAS

Justice in the Church. In the synod document, the bishops set a new agenda for themselves: to do justice if they were to preach justice. From the Hebrew and Christian scriptures, they confirmed that Christian love of neighbor and doing justice are one, essential to gospel credibility [35]. The Church therefore must respect rights of members within the Church—employee rights, juridical rights, participation in decision making at all levels, and "everyone's right to suitable freedom of expression and thought" [44]. They stressed the importance of a credible institutional and individual lifestyle for Christians, one that embodied their own solidarity with persons and nations in need.

Education for justice could also be carried out by individual example in family, school, work, and civic life, but it required conversion to recognize "sin in its individual and social manifestations" [51]. The document also called for cooperation between rich and poor churches, a concept practiced by such examples as parish or diocesan twinning. This theme of Church credibility by self-justice has been raised by both the American bishops in their pastoral letters on peace and economic justice and also pointedly by their critics.

Justice and Love. For those of us raised to consider justice a legal matter while the gospel was about "loving God and neighbor," the bishops surprised us: "Christian love of neighbor and justice cannot be separated" [34]. They grounded this connection in a post-Vatican II look to the scriptures, noting first Yahweh's demand for "faith in him and justice toward one's neighbor" [30]. To this they added Jesus' proclamation of "the intervention of God's justice on behalf of the needy and oppressed" [31]. Christian life then is summarized by the apostle Paul in "faith effecting that love and service of neighbor which involve the fulfillment of the demands of justice" [33].

This justice called for opposition to unjust systems and structures [5] and responding to victims of injustice [20]. It was to be animated by a love inspired by God's love for us [34] that calls us to turn "from concern for self to a sincere love of neighbor" [33]. Christian love "implies an absolute demand for justice, namely a recognition of the dignity and rights of one's neighbor" [34]. Justice thus "attains its inner fullness only in love" [34] and is so radically connected that the bishops spoke of "God's absolute demand for justice and love" [34]. Obviously, the Church child abuse scandal of the past year or two has eroded credibility of the bishops and underscored their own insistence on the importance of living justice and love within the Church itself.

EVANGELII NUNTIANDI, 1975
Evangelization in the Modern World
–Pope Paul VI

Setting: An exciting third synod in 1974 on evangelization had discussed a number of key issues: the nature of contemporary evangelization, the role of liberation, small or base church communities, the role of local churches, and the variety of cultures. Input from the bishops of the third world again highlighted the session, especially from the Church in Africa.[105] Unable to agree on more than a brief statement, the synod requested Pope Paul to address these issues. He did so a year later in an Apostolic Exhortation on the tenth anniversary of the closing of Vatican II.

In the United States, we were reeling from the impact of the Vietnam War including U.S. withdrawal, the My Lai massacre, and a flood of refugees. We were also stunned by disclosures of widespread CIA spying on Americans, Watergate hearings and impeachment votes, President Nixon's resignation and pardon, and numerous convictions of public officials. We also prepared to celebrate our bicentennial.

Summary: Beginning from the image of Christ the evangelizer, Pope Paul discussed the nature, content, methods, beneficiaries, workers, and spirit of evangelization. He stressed the importance of the proclamation of the Reign of God as "absolute," making everything else relative [8]. Central to Jesus' preaching was salvation, which is "liberation from everything that oppresses man but which is above all liberation from sin and the Evil One..." [9]. Paul called for a thorough Spirit-empowered evangelization of all "the strata of humanity" and all cultures by both living witness in the world and explicit proclamation of Christ. He underscored the profound links "between evangelization and human advancement–development and liberation" [31].[106]

Evangelization involved an "explicit message...about life in society, about international life, peace, justice and development–a message especially today about liberation" [29]. That message was to be adapted to different situations and cultures, involved a necessary conversion of heart and outlook, and should utilize a variety of methods, including the mass media, base ecclesial communities as both hearers and evangelizers, and ecumenical collaboration.

KEY IDEAS

Liberation.[107] Paul first cited the 1974 synod's discussion of all that condemns peoples "to remain at the margins of life: famine, chronic disease, illiteracy, poverty, injustices in international relations and especially in commercial exchanges, situations of economic and cultural neo-colonialism sometimes as cruel as the old political colonialism." In the face of these realities, Paul affirmed the Church's evangelical duty to proclaim, assist, witness to, and ensure the completion of liberation from these realities [30]. He rooted liberation deeply in the gospel proclamation of Jesus and connected it firmly to economics, politics, and social or cultural life. Yet the pope said it cannot be contained in these aspects of reality and is attached to a Christian anthropology beyond any ideology. Liberation is both in history and beyond it, a part of salvation but not the same thing [35].

Political liberation alone, he maintained, carried within itself its own destructiveness without profound motives of "justice in charity" and zeal with a spiritual dimension. Liberation requires a conversion of both structures and hearts, and Paul rejoiced that the Church is conscious of and involved in promoting liberation and providing the inspiration of faith to Christian "liberators."

Social Structural Sin. Discussions of evangelizing "all the strata of humanity" and converting "collective consciences of people, the activities in which they engage, and the lives and concrete milieux which are theirs" [18] placed a new concept before us: a social and structural concept of sin. The bishops at the 1971 synod had spoken of "the objective obstacle which social structures place in the way of conversion of hearts."[108] Paul picked up this insight in his discussion of evangelizing cultures [20], liberation from marginalizing forces [30], and even the perceptive insight that "the best structures and the most idealized systems soon become inhuman if the inhuman inclinations of the human heart are not made wholesome...a conversion of heart and outlook" [36].

There was a double understanding of the dynamic of personal and structural sin: Human beings structure the sinfulness into a social system or arrangement, and the system or structure coercively shapes the behavior of individuals, both those who oppress and those who are oppressed.[109] Paul importantly used the broad concept of "culture" from the Vatican Council to deepen his insight into the far-ranging impact of sinfulness structured into societies.

LABOREM EXERCENS, 1981
On Human Work
–Pope John Paul II

Setting: Pope John Paul's third encyclical,[110] on the ninetieth anniversary of *Rerum Novarum*, reflected his own extensive writing. He had traveled widely, including the United States, Mexico and the Puebla meeting of Latin American bishops in 1979, and Brazil and Africa in 1980.

In the seventies, the United States and Europe suffered severe recessions, followed by the oil crisis and high inflation. Third-world nations demanded monetary and trade reforms and just distribution of world income as poverty worsened. There were the new China openness; Cambodian killing fields; Soviet Afghanistan invasion; an active Polish Solidarity union; and civil wars in Northern Ireland, Lebanon, and Pakistan. Repressive conservative regimes tightened their grips on Latin America, Somoza was overthrown in Nicaragua, and civil war ravaged El Salvador.

U.S. frustrations over Iran hostages and the economy help elect Ronald Reagan president; he slashed domestic programs to substantially increase military spending and cut taxes.

Summary: The pope reiterated key themes: concern for the poor, unemployment's evil, sinful social structures, the common use of private property, and a just family wage. His theme was work, "the essential key, to the whole social question" [3]. John Paul argued that through the Genesis work mandate "to subdue the earth" humans image their Creator and share God's creative action, a font of deep spirituality.

This made people the "subjects of work" and labor was neither a tool in the productive process nor a commodity. All other facets of the economic system belonged to the "objective" order and were intended to serve humanity and their calling to be persons [6]. This deep insight into work "implies a more equitable redistribution not only of income and wealth, but also of work itself in such a way that there may be employment for all."[111] Thus, John Paul reaffirmed worker and union rights, urging "worker solidarity" for social justice, an essential mission of the "church of the poor" [8]. He deeply criticized capitalism and Marxism for reducing the worker to mere "economic man."[112]

KEY IDEAS

Workers' Rights Revisited. Moving from the priority of the person as "subject of work," Pope John Paul developed or strengthened a wide range of specific rights drawn from Catholic social teaching. The first was "suitable employment for all who are capable of it," and, when unavailable, the provision of unemployment benefits by employers or, upon their failure, the state [18]. Just remuneration for work by a head of family must "suffice for establishing and properly maintaining a family and for providing security for its future" [19]. This would mean a family wage or other social measures such as family allowances for child-raising mothers.

There must also be no age or gender discrimination and provision of social benefits such as health care, coverage of work accidents, inexpensive or free medical assistance for workers and families, old age pensions and insurance, and appropriate vacations and holidays [19]. Trade and professional unions are needed and retain the right to organize, act politically, and to strike "within just limits" [20]. The pope affirmed the dignity of agricultural labor [21], rights of disabled persons to appropriate training and work [22], and the right to emigrate to find work [23].

"Workbench Spirituality." Pope John Paul concluded his encyclical by sketching a spirituality of work developed from the first "gospel of work" in Genesis [24–27]. Since work furthers the creative design and activity of God, workers are perfecting that creative activity by their labors, whether the workbench is the factory, laboratory, home, or in the midst of the polis. John Paul cited Vatican II to the point, "They can justly consider that by their labor they are unfolding the Creator's work..." [25].

Reflection upon work can then be a source of thanksgiving, joy, and reverence. In the process of working, women and men also transform themselves, becoming more like the Creator in the creative exercise of their own gifts, talents, and energies. This not only can deepen their own sense of dignity, but it also emphasized the importance of organizing the workplace and the entire economy in ways that "harmonize with the genuine good of the human race and allow people as individuals and as members of society to pursue their total vocation and fulfill it," again quoting the council [26]. John Paul developed the insight that the carpenter Jesus belonged to "the working world," and that Jesus understood and appreciated it.

THE CHALLENGE OF PEACE: GOD'S PROMISE AND OUR RESPONSE, 1983
Pastoral Letter on War and Peace
—United States Bishops

Setting: A committee of five bishops chaired by Cardinal Joseph Bernardin wrote the document over a several-year process of three published drafts, hearings, and wide consultation, including European bishops. The bishops approved this pastoral by a vote of 238–9.

Wars raged in El Salvador, Afghanistan, Lebanon, and between Iran and Iraq. Egyptian President Anwar Sadat had been killed and President Reagan and Pope John Paul were wounded in assassination attempts. Solidarity led massive unrest in Poland. Reagan led the largest U.S. peacetime arms buildup ever, including draft registration, MX, B1, Trident, Cruise, Pershing II, neutron bomb, and Star Wars. Domestic programs suffered severely. The Nuclear Freeze movement signaled popular antinuclear sentiment, including debate over first-strike strategy and weapons systems.[113]

Summary: Writing to form consciences and influence policy in a "supreme crisis," the bishops noted that "peace is both a gift and a human work," "an enterprise in justice" [68]. They affirmed two Christian responses: the just-war approach and nonviolence [73]. However, "governments threatened by armed, unjust aggression must defend their people" [75], including armed defense as a last resort. Applying just-war criteria, the bishops declared the use of nuclear weapons against civilian populations to be immoral [147], first-strike use to be morally unjustifiable [150], and "limited" use to be morally "highly skeptical" [159].

They adopted a posture of "strictly conditioned moral acceptance" of nuclear deterrence policy, only justifiable as a step toward disarmament [173]. They described the arms race as "an act of aggression against the poor" [128] and urged reduced armaments, a ban on chemical and biological weapons, and reduced conventional forces. Real peace must be built on structural reforms and a reverence for life. They urged active church peace efforts.

KEY IDEAS

On Deterrence. Calling deterrence the "centerpiece of both United States and Soviet policy" and "the most dangerous dimension of the nuclear arms race," the bishops chose to accept, not condemn, it—a "strictly conditioned moral acceptance" [186], following Pope John Paul. Having outlawed the use of nuclear weapons in any imaginable circumstances, the bishops set forth two strict conditions for their possession-in-order-to-deter-another's-use, what we call deterrence strategy: first, "deterrence is justifiable only as a transitional strategy" to eventual disarmament; and second, "we only need for a deterrent what is necessary to see that the weapons are not used."[114]

For the bishops, deterrence preserved only "peace of a sort" and not the "genuine peace" required for international life [168]. This acceptance also yielded criteria for assessing various elements of deterrence strategy. Thus the bishops rejected proposals for first strike, prolonged nuclear strikes, or "prevailing" in nuclear war as well as the quest for nuclear superiority [188].

They supported immediate, bilateral, verifiable agreements to halt testing, production, and deployment of new weapons systems; negotiation of "deep cuts in the arsenals of both superpowers"; and a comprehensive test ban treaty [191].[115]

Nonviolence and Resistance. The bishops affirmed three modes of defending peace by refusing to bear arms: a gospel-based non-violence; gospel-based affirmative reconciliation with enemies; and an "active nonviolence" to resist aggression and undermine armed oppression [73]. Citing early and medieval saints, as well as Gandhi, Dorothy Day, and Martin Luther King, the bishops thus gave credence to the Christian "pacifist option" [119]. It complements the just-war tradition and "contributes to the full moral vision we need in pursuit of a human peace, each preserving the other from distortion" [121]. Implications included support for conscientious objection, both general and selective [233].

Such nonviolence takes many forms, the bishops declared, including diplomacy, negotiation, compromise, resistance, and peaceable noncompliance and noncooperation [222–25]. It is "not passive about injustice and the defense of the rights of others; it rather...

exemplifies what it means to resist injustice through non-violent methods" [116]. "Not the way of the weak, the cowardly or the impatient" [222], the bishops declared that nonviolent resistance may demand great sacrifice, even our lives, needs intense study, and may not succeed [223–29].[116]

ECONOMIC JUSTICE FOR ALL: CATHOLIC SOCIAL TEACHING AND THE U.S. ECONOMY, 1986
Pastoral Letter of the United States Bishops

Setting: Also written by a committee of bishops, chaired by Archbishop Rembert G. Weakland, this document originated in a resolution in 1980 to develop a letter on capitalism to complement a letter on communism issued that year. This letter went through three public drafts, hearings, consultations, and wide solicitation of ideas, including almost twenty thousand written suggestions, before overwhelming approval. It too was intended to shape Catholic consciences and influence policy. World economic problems had worsened amid major changes, including Japanese ascendancy and U.S. decline, with pollution, a widening gap between nations of the Northern and Southern hemispheres, hundreds of millions starving, and severe third-world debt and inflation.

In the United States, transitioning painfully to a post-industrial society, growing deficits and "Reaganomics" drove decisions to cut back domestic programs, implement tax cuts, and increase defense spending.

Summary: Citing both positive and negative aspects of U.S. and world economies, the bishops called for a common moral vision if the economy is to serve all people fairly [23]. What decisions do for the poor, to them, and enable them to do for themselves was the moral touchstone for judging and shaping the economy [24]. Starting from biblical justice and Catholic social teaching, they developed concepts of justice, duties, human rights, the common good, and moral priorities for the nation, including a priority concern for the poor and development of economic rights. They delineated responsibilities for workers and unions, owners and managers, citizens and governments, and all Christians.

To concretize their discussion, the bishops then considered four policy issues in specific detail: employment, poverty, food and agriculture, and relations to developing nations. One chapter calls for "a new American experiment" in economic partnership and democracy.

Finally, they challenged the Church and themselves to implement economic justice.

KEY IDEAS

"Preferential Option for the Poor." The authors clearly absorbed and applied the special option for the poor articulated by the Latin American bishops at Puebla in 1979. In a nonexclusionary context of service of the economy to all people, the bishops proclaim that the scriptures clearly "provide the basis for what today is called the 'preferential option for the poor'" [52]. That stance means speaking out for those with no one to speak for them, defending the defenseless, seeing things as the poor and powerless do, and assessing all realities from their impact on the poor. In the nation's moral priorities, "the poor have the single most urgent economic claim on the conscience of the nation" [86].

Thus, the economy and political organization must meet the basic needs of the poor [90]; increase their active participation in economic life [91]; and direct a new investment of wealth, talent, and human energy to their benefit [92]. The bishops' specific topics— employment, poverty, food and agriculture, and developing nations— reflected this priority. "The fundamental moral criterion for all economic decisions, policies, and institutions is this: They must be at the service of all people, especially the poor" [24].

"A New American Experiment."[117] The bishops called for implementation of economic rights, "to broaden the sharing of economic power and to make economic decisions more accountable to the common good" [Message, 21]. In a reformist, not radical letter, they set forth modest proposals[118] for "new forms of cooperation and partnership" [296] within businesses, in local and regional cooperation, in national policy setting, and at the international level. The bishops seemed to comprehend that if economic power equals political power, then concentrated economic power equals concentrated political power. By invoking the heroic "bold" American political experiment as a model for a new experiment in economic life, they hinted that the increasing concentration of economic power threatens our political rights as well.[119]

Earlier, the bishops observed that the loss of small farms undermines rural life in America [226]. Now, our "signs of the times" may also include the decline in U.S. voting, the rise of multinational corpo-rations, PACs (political action committees to funnel contributions to candidates) and corporate buy-outs, and the physical-emotional-psychological flight to the lifestyle enclaves of nonparticipation. Their partnership and teamwork plea confronted radical economic individualism writ large and may have signaled one last chance for us to avoid its deadly impact.

SOLLICITUDO REI SOCIALIS, 1987
The Social Concerns of the Church
—Pope John Paul II

Setting: Pope John Paul wrote this letter on the twentieth anniversary[120] of Paul VI's 1967 encyclical *Populorum Progressio,* building on the development theme of that letter. Hundreds of millions of people in the third world lived in destitution, while an enormous chasm separated the nations of the North and South. "Wars of proxy" animated by the United States and the Soviets scarred Central America, the Middle East, Southern Africa, Asia, and Afghanistan. The major powers continued massive arms spending. Debt, unemployment, recession, and inflation marked the economies of developed and so-called developing nations.

The first and second world continued to be obsessed with the East-West conflict. For example, two-thirds of U.S. foreign aid was military or security related, with Egypt and Israel the major beneficiaries. East-West leaders continued to "stonewall the Southern agenda of issues,"[121] such as development, foreign aid, and trade and debt.

Summary: John Paul contrasts Pope Paul's hopes for development with the worsening realities of underdevelopment and the division into first, second, third, and now fourth worlds, the latter being "bands of great or extreme poverty in countries of medium or high income" [14]. He blames failures by developing states and elites, neglect from affluent countries, exploitative economic, financial, and social mechanisms [16], and negative interdependence [17]. He focuses the causes of underdevelopment in the militant ideological opposition of East and West, cold war and wars of proxy, their perversion of investment and aid into neo-colonialism, turning developing countries into "cogs on a gigantic wheel" [20–23].

John Paul urged authentic development that is integral, social, and respectful of rights and the cosmos, and he develops Paul's "duty of solidarity" as the moral response to increasing interdependence. Structural sin, rooted in thirst for profit and power, calls for action by persons and institutions, criticism of capitalism and collectivism, and a preferential love for the poor [42]. Specific changes must occur in trade and monetary systems, technology transfer, and international organizations [43].

KEY IDEAS

Interdependence. "However much society worldwide shows signs of fragmentation...their interdependence remains close" [17]. In an approach similar to John XXIII's insistence on recognizing the realities of socialization, Pope John Paul developed the context of his approach as interdependence. Factually, we are more and more connected across the world in terms of media, science, economics, environment, and politics. We face both "transnational problems" and "transnational actors" in a world where so many domestic issues have foreign policy implications, and vice versa.[122] The problem is not that we are interdependent, but that the failure to attend to and tend this interdependence, "its ethical requirements," has disastrous consequences, especially for the poor. It also "triggers negative effects even in the rich countries" [17].

Examples provided by John Paul included the housing crisis, unemployment and underemployment, and international debt [18–19]. Our interconnectedness also becomes clear in the increasing awareness that development focused solely on the accumulation of goods and services produced both the miseries of underdevelopment and the destructive, obsessive consumerism of what John Paul called superdevelopment [28].

Solidarity. "...[I]f interdependence is an accurate description of the situation of our modern world, then solidarity is the appropriate Christian response to this reality."[123] The concept of solidarity had been used by John XXIII, Paul VI, the 1971 synod, and by John Paul in *On Human Work*. It achieved a new force here as the pope raised it to "a moral category," "a moral and social attitude," and, finally, a "virtue" [38]. He insisted that solidarity was not just some feeling of compassion or distress at the misfortunes around us; but it must be "a firm and persevering determination to commit oneself to the common good" [38].

As he developed it, solidarity commits the Christian to the sharing of their goods and services by the well-off, the assertion of their rights by the poor, and public demonstrations and mutual cooperation among the poor [39]. At the international level, solidarity takes the form of the moral responsibility of stronger nations to build an international system based on equality, and "the abandonment of the politics of blocs, the sacrifice of all forms of economic, military or political imperialism, and the transformation of mutual distrust into collaboration." Peace is the fruit of solidarity [39].

CENTESIMUS ANNUS, 1991
The Hundredth Anniversary
—Pope John Paul II

Setting: In the late 1980s, dramatic peaceful events led to the Soviet Union's collapse, reunification of Germany, and democratic reforms in the former U.S.S.R. and elsewhere. The cold war ended. Dictatorial and repressive regimes "fell one by one in some countries of Latin America and also of Africa and Asia" [22]. The Catholic Church and other religions played catalytic roles in Europe, Latin America, and the Middle East. U.N. forces led by the United States responded to Iraq's 1990 invasion of Kuwait. This "gulf war" drove Iraqi forces from Kuwait, created thousands of refugees, and devastated the Iraqi infrastructure.

The United States was changing from the world's leading creditor to debtor nation. U.S. deficits soared; one in five children was poor; 35 million people lacked health coverage; and drugs and violence escalated. The rich-poor gap widened within the United States and between nations.

Summary: *Centesimus Annus*[124] concluded the first century of modern social teaching by building upon the key ideas of Leo XIII. John Paul highlighted Leo's themes: social teaching as evangelization; worker rights; private property and the common good; the role of the state, limited by subsidiarity but pursuing solidarity; and the preferential option for the poor. With Leo, he underscored socialism's fatal flaws,[125] hailing the collapse of "real socialism" and the nonviolent uprisings that caused it. Warning against an "impossible compromise between Marxism and Christianity," John Paul reaffirmed "an authentic theology of integral human liberation" [26]. He cautioned against deep European injustices and called for arbitration and aid, without reducing third-world assistance.

"New property" existed in know-how, technology, and entrepreneurial organization [32]. The pope bemoaned exclusion of many peoples from productive systems and capitalism's "ruthlessness" for much of the third world [33]. He acknowledged free-market efficiency, with limits and failures. He called for reducing third-world debt, rejecting consumerism, protecting natural and human ecology and collective goods against the new capitalism, and state provision for nonmarket human needs.[126]

KEY IDEAS

Nonviolence Revisited. *Centesimus Annus* raised the ante in the debate between justifiable war adherents and Christian pacifists, contrasting two recent events. First, in the face of Marxism's emphasis on violent struggle, "the protests which led to the collapse of Marxism tenaciously insisted on trying every avenue of negotiation, dialogue and witness to the truth, appealing to the conscience of the adversary..." [23]. Violence "always needs to justify itself through deceit and to appear, however falsely, to be defending a right or responding to a threat..." [23]. Trust in God enabled the "miracle of peace" and discernment of "the narrow path between the cowardice which gives in to evil and the violence which, under the illusion of fighting evil, only makes it worse" [25].

John Paul then cited the "tragic war in the Persian Gulf," repeating the earlier papal cry of "Never again war!" War destroys innocent lives, teaches killing, upsets those who kill, and "leaves behind a trail of resentment and hatred, thus making it all the more difficult to find a just solution of the very problems which provoked the war" [52].

The pope urged U.N. development of nonviolent conflict resolution, dialogue rather than violent struggle, arbitration in Europe, conversion of resources by disarming both "huge military machines" [28], arms reductions and trade restraints, and genuine economic development.

Free but Fair Markets. John Paul declared, "It would appear that...the free market is the most efficient instrument for utilizing resources and effectively responding to needs." What he affirmed almost in the abstract, he immediately qualified: "But this is true only for those needs which are 'solvent' insofar as they are endowed with purchasing power and for those resources which are 'marketable' insofar as they are capable of obtaining a satisfactory price. But there are many needs which find no place on the market" [34]. Marketplace autonomy is qualified by a dual state role: setting the juridical framework for economic affairs and insuring "a certain equality between the parties..." [15]. He enumerated market constraints—to be exercised by subsidiary institutions, strong unions, and by public authorities— in at least three categories: prior constraints of basic human needs and rights, participation in society and the economy, and protection of "common goods such as the natural and human environments" [40]; outside constraints of human needs not met by markets, regions controlled by foreign companies and "ruthless" capitalism,[127] and the fourth world of those marginalized within developed countries, such as the elderly, young people, and many women; and inside constraints of workers' rights, including participation in enterprises, and the need for controls on grave imbalances between nations, on monopolies, and on illegitimate ownership and profits.[128]

OTHER DOCUMENTS

Catholic social teaching by the Vatican and the hierarchy is not contained solely in the so-called social encyclicals. It arises and is developed as well in other documents of the magisterium and, as discussed above, in the work of many other Church members as well. In this section are a few important documents of the last decade that further addressed issues that we associate with the social tradition of the Church.

Tertio Millennio Adveniente (1994)[129] was Pope John Paul's apostolic letter calling for preparation across the world for the jubilee year 2000. In the letter, the pope described and discussed the scriptural tradition of the jubilee year and its implications for justice, protection of the weak, and stewardship of creation for all [11–16]. John Paul urged an intense preparation in the three years immediately preceding the jubilee, highlighting social themes for each year, including: solidarity with neighbor, especially the most needy, in 1997 [42]; respect for the environment, work for peace and justice, and reconciliation and solidarity in 1998 [46]; and charity, the preferential option for the poor, inequality, debt relief, and women's rights in 1999 [50–51]. In his 1998 Bull of Indiction[130] of the jubilee year he returned to important social themes of charity, vast sectors of poverty and exclusion around the world, debt relief, abuse of power, and the "need to create a new culture of international solidarity and cooperation, where all—particularly the wealthy nations and the private sector—accept responsibility for an economic model which serves everyone" [12]. He called for conversion and a change of life to eliminate the scandal of extreme poverty, using his favorite image of the rich man and the poor Lazarus (Luke 16:19–31) to underscore his point.

Evangelium Vitae (1995),[131] the eleventh encyclical letter of Pope John Paul II, focused on the inviolability of human life and proclaimed a gospel of life in the face of what the pope called a culture of death [12]. The pontiff argued that the right to life was the most basic of human rights [2] and that its corruption represents "a direct threat to the entire culture of human rights" [18]. Without acknowledging and defending the right to life, it is impossible to further the common good since it is the right to life "upon which all the other inalienable rights of individuals are founded and from which they develop" [101]. In strong terms John Paul condemned murder [57], procured abortion [58], euthanasia [65], and capital punishment (except in cases where the death penalty is the only way to defend society, but "such cases are very rare if not practically nonexistent" [56]). He also faulted policy makers and the media for sanctioning or encouraging abortion and euthanasia, international organizations for promoting artificial contraception and abortion as forms of population control [91], and "those who should have ensured—but did not—effective family and social policies in support of families, especially larger families and those with particular financial and educational needs" [59]. From the right to life John Paul also affirmed our basic ecological responsibility [42], the care of parents for children with disabilities [63, 93], adoption of children who are rejected by others [63], a duty of conscientious objection to abortion and euthanasia [73–74, 89], and the service of charity through a wide range of social services and health care and other institutions that care for people from birth to death [87–90]. Acknowledging that modern social, economic, and cultural conditions make it more difficult for families to care for children, the sick, and the elderly, the pope called for the development of positive family policy [90]. "Communities and states must guarantee all the support, including economic support, which families need in order to meet their problems in a truly human way" [94].

Ecclesia in America (1999)[132] came as an address in Mexico City to the assembled representatives of the hierarchy of North and South America but directed to "the bishops, priests and deacons, men and women religious, and all the lay faithful on the encounter with the living Jesus Christ: the way to conversion, communion and solidarity in America." It was a response to concerns raised in the December 1997 Special Assembly for America of the Synod of Bishops, especially the cry of the poor.[133] Pope John Paul underscored the place of encounter with Christ in "the persons, especially the poor, with whom Christ identifies himself" [12]. He acknowledged the important presence of the Church in social and charitable work across the Americas [18], a growing respect for human rights [19], and the positive and negative impact of globalization [20]. He then underscored the challenges of growing urbanization [21], the external debt burden [22, 59], widespread corruption [23, 60], the drug trade [24, 61], ecological abuse and destruction [25], the arms race [62], discrimination against indigenous peoples and Americans of African descent [64], immigrants and migrants [65], and the dominance of the powerful in eliminating the powerless in a growing culture of death [63].

John Paul urged his listeners to a solidarity that is "the fruit of the communion which is grounded in the mystery of the triune God, and in the Son of God who took flesh and died for all" [52]. He underscored the Church's social doctrine as a starting place in the search for practical solutions [54] and called them to analyze the "globalized economy" in light of the principles of social justice, especially the preferential but not exclusive option for the poor [55, 58, 67]. The pope called for the promotion of solidarity and peace to confront social sins and the dominant system of "neoliberalism" that "considers profit and the law of the market as its only parameters, to the detriment of the dignity of and the respect due to individuals and peoples" and becomes the ideological justification for "neglect of the weaker members of society" [56]. Finally, he called for a new evangelization, including evangelization of the poor themselves and insistence on formation of all consciences on the basis of the Church's social doctrine [67].

Catechism of the Catholic Church (1992)[134] groups many of the major themes of Catholic social teaching in two places in Part Three on life in Christ—under the heading "The Human Community" and in the treatment of the seventh commandment. In the listing below are presented some key themes from the first treatment (with paragraph numbers indicated):

Part Three, Section One, Chapter Two: The Human Community

a. Voluntary associations and institutions; socialization [1882].

b. Socialization and subsidiarity [1883].

c. Charity, the greatest social commandment, and justice [1889].

d. Diversity of political regimes is morally acceptable [1901].

e. The common good defined [1906] and contains three essential elements: respect for the person [1907], social well-being and development [1908], and peace [1909].[135]

f. The role of the state is to defend and promote the common good [1910].

g. Interdependence and the universal common good; social needs; refugees and migrants [1911].

h. The duty of participation in society [1913], including personal responsibility for family and work [1914] and active citizenship [1915].

i. Social justice [1928].

j. Dignity of the human person [1929] and respect for the rights that flow from that dignity [1930].

k. Equal dignity for all [1934] and the rejection of discrimination among people on the grounds of sex, race, color, social conditions, language, or religion [1935].

l. Sinful inequalities in excessive economic and social disparities between individuals and peoples [1938].

m. The principle of solidarity [1939] is manifested first by the distribution of goods and remuneration for work [1940]; and socioeconomic problems can be resolved only through all forms of solidarity [1941].

In *Ecclesia in America,* Pope John Paul II observed the need for a "Catechism of Catholic Social Doctrine" and that the treatment of the seventh commandment in the Catechism could serve as a starting point for developing such a social catechism.[136] Listed below are some of the key themes from the treatment of the seventh commandment (again, with paragraph numbers indicated):

**Part Three, Section Two, Chapter Two, Article 7:
The Seventh Commandment**

a. The universal destination of goods [2402] and the right to private property [2403] are both confirmed, with the understanding that the universal destination of goods remains primordial, "even if the promotion of the common good requires respect for the right to private property and its exercise" [2403].

b. The right and duty of political authority to regulate the legitimate exercise of the right of ownership for the sake of the common good [2406].

c. Theft of another's property is forbidden, but there is no theft in the case of the use of another's property in circumstances of urgent necessity and it is the only way to meet essential needs [2408]. The commandment also forbids business fraud, unjust wages, and artificial price manipulation [2409].

d. Commutative justice applies to exchanges between persons [2411] and requires restitution of stolen goods as reparation for injustice [2412].

e. The commandment requires respect for creation and its use is limited by the quality of life of one's neighbor, including generations to come [2415].

f. The social doctrine of the Church involves moral judgments about economic and social matters [2420] and provides principles for reflection, criteria for judgment, and guidelines for action [2423].

g. Any theory that makes profit the exclusive norm and ultimate end of economic activity is morally unacceptable, as is any system that subordinates the basic rights of individuals and groups to the collective organization of production [2424].

h. The Church has rejected the totalitarian and atheistic ideologies of communism or socialism and also capitalism's individualism and the absolute primacy of the law of the marketplace over human labor. "Reasonable regulation of the marketplace and economic initiatives, in keeping with a just hierarchy of values and a view to the common good, is to be commended" [2425].

i. Economic activity is meant to provide for the needs of human beings [2426]; and human work is a duty [2427] that fulfills in part the nature of the human person [2428].

j. Everyone has a right of economic initiative [2429]; access to employment and the professions must be open to all without unjust discrimination [2433]; recourse to strike is morally legitimate [2435]; and a just family wage must be paid that guarantees "the opportunity to provide a dignified livelihood for himself and his family on the material, social, cultural, and spiritual level, taking into account the role and productivity of each, the state of the business, and the common good" [2434].

k. The state has the responsibility to guarantee individual freedom and private property, a stable currency and efficient public services, and, with individuals and associations, the task of overseeing and directing the exercise of human rights in the economic sector [2431].

l. Solidarity must extend to relations among nations, doing away with abusive if not usurious financial systems, iniquitous commercial relations among nations, and the arms race. In their place must come a common effort to mobilize resources toward moral, cultural, and economic development [2438].

m. Rich nations have a grave moral responsibility in solidarity and charity to ensure the means of development [2439], including direct aid, necessary reforms in international economic and financial institutions, and support for efforts toward growth and liberation of poor countries, especially in the area of agricultural labor [2440].

n. Love for the poor is part of the Church's tradition [2444] and is incompatible with immoderate love of riches or their selfish use [2445]. What is due in justice is not to be offered as a gift of charity [2446]. The works of mercy are affirmed [2447] as is the preferential love on the part of the Church for "those who are oppressed by poverty" [2448].

o. "The decisive point of the social question is that goods created by God for everyone should in fact reach everyone in accordance with justice and with the help of charity" [2459].

The two areas of the Catechism discussed above do not exhaust its coverage of themes from Catholic social teaching. One must look elsewhere to find important discussions, including: our relationship to, and responsibility for, creation [339, 344, 373]; religious freedom [1738]; the family and society [2207-13]; the duties of civil authorities [2235-37] and citizens [2238-40, 42-43]; the duty to welcome immigrants by prosperous nations [2241]; the right to armed resistance to oppression [2243]; human life and assaults on it [2258-83]; and the duty to safeguard peace [2302-17].

Key Themes or Principles in Catholic Social Teaching

Several authors recently have attempted to summarize the key themes or principles of Catholic social teaching in ways that will be helpful for understanding and action. One or more may provide a useful framework for the ideas contained in the above review of the key documents in the tradition. First, economist William J. Byron, writing in *America* several years ago, offered "ten building blocks of Catholic social teaching."[137] Stating the key themes in the form of principles, Byron's list follows:

1. The principle of human dignity.
2. The principle of respect for human life.
3. The principle of association.
4. The principle of participation.
5. The principle of preferential protection for the poor and vulnerable.
6. The principle of solidarity.
7. The principle of stewardship.
8. The principle of subsidiarity.
9. The principle of human equality.
10. The principle of the common good.

Byron suggests that these ten principles can accommodate every conceivable social issue, provide categories for developing lectures or class materials, or provide a framework for storing and retrieving materials on the tradition.

Second, in a recent book on Catholic social teaching in action, theologian Thomas Massaro offers nine themes around which to organize the key texts within the tradition. His list has some similarities to that offered by Byron:

1. The dignity of every person and human rights.
2. Solidarity, common good, and participation.
3. Family life.
4. Subsidiarity and the proper role of government.
5. Property ownership in modern society: rights and responsibilities.
6. The dignity of work, rights of workers, and support for labor unions.
7. Colonialism and economic development.
8. Peace and disarmament.
9. Option for the poor and vulnerable.[138]

Massaro, in introducing his list of key themes, observes that, while similar lists offered by others rarely match perfectly, there seems to be a general agreement about the basic items that belong on such a list.

Third, the bishops of the United States also have worked to develop summaries of major themes from Catholic social teaching. Their efforts also demonstrate how summaries can evolve over time, as Catholic social teaching itself evolves. In 1991, on the hundredth anniversary of *Rerum Novarum*, the bishops wrote a short pastoral message in which they highlighted the following six themes from the tradition:

1. The life and dignity of the human person.
2. The rights and responsibilities of the human person.
3. The call to family, community, and participation.
4. The dignity of work and the rights of workers.
5. The option for the poor and vulnerable.
6. Solidarity.[139]

Seven years later, in a new document on the teaching of Catholic social teaching, the bishops reiterated the above six themes, but added a seventh:

7. Care for God's creation.[140]

This addition reflected an increasing concern from both the Vatican and bishops around the world about the condition of our natural and human ecology and a growing awareness that the duties of steward-ship of the earth needed more articulation as an intrinsic component of the tradition. It also underscored the difficulty faced by those who attempt to summarize a complex and evolving tradition in a short list of themes, that, frozen in time, may be inadequate to reflect the tradition or to respond to changing needs or conditions. The bishops' list, however, probably will have the longest shelf life in the United States since educational materials are being promoted by Catholic educators and publishers organized around these seven themes. An interesting question would be whether the recent terrorist attacks on New York and Washington and the wars in Afghanistan and Iraq would prompt the addition of another theme better reflecting the war and peace component of the tradition (similar to Massaro's seventh item).

Some Trends in the Tradition

This survey of major developments in modern Catholic social thought shows that a wide variety of concerns have been woven into a rich tapestry of teaching: worker rights, development, church-state relations, military spending, deterrence policy, liberation, and the option for the poor. This summary presentation also betrays the shifts and developments of a reflective church leadership over a century-plus of radically and rapidly changing social and political realities. Various commentators have analyzed those trends at length, far beyond the scope of this study. A few key developments, however, need emphasis here for purposes of better understanding the modern roots of faithjustice.

A World Perspective. First, it is abundantly clear that, as the Church included more and more third-world bishops in its leadership, it also opened its eyes to the wider world. Under the influence of media and economic and social forces, citizens across the world likewise were opening their eyes. The focus of Catholic social thought upon the plight of the industrial workers of Europe and North America in the earlier decades has shifted. It has now turned to the nations of the Southern hemisphere, so much so that, "What was the periphery, the southern or third world, has become the center, the criterion by which other realities are judged."[141] In addition, with the fall of the U.S.S.R., the acute development needs of the countries of Eastern Europe joined those of the Southern half of the world as priority concerns.

With that broadening in vision and concerns came a shift from acceptance of a relatively static and autocratic European society in the late nineteenth century to call for a new world economic order.

That new order would require structural changes to effect international equity and justice between nations, as well as an end to neo-colonial arrangements within nations of the South. New imperatives rose for changes in international trade, arms reduction and control of the arms trade, alleviation of third-world debt, and attention to the growing problems associated with globalization of the economy and culture.

Communism and Capitalism. Second, there is also a shift from an "acceptance," without formal endorsement, of capitalism by Pope Leo XIII in the beginning of this period. This initial acceptance is gradually changed by the doubts of Pius XI, by Pius XII's recognition of capitalism's tie to egoism, and John XXIII's call for its reform. Paul VI then seems to take a posture of greater neutrality on both capitalism and communism, allowing local church affirmation of the good and criticism of the evil in a plurality of economic and political models operative in local situations. Pope John Paul II in his earlier writing then attempts to distance the Church from the dominant political and economic schools of both East and West. He harshly criticizes the underlying ideologies of both liberal capitalism and Marxist collectivism and the devastating evil and destructiveness of their interaction.

Then, in *Centensimus Annus,* Pope John Paul reflects on both socialism and liberalism in light of the fall of the U.S.S.R. and the dominance of capitalism on the world stage. He contends that Pope Leo foresaw the negative political, social, and economic consequences of the social order proposed by socialism, including its suppression of private property [12]. Socialism's flawed anthropology subordinates persons to socioeconomic mechanisms [13] and is rooted primarily in atheism [13] and class struggle [14]. "Real socialism" was embodied in the oppressive regimes that fell in 1989. Their fall, John Paul says, was due to violations of the rights of workers (private initiative, ownership of property, and economic freedom) [23], the inefficiency of the economic system as a consequence of violating human rights [24], and the spiritual void created by atheism [24].

Turning to capitalism and in the context of affirming the efficiency of "the free market," John Paul writes:

> We have seen that it is unacceptable to say that the defeat of so-called "real socialism" leaves capitalism as the only model of economic organization. It is necessary to break down the barriers and monopolies which leave so many countries on the margins of development and to provide

all individuals and nations with the basic conditions which
will enable them to share in development.[142]

Again, he asks whether "capitalism should be the goal of the countries now making efforts to rebuild their economy and society?" John
Paul's answer is:

> The answer is obviously complex. If by *capitalism* is meant
> an economic system which recognizes the fundamental
> and positive role of business, the market, private property
> and the resulting responsibility for the means of produc-
> tion as well as free human creativity in the economic sec-
> tor, then the answer is certainly in the affirmative even
> though it would perhaps be more appropriate to speak of
> a *business economy, market economy,* or simply *free economy.*
> But if by capitalism is meant a system in which freedom in
> the economic sector is not circumscribed within a strong
> juridical framework which places it at the service of
> human freedom in its totality and which sees it as a par-
> ticular aspect of that freedom, the core of which is ethical
> and religious, then the reply is certainly negative.[143]

It is important to read this statement in full. Many commentators quoted it in part and out of context, even going so far as to
reverse the two alternative "if" sentences to end with the affirmative
(Richard John Neuhaus).[144] Ringing praises of capitalism, as some
claimed, or "the moral vision of a political economy such as that of
the United States" (Michael Novak)[145] were at best a new form of theological spin control and at worst a form of "market idolatry" [40]
when judged in the encyclical's full complexity. As John Paul
explained at an audience on the day *Centesimus* was released, the
Catholic Church "has always refused and still refuses today to make
the market the supreme regulator or almost the model or synthesis of
social life."[146]

John Paul's position, consistent with the tradition, has been to
criticize both socialism and capitalism, even the "new capitalism." As
if to respond to the wishful thinking of some free-market commentators, the pope once more made clear in a 1993 address in Latvia his
criticism of both communism and capitalism:

> Besides, Catholic social doctrine is not a surrogate for cap-
> italism. In fact, although decisively condemning "social-

ism," the church, since Leo XIII's *Rerum Novarum,* has always distanced itself from capitalistic ideology, holding it responsible for grave social injustices (cf. *Rerum Novarum,* 2). In *Quadragesimo Anno* Pius XI, for his part, used clear and strong words to stigmatize the international imperialism of money (*Quadragesimo Anno,* 109). This line is also confirmed in the more recent magisterium, and I myself, after the historical failure of communism, did not hesitate to raise serious doubts on the validity of capitalism, if by this expression one means not simply the "market economy" but "a system in which freedom in the economic sector is not circumscribed within a strong juridical framework which places it at the service of human freedom in its totality" (*Centesimus Annus,* 42).[147]

The pope endorses neither capitalism nor communism, nor does he propose some third way between the two or some economic model of its own. The Church's proper contribution is Catholic social teaching that, in the prophetic mode, "recognizes the positive value of the market and of enterprise, but which at the same time points out that these need to be oriented toward the common good" [43]. The 1999 discussion of "neoliberalism" in *Ecclesia in America* [56] adds further weight to the argument that Catholic social teaching remains profoundly critical of current market-driven societies and the injustices which they perpetuate.

Private Property and Universal Destination. Third, the Church's stance toward private property and, importantly, its concept of the nature of property evolve across the modern tradition. Initially, the popes are strong in their support for the right of private property, though they call upon owners to exercise their own social responsibility in sharing especially surplus property with those in need around them. Gradually, perhaps influenced more by the rediscovery of the biblical tradition as refining the natural law tradition, the Church stresses the social mortgage on private property. Individual property rights are then conceptualized and affirmed in a socialized context where property must serve the common good and where the state has a duty to insist that it does, even to appropriate it to its common purposes. The right of private property, however, remains intact, especially seen as a way for the poor themselves to acquire and exercise economic rights, freedoms, and human dignity.

In keeping with the tradition, Pope John Paul II in *Centesimus Annus* affirms the importance of the right to private property and the understanding that these rights were not absolute, modified by com-plementary principles such as the universal destination of all goods [6]. In his own treatment, he roots the common destination of goods in cre-ation and in the gospel of Jesus [30–31], and clarifies its meaning:

> Ownership of the means of production, whether in indus-try or agriculture, is just and legitimate if it serves useful work. It becomes illegitimate, however, when it is not uti-lized or when it serves to impede the work of others in an effort to gain a profit which is not the result of the overall expansion of work and the wealth of society, but rather is the result of curbing them or of illicit exploitation, specu-lation or the breaking of solidarity among working people. Ownership of this kind has no justification and represents an abuse in the sight of God and man.[148]

John Paul further explains that "ownership morally justifies itself in the creation...of opportunities for work and human growth for all" [43].

The pope also notes an important development in the nature of property, shifting from land to capital to know-how, technology, and skill.

> Whereas at one time the decisive factor of production was the land and later capital—understood as a total complex of the instruments of production—today the decisive factor is increasingly man himself, that is, his knowledge, espe-cially his scientific knowledge, his capacity for interrelated and compact organization as well as his ability to perceive the needs of others and to satisfy them.[149]

Hailed by some commentators as paean to the entrepreneur, the encyclical rightfully highlights the key role of disciplined, creative human work, economic organization, and initiative and entrepre-neurial ability. The pope affirms important virtues associated with this economic role, namely, diligence, industriousness, reasonable risk taking, reliability and fidelity in relationships, and courage in decision-making leadership [32]. These are ultimately rooted in free-dom, dependent on protection of "the right to freedom as well as the duty of making responsible use of freedom" [32].

By the same token, however, this insight into the nature of prop-erty in a highly technical and organized economic society prompts

John Paul to a deeper insight into the nature of poverty and marginalization within this same national or international society.

> The fact is that many people, perhaps the majority today, do not have the means which would enable them to take their place in an effective and humanly dignified way within a productive system in which work is truly central. They have no possibility of acquiring the basic knowledge which would enable them to express their creativity and develop their potential. They have no way of entering the network of knowledge and intercommunication which would enable them to see their qualities appreciated and utilized. Thus, if not actually exploited, they are to a great extent marginalized; economic development takes place over their heads, so to speak, when it does not actually reduce the already narrow scope of their old subsistence economies.[150]

These people are thus unable to compete effectively or to meet needs formerly satisfied by traditional means of production. Intensification of their poverty, powerlessness, and marginalization then results. In his words, "In fact, for the poor, to the lack of material goods has been added a lack of knowledge and training which prevents them from escaping their state of humiliating subjection" [33]. This, the pontiff says, is the condition of the majority of the third world.

This inability of so many people to access the productive system and the "free market" is another indication of the limited scope of the pope's acknowledgement of the efficiency of the market. It also signals yet another area where government and subsidiary institutions must act in solidarity with the poor to insure the common good. Efforts to meet immediate basic human needs must be combined then with basic and advanced education, technical training, economic and development assistance, sharing of technology, and other efforts to remove the barriers to access and to insure equality of opportunity and participation within institutions, markets, and productive systems.

Both this expanded sense of property and the heightened sense of poverty also underscore the importance of property holding by the widest number of citizens and participation in the control and ownership of productive enterprises by workers as well as those traditionally called owners and managers. These ideas also support creative efforts, such as the Catholic Campaign for Human Development created by the U.S. bishops, which focus on empowerment and economic

development among communities traditionally thought to be powerless and asset deficient. The importance of property, participation,
and ownership has been part of the Catholic social tradition for
almost a century; but these ideas receive new importance here.

Justice and Evangelization. The fourth trend concerns the connection of faith, evangelization, and the social question. Initially, the
Church viewed the problems of industrial society as ones of the application of faith and the pastoral needs of workers. The Church was primarily concerned about workers' well-being and even their loss of
faith due to hardships or their involvement in social movements and
ideologies outside the Church. In the wake of Vatican II and the
Synod of 1971, the social reality then shifts to the center of the faith
question. Justice is seen as central to the gospel and its proclamation
and implementation by the Church as central to its evangelizing mission, which is also its liberating mission. The preferential love of the
poor stands at the heart of the Church's understanding of who God
and Christ are. Political apathy by Christians is then unacceptable
because "the Church shares responsibility for secular as well as religious history."[151] Doing justice is a credibility test.

Later, in *Centesimus Annus,* Pope John Paul II indicates that social
teaching is not only part of the evangelizing mission of the Church but
"social teaching is itself a valid instrument of evangelization" [54]. The
credibility of the Church's social message, the pope adds, must come
"more immediately from the witness of actions than as a result of its
internal logic and consistency" [57]. The love of Christ in the poor is
made concrete in the promotion of justice [58]. He also reiterates that
oppressive social institutions are "structures of sin." To destroy such
structures and to replace them with more authentic forms of living in
community requires both courage and patience [38].

The Role of Workers and the Poor. Fifth, there is a shift, growing
but not yet mature, from an attitude of protecting workers and the
poor to an understanding that they must be the artisans of their own
destiny—individually, as workers and citizens, and as poor nations.
The language of empowering and enabling, solidarity and interdependence, and preferential love all contribute to this growing awareness. Its full meaning, however, especially in ways that can involve the
poor and nonpoor in mutuality in first, second, third, and fourth
worlds, is still unfolding.

One longstanding vehicle for such empowerment in Catholic
teaching and in historical reality has been the labor union. Rather
than to consider unions as organizations in decline and no longer to
be promoted and defended by the Church, in *Centesimus Annus,* Pope

John Paul II affirms their importance in defending workers' rights and interests, as well as providing a vital cultural role of enabling workers to participate more fully in the life of their nation and assisting in their own development [35]. John Paul also introduces new thinking about the workplace when he notes that work has become increasingly social. He attributes this to the economic system where successful work combines increasing knowledge of the potentialities of the earth with a better grasp of the needs of those for whom one does one's work [31]. This is a "community of work" that "embraces ever widening circles" [32].

If work is essentially communitarian, there are significant implications for owners, managers, and workers. Good managers know that employees' morale and well-being is critical to the status of any enterprise and that policies destructive of workers' rights and dignity eventually undermine the firm itself. What John Paul does, however, is to give a more reasoned and ethical foundation to a priority concern for the "community of persons" comprising any productive enterprise. This is true in the profit, not-for-profit, voluntary, or religious sector.

The role of workers, in turn, is transformed by this social understanding of the workplace:

> This teaching also recognizes the legitimacy of workers' efforts to obtain full respect for their dignity and to gain broader areas of participation in the life of industrial enterprises so that, while cooperating with others and under the direction of others, they can in a certain sense "work for themselves" through the exercise of their intelligence and freedom.[152]

John Paul adds that, even though integral development of persons through work may weaken consolidated power structures, it will promote the greater productivity and efficiency of work.

One hears echoes here of the U.S. bishops' 1986 pastoral letter on economic justice and their call for a "new American experiment" in economic rights. Cooperatives, worker ownership, and other shared decision-making models were recommended "to broaden the sharing of economic power and to make economic decisions more accountable to the common good." (See pp. 113–15, above.)

John Paul's reflections on the workplace hardly exhaust the areas in which increased participation, self-determination, empowerment, democracy, and leadership are to be exercised by those whom society has traditionally marginalized in poverty and obscurity. While church documents continue to stress the preferential love for individuals and groups who are poor, imaginative vehicles for them to become artisans of their own destiny need further development in economic, political, and social reality.

Urgency. The final trend comes most easily from studying the historical chart on the following page, which overviews the history of the last one hundred years of Catholic social teaching. Developed from a presentation by Jim Jennings of the U.S. bishops' Catholic Campaign for Human Development, the chart[153] makes one preeminent point: the urgency of the Church's social concern! From a forty-year interval between *Rerum Novarum* and *Quadragesimo Anno* to a twenty-year interval preceding *Mater et Magistra*, we have now entered an epoch of major and intensifying proclamations of church leadership on social concerns. It is reflected as well in the action of Christians across the world in addressing social injustice. The authors of these documents repeatedly insist, as the cries of the poor proclaim to all who will listen, that the social reality is worse. The gospel of love and justice is more and more shut out by the noise of intensifying consumption and worsening oppression; and the call of the Christ of the poor is more and more plaintive.

The Ongoing Task

Before leaving this topic, it is important to note that, if this is an organic tradition, as noted earlier, then there is more to be done. There are a number of questions either not addressed, or not adequately addressed, by the main documents in the tradition. Moreover, social and economic changes in the future will give rise to the need for new reflection from the perspective of faith. Among these topics is the care of the environment, although many commentators see good progress begun in Pope John Paul's 1990 world day of peace message *Peace with God the Creator, Peace with All of Creation* and in a number of statements from national and regional conferences of bishops in recent years.[154] One challenge for the future will be to move from the "stewardship model," which positions humans over-against the rest of creation, to a more adequate and updated approach that would take seriously the solidarity that extends beyond the human species to other forms of life and their habitats.[155]

Another important issue for many people is the role of women both in rapidly changing societies of industrial and developing

THE FAITHJUSTICE CENTENNIAL

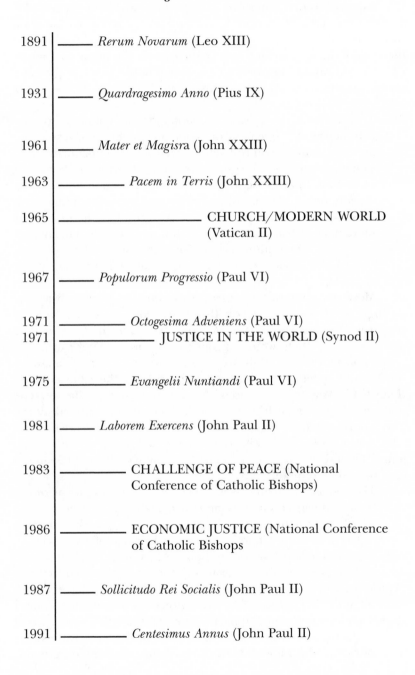

1891 —— *Rerum Novarum* (Leo XIII)

1931 —— *Quardragesimo Anno* (Pius IX)

1961 —— *Mater et Magisra* (John XXIII)

1963 ———— *Pacem in Terris* (John XXIII)

1965 ———————— CHURCH/MODERN WORLD
(Vatican II)

1967 —— *Populorum Progressio* (Paul VI)

1971 ———— *Octogesima Adveniens* (Paul VI)
1971 ————— JUSTICE IN THE WORLD (Synod II)

1975 ———— *Evangelii Nuntiandi* (Paul VI)

1981 —— *Laborem Exercens* (John Paul II)

1983 ———— CHALLENGE OF PEACE (National
Conference of Catholic Bishops)

1986 ———— ECONOMIC JUSTICE (National Conference
of Catholic Bishops

1987 —— *Sollicitudo Rei Socialis* (John Paul II)

1991 ———— *Centesimus Annus* (John Paul II)

nations and within the Church itself. That is the subject of the 1990 U.S. bishops' pastoral letter *One in Christ Jesus,* which attempts to dialogue with women's concerns. The controversial course of that letter, with many commentators urging that it not be published, highlighted the continuing complexity and challenge of this question for the Church. As Cardinal Bernardin commented to the U.S. bishops gathered for their retreat meeting in June 1990:

> The difficulties we have encountered and continue to experience with our pastoral letter on women's concerns are a sign of the unrest and alienation affecting many women, even as some support the more traditional roles of women. In any case, the issues of ordination and jurisdiction, or the exercise of authority, as they relate to ministry will not simply go away by fiat. The feminist movement impacts the church. How can the church, in light of its constitution and mission, best address the aspirations of women? There is no doubt that we must.[156]

Most disappointing in *Centesimus Annus,* certainly, was the incongruous near-muteness on the oppression of women and the concerns of women both in secular society and in the Church. The overall insensitivity to women's concerns was manifest, for instance, in the constant use of exclusive language (in the English language version and others)—culminating in the title of the final chapter, "Man Is the Way of the Church." Vatican staffers know better. The insult to many women inside of the Church is compounded by the lost opportunity to evangelize women outside the Church who have many concerns common with this otherwise strong document. Pope John Paul and the cause of modern Catholic social teaching should have been served better.

The so-called women's issue, touching as it does so many of the church and human community and so many of those who are the *anawim,* will require further and deeper consideration both in the universal reflection of the Church and in a wide range of local cultures and churches, including various bishops' conferences.

A third issue pushing its way into the forefront of church discussions of social teaching is globalization. Although it has received some attention in *Centesimus Annus,* regional synods of bishops, and elsewhere, its far-reaching impact demands a searching analysis and clear reflection in faith. Its pervasiveness and power raise questions of the need for a world authority of comparable strength and oversight, a suitable juridical framework of trade agreements and more, and the development and strengthening of world labor movements to confront the challenges of transnational corporate power.[157]

In the wake of the collapse of the major confrontation between East and West, the 1990s were dominated by a series of conflicts which philosopher John P. Langan describes as "waged by nations, races and empires for the exercise of domination by groups defined in ethnic, linguistic, religious and cultural terms."[158] While these conflicts were not limited to the past decade, they and their roots became clearer—in such places as the former Yugoslavia, Rwanda and Burundi, Northern Ireland, and Sudan. Langan articulates this fourth challenge to Catholic social teaching as the need for a "more penetrating and discerning sense of the ways in which the lesser solidarities of race and neighborhood, of clan and state, of tribe and Gemeinschaft come to obstruct the call to the greater solidarity of our common humanity."[159] The September 11, 2001, terrorist attacks on the United States and the subsequent wars in Afghanistan and Iraq might well fall under this same challenge, pushing us as well to respond both to the underlying causes of conflict and the rules of engagement in fighting terrorism.

A fifth issue was raised by Archbishop Rembert G. Weakland in his revisit to the pastoral letter on economic justice ten years after its publication. Noting the concerns of the U.S. bishops about the economy, Weakland named the relationship of wealth and power as one of the critical issues that was not treated in the 1986 pastoral letter, but that has become more and more important with the passage of time. With some corporations now wielding more economic power than entire nation-states and the insidious power of money increasingly evident in the decisions of our own government, Weakland questioned the effects of unbridled capitalism on democracy itself.[160] And, to the extent that democracy is undermined by wealth, we can assume that there will not be the appropriate juridical framework to constrain free-market capitalism in the interest of justice and the common good, with the resultant social evils that already are evident worldwide.

The sixth priority concern for the future is the rising disparity between rich and poor occurring both within the United States and across the world. Besides the vivid injustice of some living in excessive luxury while so many others literally starve to death, these acute disparities between individuals and nations can seriously undermine the legitimacy of governments and sharply threaten the world's peace. The urgency in Catholic social teaching noted above will continue and escalate as the sufferings of the poor are exacerbated by the negative forces of globalization and social injustice; and the condemnations of the excesses of free-market capitalism should intensify as well as the search for alternative economic and regulatory structures.

Other issues needing further treatment include: the role of technology in post-industrial societies, as in health care; the continuing plight of millions of refugees worldwide; consumerism, advertising, and the electronic media and their devastating impact on human dignity and community; the role of the poor as agents of social change, including further deliberation on the use of armed resistance to oppression and injustice.

Centesimus Annus concluded the first one hundred years of modern Catholic social teaching strongly by building firmly on that tradition. It opened the second century with a vigorous challenge to market economics and the international community to construct a future that draws all peoples and nations into a full share in creation and its new property. The letter challenged the Church to a renewed evangelization in action for social and international justice and the promotion of authentic democracy. Our next two chapters will focus on two critical themes that are at the center of this renewed evangelization: the preferential love of the poor and the movement from individual action to structural change in the service of charity and justice.

QUESTIONS FOR REFLECTION AND DISCUSSION

1. When and how did you first learn about Catholic social teaching?

2. What were the most important developments in the history of the Church in giving birth to its social teaching?

3. What key idea(s) in the tradition most pleased you? Upset you? Surprised you?

4. What issues have been ignored in the development of the tradition?

5. What social issues need more work by the Church?

6. What viewpoints or perspectives seem overlooked?

7. Which summary of the key themes in Catholic social teaching seems most comprehensive? Construct your own summary (individually or with others in your group).

CHAPTER FOUR

Standing with the Poor

> Atticus was right. One time he said you never really know
> a man until you stand in his shoes and walk around in
> them.
>
> Jean Louise "Scout" Finch
> *To Kill A Mockingbird*[1]

*During my last semester of philosophy studies in Mobile in the Spring of
1967, I volunteered one day a week in the counselor's office in a large Black
inner-city public high school in an area called Toulminville. On my first day,
I was led to the cafeteria near the end of the first half of the lunch period and
sat down to eat at one of the faculty tables in the front. In a few minutes, those
I had been introduced to at the table had finished lunch and left for other
duties. No one else sat down to eat with me as the second lunch period began,
and I found myself alone staring at hundreds of strangers of another race,
who politely ignored me and enjoyed their lunches and one another in the typical roar of school cafeterias.*

*In that very brief moment of isolation, I felt I had some glimpse of the
alienating experience taking place all over the South and elsewhere as young
Black students were being asked by society, their families, and the law to
break the color barrier at our all-white grammar schools, high schools, and
colleges. Mine was hardly traumatic, but it seemed to me that theirs was surely
a terrifying and heroic experience, especially with the hostility and violence
which were all too common then.*

❖ ❖ ❖

*At the end of my first year of legal services practice in Atlanta, a group
of us were sent to a consumer law training conference in Cincinnati. It was
1973 and my first trip to a new city in some time. In the taxi from the air-
port to our downtown hotel, I found my attention drawn irresistibly to the*

142

interest rates displayed in loan company windows, the eighteen-months-to-pay signs posted by what my Jewish friends called "schlock merchants," storefront day-labor marketeers, AFDC and Food Stamp offices, and transient hotels. No matter how hard I tried to be just another tourist enjoying new sights in a new town, the signposts of the world of the poor, which I thought I had left at the Atlanta Legal Aid Society office, glared out at me. I could not turn my eyes away from the sadness.

❖ ❖ ❖

Each semester, twice a year for the past twenty-five years, a painful drama has been played out in the Catholic theology schools in the United States, which have admitted both women and men to study for their divinity and theology degrees in preparation for various ministries in the Church. This was the case for us in Chicago in the mid-seventies as well. As the time of our ordinations approached, classmates who shared three or four years of classroom and term-paper grind, theological reflection groups, informal bull sessions, ministerial internships, genuine friendships, and all that makes up the formal and informal ways of education often found themselves torn apart by one reality of our Church: Only the men could be ordained.

The men had to choose to support, accept, rationalize, explain, tolerate, or protest, not just to their religious superiors or to their families, who were often unaware of the problem, but also to their female classmates and ultimately to themselves. The women, in turn, even if they did not seek ordination, chose to support their male classmates, accept, rationalize, explain, tolerate, protest, or, as some friends of mine did, slip away on ordination weekend to nurse their grief and anger in solitude. Few passed through this experience without strong feelings of one kind or another, not the least of which was powerlessness before larger forces and the frustration, guilt, anger, blaming, and even rage which it engendered.

❖ ❖ ❖

Back in Atlanta in the late seventies, even though I directed the Senior Citizens Law Project of the Atlanta Legal Aid Society, I still had some opportunities to spend time with clients. One morning in a small home in a near northwest neighborhood, I waited with two elderly Black gentlemen for a delayed witness to a will signing. While we sat in an overheated room, one, a bricklayer, told the story of riding out of north Georgia as a boy on the back of their family wagon at a time when all the Black families in that particular county had been driven out. He then had worked a long and productive life and raised his own family in Atlanta.

The other, a carpenter, told stories of how he had gone back to north Georgia as an adult to work, but how he had to be sure of a secure place to stay each night or be out of those rural counties when the sun set–or else!

They talked without rancor, in the mellowness of old age and the security of hard work and honest living. I could not help but like them and feel at ease with them. I was honored by their reminiscing with me there, and almost felt myself an intruder. They caused me to reflect that our work was with persons, not clients or the poor. Later, I resented those who would try to restrict the scope of what I, as a legal services attorney, could do in representing these persons. I even more deeply detested the no-nothingness of those who would dare to pretend to distinguish the truly needy among America's poor persons without one whit of experience among them.

❖ ❖ ❖

Some time ago, I had lunch with a young woman who had a very responsible job in Washington working with the United States Catholic Conference, the bishops' national offices. She had a deep commitment to social justice, a more than full-time job promoting the bishops' vision of a more caring society, and was newly married. As we talked, she explained that, no matter how important her work or her objectives there, she missed the direct contact with poor persons that she had in her previous position back in her home city. Because of this, and her fear that job responsibilities could detach her from the very people she set out to help, she had volunteered in one of Washington's homeless shelters a night a week. There, for a few hours a week, she helped the occupants fill out their Social Security applications.

❖ ❖ ❖

During my time working at Catholic Charities USA, the nation engaged in an intense political debate about welfare reform. We produced our own welfare reform plan in 1993 entitled, Transforming the Welfare System. *Although we believed the system needed to be transformed to provide a focused investment in low-income families, we opposed much of the plan developed by President Clinton's administration and most of that subsequently developed by the Newt Gingrich-led Congress and signed by President Clinton in 1996. Because of our outspoken opposition, we were attacked in turn by George Weigel, Republican Senator Rick Santorum of Pennsylvania, the Capital Research Center, the Manhattan Institute, Michael Novak, George Will, the*

Heritage Foundation, and others in the pantheon of conservative commentators. Their main charge was that we were "not Catholic" because of our opposition to welfare reform and because of our partnership with government in many programs operated by Catholic Charities agencies across the country. They were silent, strangely, about the fact that the U.S. Conference of Catholic Bishops had raised the same questions about the so-called welfare reform law passed by Congress.

One of my favorite heroic scenes occurs in the defense of the Alamo against General Santa Anna's Mexican army. Colonel William Barret Travis gathers the small band of defenders together, reminds them of their family responsibilities and their likely fate if they remain in the mission fort, and invites them to choose for themselves what they will do. He does so by drawing a line on the ground with a sword and challenging those who will stay to cross the line. U.S. moviegoers swell with pride and excitement as Davy Crockett, a wounded Jim Bowie, and all but one or two of the men cross the line to join Travis in heroic martyrdom for the Lone Star Republic. This chapter is about crossing the line.

Despite the long list of key ideas from modern Catholic social thought developed in the last chapter, a contemporary life of *faithjustice* essentially revolves around two nuclei. These two key considerations shaped much of the late twentieth-century Roman Catholic reflection upon *faithjustice*, and they form the dual themes for the rest of this book. The first of these is the option for the poor. It is a controversial phrase with its roots in the Medellin Conference of Latin American bishops in 1968.[2]

For some people the option for the poor is a strong phrase "which has become a powerful summary and symbol of the new approach"[3] of the Church to the social question. For others it has smacked of a Marxist class option, which suggests that the Church has taken sides in a class struggle.[4] For still others, words like *option* suggest "optional" and, in English at least, belie the strength of the underlying and fundamental scriptural commitment.[5]

The option for the poor actually reflects Pope John's emphasis one month before the Vatican Council that the Church present itself to the underdeveloped world as it is, "the Church of all, and especially *the Church of the poor.*"[6] His point has been emphasized again by both Pope Paul VI and Pope John Paul II. John Paul also uses an apparent alternative "a preferential love of the poor." John Paul has further restated it as, "preferential yet not exclusive love of the poor," apparently to correct whatever he thinks may be misleading about the

uses of the phrase. Even in doing so, however, John Paul has taken
pains to make it clear that he does not retreat from the point of the
preference.[7] He himself has preached most strongly on this in his trav-
els, including frequent use of Pope John's phrase "the Church of the
poor."[8] More recently, in *Ecclesia in Asia,* the pope again affirmed this
preference and explained:

> In seeking to promote human dignity, the church shows a
> preferential love of the poor and the voiceless, because the
> Lord has identified himself with them in a special way (cf.
> Mt. 25:40). This love excludes no one, but simply embod-
> ies a priority of service to which the whole Christian tra-
> dition bears witness.[9]

The appropriateness and tenacity of this concept in Catholic social
teaching in the past half century invite us to take this chapter to
understand more deeply the concept and its application.

I use "standing with the poor" to get at the underlying thrust of
both "option for the poor" and "preferential love." Standing with the
poor carries the sense of an active stance, a definite choice, and a
decision to cross over the line drawn between most of us and the marginalized pushed to society's periphery. Standing with the poor
recalls the Lord Yahweh who pitches a tent in the midst of God's chosen people, who makes their suffering and hopes God's own suffering and hopes. It suggests the Emmanuel of Jesus, God choosing to
be one of us and then identifying with "the least among us."

Standing with the poor does not involve a class-struggle rejection of those not poor; but, as we shall see, this decision inevitably
draws down upon those who stand with the poor not only the oppression experienced by the poor themselves but also a special bitterness
reserved by the powerful for the prophets. To understand the thrust
and scope of this preferential love, it is necessary to look at who are
the poor, why they are to be preferred, and what this means for contemporary Christians. In so doing we can also come to a better understanding of the biblical and spiritual "poor in spirit," another way of
describing those who stand with the poor.[10]

Poverty of spirit is sometimes discussed as a kind of spiritual
detachment from one's wealth of whatever magnitude that somehow
mysteriously connects us to the poor and to the poor Christ. As such,
it can seem to excuse us from the substantive demands of social justice. On the contrary, as John Paul himself made clear in preaching
in Brazil in 1980, to be "poor in spirit" is to be open to God, ready to

receive God's gifts, aware that all is gift, *and thus to be merciful and generous.* While deeply spiritual in its profound insight into self and into our relationship to God and neighbor, "poor in spirit" has specific content, the pontiff insists.

For the poor, John Paul continues, poverty of spirit means that, because of their closeness to God, they must maintain their human dignity and their openness to others around them. For those who are somewhat better off, it means thinking of those poorer than themselves and sharing with them "in a systematic way...." The meaning of poverty of spirit for the wealthy, the pope declares, is that they constantly give themselves and serve others in proportion to their riches. He clearly links openness to God to giving generously and to working for structural change in society, namely: "how to organize socio-economic life...in such a way that it will tend to bring about equality between people, rather than putting a yawning gap between them."[11]

Who Are the Poor?

We ask the who-question because of a reaction among well-meaning churchpeople against the concept of a love that would seem to prefer one group as opposed to others. For example, in the wake of the renewed call of the Church since Vatican II to stand with the poor, Jesuits around the world have had a number of meetings to explore its implications for the direction of our schools, parishes, and retreat houses. Questions have arisen about whom we serve through these institutions, what values we convey, and what the institutional impact of our works is upon structural justice and injustice. Strong challenges have arisen against continuing the status quo in many institutions where few of the economically poor can afford to participate. In our formal and informal deliberations, these challenges have certainly generated "resistance"[12] in our communities and among our school and pastoral staffs.

Jesuits are by no means the only ones to react this way. Widespread difficulties with this concept of standing with the poor, including fears that it might have implications about the clientele served by church-sponsored schools, parishes, hospitals, or diocesan services, have been framed in terms of a concern that one group was somehow better in God's eyes than others.[13] Clergy and laity alike have sometimes tried to generalize by saying that all of us are poor. In itself, of course, without historical referent, this statement is true enough as a description of our sinful state and everyone's need for God's grace.[14]

Frankly though, many of us are not now poor, and never have been.[15] This ahistorical generalization that would widen the sweep of the net of the poor to include us all therefore must be tested against the tradition of *faithjustice* itself. In fact, that tradition, discussed in the preceding chapters, is usually repeated and spelled out in each of the contemporary Church documents that call Christians to stand with the poor. To understand the poor on the lips of Church leaders now, the first touchstone is the *anawim* of the Old Testament: the widows, orphans, and strangers who comprised God's beloved poor. They were those oppressed by a combination of poverty, powerlessness, and exclusion from the community. As the U.S. bishops put it, "What these groups have in common is their vulnerability and lack of power. They are often alone and have no protector or advocate."[16]As a group they are pushed or drop out of the community of the covenant, excluded from a decent share in the original goodness of God's creation.

We next look to Jesus for indications of who are the poor of this preferential love. Jesus tells the story of the rich man, Dives, ignoring the poor Lazarus who is described as being without the most basic economic resource: food (Luke 16:19–31). This is Pope John Paul's favorite parable for U.S. audiences. Jesus also repeatedly warns his listeners against greed and reliance on material possessions (Luke 6:24). Then, in that dramatic judgment scene from Matthew, Jesus names the *anawim* of his own time and place: the hungry, thirsty, naked, sick, and those in jail, often imprisoned for debt.[17]

The Old and New Testament scriptural terms for the poor primarily describe lack of material goods, but they also suggest dependence and powerlessness.[18] In this regard, the related term, *the lowly,* sometimes seems to suggest class status rather than mere absence of economic resources. However, there is a direct correlation in the same scriptures between the absence of possessions, the lack of status in the community, and the right to participate in community decision making. By analogy, we might consider, from the American experience, the use of property holding as a voting requirement and the infamous poll tax used to disqualify poor, Black voters.

The poor, except for those who might elect voluntary poverty for religious or other motivations, are almost always looked down upon and excluded from the decision and power centers of most societies. *Rarely is a group with wealth so excluded.* When such exclusion of a wealthy group does occur, powerfully held biases against ethnic or other group characteristics must be operative. More often than not, however, the same biases will also be operative in the economic sphere to make the group poor as well.

Poverty is clearly tied to issues of power and participation in society, profoundly assaulting human dignity. Theologian Thomas E. Clarke explains this assault and connects it to the destructive nature of oppression:

> Human dignity is most tragically affronted, not by material deprivation as such, but by every projection of contempt onto individuals and especially onto groups, on whatever basis. Oppression in its most dehumanizing form happens when a dominant culture says to whatever group it has chosen for scapegoating, "You are of lesser worth—of little worth—of no worth."
>
> The economic pastoral, despite its focus on economic oppression, moves toward this understanding of poverty, I believe, when it makes participation, not provision of material goods, the key to justice for the poor. "The ultimate injustice is for a person or group to be actively treated or passively abandoned as if they were nonmembers of the human race. To treat people this way is effectively to say that they simply do not count as human beings. This can take many forms, all of which can be described as varieties of marginalization or exclusion from social life" (No. 77).[19]

For Clarke, "What brings cultural disparagement to its peak as a truly demonic evil is its acceptance and interiorization by the scapegoated group." Citing Native Americans and Black males as prime examples of scapegoating in contemporary U.S. society, Clarke says that, when a marginalized group yields to the overwhelming pressure, it is then "fully constituted as oppressed and impotent."[20] This radical impoverishment is profoundly destructive of self-esteem, self-love, and self-acceptance.

Seen against this background and an analysis of recent Church documents as well, the poor with whom Christians are called to stand are generally those without the material resources for meeting life's needs and for inclusion in the ordinary life and processes of the society in which they are found.[21] Former Catholic University president and economist William Byron gives us a fuller sense of this:

I understand poverty to be sustained deprivation, and economic poverty to be sustained deprivation of income and
wealth (and, derivatively, deprivation of health, shelter,
food, education, employment and human dignity to the
extent that this last derives from all the rest).[22]

Efforts to render us all poor as a response to the call to stand with the
poor are simply untrue to the Judaeo-Christian tradition of *faithjustice*. In addition, such efforts would render the call for a special love
meaningless as well.

Ironically, what also sustains the reliance upon the overall tradition in defining the poor at this point is that the three primary
groups constituting the biblical *anawim*—widows, orphans, and
strangers—continue to be core groups within the contemporary
world's economically poor, politically powerless, and culturally marginalized, even in the United States.

Widows and Other Women Alone

The place of the biblical widow is held in our society by a number of women alone, many raising children as a result of an astonishing transformation in family units wrought by a variety of social and
economic forces. Not the least of these is desertion by husbands and
fathers. An astonishing number of these women live in poverty,
around the world and increasingly in the United States as well. Over
30 percent of all U.S. families headed by women are poor; and,
among minority families headed by women, the poverty rate for Black
families is almost 40 percent and that for Hispanic families exceeds
45 percent.[23]

In their discussion of women's poverty, the U.S. bishops
included among the causes: wage discrimination, for example,
women working full time outside the home earn only 75 percent of
what men earned;[24] discrimination in advancement and benefits;
weak unionization; and grossly insufficient alimony and child support.[25] Older women in the United States suffer the results of longer
life, with resultant increased health costs, and inadequate income,
assets, or coverage in private and public pension plans and under
social security. As a result, 73 percent of the elderly poor in the
United States were women.[26]

Across the world, the situation of women alone or raising families is often much worse. Inadequate income, backbreaking physical

labor, grossly inadequate health care, responsibilities for rearing large numbers of children, and other hardships are often combined with the denial of basic political, civil, and human rights. One report puts it this way:

> There are many ways of summarizing women's status relative to men's. One is economic, and here the well known United Nations quote from 1980 is still relevant: "Women constitute half the world's population, perform nearly two-thirds of its work hours, receive one-tenth of the world's income, and own less than one-hundredth of the world's property."
>
> Another indicator is women's legal status: nowhere in the world do women have the same legal or constitutional rights as men. The legal provision of rights does not guarantee "equality", but it is an essential prerequisite for women's full participation in political, economic, social and cultural development—from which equality can follow.[27]

Women continue to be considered as property in many cultures and/or to be severely restricted in their activities in others. Their contemporary condition only reiterates the privileged status called for in the scriptures.

Orphans and Other Children without Support

Despite the efforts of many women and men to the contrary, society continues to deem women to be the primary child-care providers. Considering their general economic, social, and political status sketched above, it comes as no surprise that large numbers of poor children come from families without one parent or both. The bishops presented an overview of child poverty in the United States in their 1986 pastoral letter:

> Poverty strikes some groups more severely than others. Perhaps most distressing is the growing number of children who are poor. Today one in every four American children under the age of 6 and one in every two black children under 6 are poor. The number of children in poverty rose by 4 million over the decade between 1973–83,

with the result that there are now more poor children in
the United States than at any time since 1965. The problem is particularly severe among female-headed families,
where more than half of all children are poor. Two-thirds
of black children and nearly three-quarters of Hispanic
children in such families are poor.[28]

The reasons relate to the breakdown of family structures, gender discrimination, economic deterioration, and cutbacks in governmental
assistance to families in the eighties. In the nineties, with an economic boom and improvements in employment and earnings among
low-income families, the percentage of children in poverty—after
counting government benefits and taxes—declined from 18 percent in
1989 to 14.3 percent in 1998, or 11.8 million in 1989 to 10.2 million
in 1998.[29] The recession of 2001 and the sharp rise in unemployment
will reverse these positive trends and drive the number of children in
poverty back up again; but, even in time of economic prosperity,
more than ten million U.S. children were living in poverty.

    Children's poverty is symptomatic of the poverty of their par-
ents. The disadvantages of poor children begin even before their
births as inadequate prenatal care exposes them to "much greater risk
of premature birth, low birth rates, physical and mental impairment,
and death before their first birthday."[30]

    The Children's Defense Fund provides a vivid picture of the sta-
tus of U.S. children in a frequently updated report entitled *Every Day
in America*. As of April 2001:

Every Day in America
- 1 young person under 25 dies from HIV infection.
- 6 children and youth under 20 commit suicide.
- 10 children and youth under 20 are homicide
  victims.
- 10 children and youth under 20 die from firearms.
- 34 children and youth under 20 die from accidents.
- 78 babies die.
- 156 babies are born at very low birthrate (less than
  3 lbs., 4 oz.).
- 186 children are arrested for violent crimes.
- 351 children are arrested for drug abuse
- 410 babies are born to mothers who had late or no
  prenatal care.

817   babies are born at low birthrate (less than 5 lbs., 8 oz).

1,310   babies are born without health insurance.

1,354   babies are born to teen mothers.

1,951   babies are born into poverty.

2,324   babies are born to mothers who are not high school graduates.

2,911   high school students drop out.

3,544   babies are born to unmarried mothers.

17,297   students are suspended from school.[31]

Children across the world suffer more acutely than adults from the ravages of poverty, famine, war, economic injustices, and the shocking individual and family dislocation experienced in countries undergoing "development." The Pontifical Justice and Peace Commission reported in 1987 that, "In Latin America, it is estimated that 20 million children sleep in the streets."[32]

Sojourners and Others without Homes

Today, the modern sojourners are the immigrants, migrants, refugees, and others dislocated from their homes and homelands by a variety of political, economic, social, and natural forces. One can hardly walk across the downtown of any large or small American city without encountering the homeless poor of our prosperous nation. Food lines and food banks have become the primary business of a variety of church and social agencies that once dealt with a wide range of other human and social needs. An increasing number of the homeless are families jettisoned from our economic and social system as some new form of debris.

The reality of America's homeless is also substantially linked to government cutbacks of support for housing rentals and purchases by 77 percent from $32 billion dollars in 1981 to less than $8 billion in 1989.[33] New units of Section 8 rental certificates, which assist in renting apartments in the private sector, and public housing rental subsidies continued to decline into the nineties, including four years—1995 to 1998—when no additional units or subsidies were funded by Congress.[34] Waiting time to be placed in public housing had risen to eleven months in 1998 and the average Section 8 waiting time had risen to twenty-eight months.[35] In March 2000, the Department of Housing and Urban Development (HUD) released its report entitled

Rental Housing Assistance–The Worsening Crisis, highlighting the following four points:

- *Despite continued economic expansion, worst case housing needs have reached an all-time high of 5.4 million families, increasing by 4 percent between 1995 and 1997.* Households with worst case needs are defined as unassisted renters with incomes below 50 percent of the local median, who pay more than half of their income for rent or live in severely substandard housing.

- *Families with worst case needs are working harder than ever.* Between 1991 and 1997, worst case needs increased more than three times as fast for very-low-income families with full-time wage earners than for all other very low-income families.

- *Housing that is affordable to the lowest income Americans continues to shrink.* The number of rental units affordable to extremely low-income families decreased by 5 percent since 1991—a loss of over 370,000 units.

- *The concentration of worst case housing needs among the poorest families continues to rise.* Between 1991 and 1997, worst case housing needs became increasingly concentrated among households with extremely low incomes. By 1997, over three-fourths of those with worst case needs had incomes below 30 percent of area median.[36]

One of the perverse impacts of the economic boom of the nineties was to drive up the cost of housing, making it more unaffordable for low-income families and worsening the homelessness situation in many U.S. communities.

While 20–25 percent of the single adult homeless population suffers from persistent mental illness, the National Coalition for the Homeless reports that children under 18 account for 25 percent, single women comprise 14 percent, and single men 45 percent of the urban homeless. Families with children are considered to be the fastest growing segment of the total homeless population, comprising 38–40 percent, with higher proportions reported in rural areas.[37]

Worldwide, some twenty-one million persons are counted officially as refugees,[38] and an uncounted number of immigrants and migrants are also without home and community. But the U.S. bishops noted a recent trend in U.S. receptiveness to refugees:

> Notwithstanding our nation's historic generosity in welcoming refugees, we are concerned with recent trends which indicate that the United States' commitment to refugee protection is waning. Since 1992, refugee admissions into the United States have dropped by forty-two percent, while U.S. overseas assistance to refugees has failed to keep pace with inflation. [39]

The bishops stated their concern in June 2001. We have already seen a fruther negative impact on refugee admissions and refugee concerns from the September 11, 2001, terrorist attacks on the United States. Overall, under the heading of homeless, "One hundred million quite literally do not have a roof over their head."[40] From the favelas of Rio to the inner city of Chicago to the streets of Calcutta, one billion persons—one-fifth of the human race—has inadequate housing.

Among the numbers of those without homes, those yet unwelcomed into the community, the United States must still count the vast majority of its racial minorities. Persistent racism leveled against Black, Hispanic, Native American, and other groups has resulted in widely reported and substantial economic impact, social cost, psychological damage, and political inequalities among minorities in this country. The obvious data can be counted in illiteracy, poverty, sickness, crime, and homelessness. The more subtle price is paid in alienation, anger, rage, and damaged self-esteem.

In the majority community, the cost is cultural deprivation, fear, guilt, and the shameful negative politics of backlash. Majority-race Americans have increasingly reacted against efforts on the part of government, universities, and other institutions to right the wrongs of slavery, segregation, discrimination, and racism, predominantly affecting African Americans in this country. The claim of those opposing affirmative action efforts of various kinds is that the days of segregation and discrimination are over and that there should be a level playing field for all people of all races. Unfortunately, racist values and racist attitudes are all too often found at the core of major American institutions and policies that impact negatively, with devastating effects, on persons of color. For example:

- HUD reports racial discrimination in mortgage lending, from pre-application inquiries to loan denial rates, denying young families the opportunity to invest in property in order to build financial equity and stability for the future.[41]

• A Georgetown University study indicates that doctors are far less likely to recommend sophisticated cardiac tests for Blacks and women than for White men with identical complaints of chest pain and the differences are caused by race and gender bias.[42]

• A 2001 Harvard University study shows that Black and Latino students have become more segregated in impoverished school districts than at any time in the last thirty years, as a result of the rescinding of federal court desegregation orders, White flight, persistent housing segregation, loss of tax base in center cities, and the growing number of Hispanic students in the schools. More than 70 percent of the nation's Black students attend predominantly minority schools that suffer from poor funding, the survey found.

• In June 2000, a group of state insurance commissioners announced a $206 million dollar agreement with a Nashville-based insurance company to settle allegations that the company charged Blacks more than Whites for small life insurance policies, often called burial insurance by those who purchased them; the settlement involved compensation for two million Black customers and their families.[43]

• Blacks account for 26 percent of all juvenile arrests, but they account for 44 percent of juveniles who are detained, 46 percent of those who go to an adult court, and 58 percent of those who end up in an adult prison. Whites account for 71 percent of all juvenile arrests, 50 percent of those going to adult court, and 25 percent of those going to adult prisons.[44]

• A General Accounting Office report indicated that Black women were nearly twice as likely as White men or women to be strip-searched by the U.S. Customs Service on suspicion of smuggling upon reentering the

United States. The intrusive searches were not justified by a higher rate of discovery of contraband among minority groups, according to the report.[45]

- A 2000 report by the United States Conference of Catholic Bishops indicated that Hispanics were twice as likely as other Catholics to worship in "separate and unequal settings."[46]

Furthermore, the bitter fruits of America's past have been horribly reincarnated in recent racially motivated murders in Oklahoma City, Oklahoma; Jaspers, Texas; Columbine, Colorado; Springfield, Virginia; and in the epidemic of fire bombings of African American churches. As Bishop Sean O'Malley of Fall River, Massachusetts, noted in a 2000 pastoral letter on racism, "In the last year, 220 articles on racial violence appeared on the pages of the *New York Times,* including the tragic high-profile accounts of the torture of Abner Louima and the killing of Amadou Diallo."[47]

Why Stand with the Poor?

One of the nagging questions lying beneath the call to stand with the poor, this love of preference of Pope John Paul, is whether poor people are somehow better than middle-class or rich people. Such an interpretation of the preferential option is not really necessary to understand this call. In fact, that particular implication may be partly responsible for the resistance of many people to standing with the poor. Those who are poor or who have lived or worked among the poor have all experienced evil and good there, just as there is evil and good among middle-class and rich people. Our experience in fact is that poverty can brutalize, warp, and twist. It can also ennoble and dignify. Poverty is generally considered a negative condition in most societies and among Christians as well.[48]

So why the preferential option for the poor, who are even called "blessed" by Jesus?[49] If the answer is not found in the poor themselves, then perhaps we need to look to God and the revelation in Jesus of Nazareth, who himself embodied the preferential love of Yahweh for the poor. God's predilection for the poor is not because they have some special knowledge or insight. On the contrary, "No, their special place is because of their *need*, the inhumanity of their situation is what draws God close in hiddenness, shared suffering and the power of the kingdom."[50] Peruvian Gustavo Gutiérrez underscored this in a talk in Cambridge, England. First, he denied that the reason for our commitment to the poor lies in social analysis, human compassion, or in our own experience of poverty.

> Having said all that, I must strongly emphasise that the ultimate reason for a Christian is the God of Jesus Christ. We must be committed to the poor because we believe in the God of the Kingdom. The preferential option for the poor is a *theocentric* option. We must be committed to the poor, not necessarily because they are good, but because God is good. According to Karl Barth, God always takes the side of the lowly. As Bishop Desmond Tutu said..., "God is not neutral."[51]

Pope John Paul put it in similar words, "The poor are, in fact, God's favorites."[52] The preferential option comes not from the poor or from ourselves but from Christ Jesus, because we Christians are called to be like this Christ the King. We are called to royal sovereignty over this earth. We are anointed at baptism as priests, prophets, and rulers. One aspect of that royal status is that found in the tablets at Ebla and in the pages of the Old Testament: The special responsibility that the king had for the poor. It is one of the few aspects of royalty making any sense in a democratic society where sovereignty resides in the people.

As Jesus then takes upon himself Yahweh's special love for the poor as Christ the King, so too we now have that duty as a priestly, royal people. In effect, we are asked to go back even earlier to the first part of Genesis and to be like God...because Abba God loved us first. We are invited and challenged to love the poor without reason or profit or return, to be the initiator of love and concern, as Yahweh is. The competing choices, then, are to be like the Baals who shut up their eyes, ears, mouth, and to have unfeeling hearts of stone or...to be like our God who moves first to love passionately in a special care for the *anawim*.

The New Testament revelation of Jesus has also made clear to us that standing with the poor, which includes feeding the hungry, clothing the naked, and visiting the sick and imprisoned, is the privileged place for us to find and come to know Jesus. In theological terms, the poor, whether good or bad, rude or gracious, beautiful or ugly, are *sacraments* for us. As the judgment scene in Matthew 25 explained, the poor are blessed encounters with Christ Jesus who has hidden himself in their midst, wrapping himself in their hunger, nakedness, pain, sorrow, and suffering. Saints like Vincent de Paul, Louise de Marillac, and Peter Claver understood this and taught it to their followers. Teresa of Calcutta has taught the same lesson to a new generation of followers.

Another reason for this call to the preferential option is that it serves as a freedom-check in our own spiritual life. The poor become for us a test of how we understand ourselves and who our God is. They provide an opportunity for us to discern where we are in the cycle of Baal, whether we are imbued with a deep sense of the complete grace of creation and of our own gifts, as in the original blessing, or whether we have become owners, holding on to what we have as mine because our self-value and identity are so invested in these things. The poor help us to see whether we are free to share gratuitously, or are hooked by our gifts.

Our encounters with the rich, powerful, and beautiful are always suspect, subject to the taint of what we can get from them in return. Jesus cautioned a leading Pharisee who had invited him to dinner:

> When you hold a lunch or a dinner, do not invite your friends or your brothers or your relatives or your wealthy neighbors, in case they may invite you back and you have repayment. Rather, when you hold a banquet, invite the poor, the crippled, the lame, the blind; blessed indeed will you be because of their inability to repay you. (Luke 14:12–14)

Standing with the poor, then, can give us the opportunity to know who God really is and to be free of the entrapment of the gifts that we hold in trust. It is a gift that can be given to us only by the poor.

Is Standing with the Poor Unfair?

Some may object, "Is not standing with the poor a choice against others who are not poor?"

Before answering, consider our context in America. It seems clear that as Americans we have a bias toward the rich, a radical pre-rational admiration for the rich and powerful. In contradiction to the scriptural mandate, our culture has made a fundamental option for the rich. Our economy, arts, politics, media, and personal ambitions worship at the altar of wealth and power. Even our churches are biased toward the rich, who are honored with positions within church institutions, honorary ecclesiastical accolades, and real decision-making power.

Whom do we call the beautiful people, whose homes, cars and stories grace the pages of *People* magazine? When we wait in the checkout line at the supermarket, the tabloids at our elbow are not covering the lives of the poor and starving, the sick and the down-and-out, the welfare mother, or the old person barely surviving on several hundred dollars of Supplemental Security Income per month.

The TV show that epitomized our attitudes toward economic status was not entitled, "Lifestyles of the Poor and Unknown." It did not take us into the rundown, rat-infested tenements, the shotgun duplexes in the ghetto, the overcrowded housing projects, or the group home for persons with disabilities. "Lifestyles of the Rich and Famous" television program did far more than provide us with human-interest stories or noble character studies. It embodied and underscored for every American viewer our culture's "preferential option for the rich." We need not take offense at this observation, as if it were aimed only at U.S. culture. When Jesus tells the disciples in Luke's Gospel how hard it will be for the rich to enter the Reign of God, they ask in shock, "Then who can be saved?" (Luke 18:26). In doing so, they are expressing their own social and religious expectation that a wealth of possessions is "a sure sign of God's blessings both now and hereafter."[53]

A friend of mine was sent out into the streets of Chicago in the sixties as a social work student to interview Americans about two news stories. The first story was about a British duchess booked first class on a flight to Canada who insisted on taking her poodle on board the plane with her. When the airline personnel refused her request, insisting that the duchess's dog had to ride in the pet compartment with other canines, this lady simply rented an entire full-size commercial jetliner for herself and her dog to make the flight. The cost was tens of thousands of dollars.

The second news story was about a woman who had cheated on welfare or food stamps for herself and her family, gaining several thousand dollars of illegal benefits (additional food) from her misrepresentations over a period of some months. She was to be sentenced to jail for her offense.

The popular reaction to the two stories was that the welfare mother should be sentenced to serious hard time in prison (and throw the key away!), but the duchess was admired for her independence and her persistence, no matter what the cost.

In America and much of rest of the world as well, we judge the wealthy in one way and the poor in another. To get a more complete sense of what this means, consider this question: What do we get irate about, maddest at, tend to forgive less easily? Like these people interviewed on the streets of Chicago, our spontaneous reactions to the duchess and the welfare mother may well surprise us. One researcher recently suggested that a surprisingly large number of Americans hate the poor because they are deeply threatening to our national character and values and because we fear we may become poor ourselves.[54] A recent *Washington Post* survey revealed that 46 percent of Americans said a person was poor because of "a lack of effort" and 47 percent said that poverty was due to circumstances beyond the control of those who are poor.[55] Surveys for several decades have revealed this basically even split in U.S. attitudes toward poverty and its primary causes, roughly half blaming the poor and the other half faulting other social causes.

When we try to get in touch with our spontaneous and deeply felt answers, we find other indicators that our culture is hardest on the poor. Look at our criminal justice system, at who gets the longer sentences. It is not the so-called white-collar criminals, embezzling millions of dollars and using public office and trust for personal gain, as in the savings and loan scandal with its hundreds of billions of dollars lost to the nation. Instead, it is often the small-time or street criminals, whose crimes total far less. Look at who is in our jails and prisons and who is sentenced to death in America. It is invariably the poor and members of racial and ethnic minority groups.

In savoring our popular attitudes, one of the groups most harshly judged by Americans are those most representative of the poor in our society, namely those who receive welfare. President Clinton ran his 1992 campaign for president pledging to "end welfare as we know it"; two years later, Republicans took control of the Congress promising, in their "Contract with America," to change welfare radically, which they accomplished in 1996, with Bill Clinton's assent. To understand this antipathy for welfare and people on welfare, some background is necessary. Prior to 1996, there are two main financial support programs for the poor in America, both of which began during the Roosevelt New Deal. One was originally a federal-state program called Aid to the Aged, Blind, and Disabled (AABD); it is now the federal Supplemental Security Income (SSI) program on which many of the poor elderly and disabled rely for subsistence income. In 1990, for households having no other income, the basic federal SSI payment for an individual was $472 a month or $5,664 yearly. The grant for a poor couple was $681.50 a month or $8,178 yearly. States could choose to supplement this low amount, but almost half did not; even with a state supplement most recipients still had incomes below the poverty line.[56]

The second major welfare program from the New Deal era was called Aid to Families with Dependent Children (AFDC or ADC). This was a federal-state program that assisted children and mostly female single parents deprived of the support of a spouse by death, divorce, desertion, or, as of 1990, unemployment of the principal earner. The federal budget supplied over half of the AFDC grant funds, but the states set the grant amounts. States first determined a standard of need for families of various sizes: "the amount of income needed for a minimally adequate standard of living in that state."[57]

After setting the need standard, the states determined how much actual benefits would be: *in the median or typical state, in January 1990 a single parent with two children and no other income received $364 per month, 44 percent of the poverty line.* Under AFDC laws, if the family had other income, the grant was normally reduced. In forty-six states, the maximum AFDC cash benefit was less than 75 percent of the poverty level. In thirty-two states, it was less than 50 percent. Thirty-one states did not meet their own standard of need and ten states had benefits less than one-half of their own standards. The benefit in some states barely exceeded one hundred dollars a month. Food stamps did increase the support a poor family could receive, but, together with AFDC in the median state, it only raised family income to 73 percent of the poverty line.[58]

Welfare, as Americans referred primarily to AFDC, met essential human needs, was critical to survival for people in particularly hard times, and was usually transitional for most families. Fewer than 1 percent of AFDC families remained grant recipients over a ten-year period.[59] Recent studies have also indicated that many parents who are current or former welfare recipients have physical or mental disabilities or other medical conditions, learning disabilities, low IQs, and substance abuse problems.[60] Despite the fact that many welfare families had members who worked and fraud figures were actually low, public attitudes about welfare recipients, the most visible of the poor, were so notably punitive that the bishops made a particular plea in 1986 in that regard:

> We ask everyone to refrain from actions, words or attitudes that stigmatize the poor, that exaggerate the bene-

fits received by the poor and that inflate the amount of fraud in welfare payments. These are symptoms of a punitive attitude toward the poor. The belief persists in this country that the poor are poor by choice or through laziness, that anyone can escape poverty by hard work, and that welfare programs make it easier for people to avoid work. Thus public attitudes toward programs for the poor tend to differ sharply from attitudes about other benefits and programs. Some of the most generous subsidies for individuals and corporations are taken for granted and are not even called benefits, but entitlements. In contrast, programs for the poor are called handouts and receive a great deal of critical attention, even though they account for less than 10 percent of the federal budget.[61]

The bishops' plea largely fell on deaf ears and thus both parties used welfare for political gain in the nineties and eventually signed off on the more punitive changes put forward by the new Republican majorities in the Congress.

AFDC was transformed in 1996 to Temporary Assistance to Needy Families (TANF). Critical changes were a shift in focus from family support of the needy to "work first" programming concentrating primarily on placement in work. A federal lifetime limit of five years on TANF was established, coming due in 2002, and a work-within-two-years-or-be-cut-off requirement was implemented, although states could shorten both time periods. States were also allowed to keep federal funding in "block grants," no matter how many people were on TANF, and to significantly cut state matching contributions to the program. In addition the 1996 legislation made major cuts in food stamps, SSI, and other programs. In the next several years, welfare rolls plunged by more than 40 percent, giving the proponents of the changes a claim to great success. With some exceptions, states piled up billions of dollars in unspent TANF funds for a "rainy day," replaced state funds in social programs with federal surpluses, and moved those recipients who were easiest to place into jobs which were being created in a booming economy. The levels of state TANF grants to individual families remained largely well below the poverty line.

Many commentators have noted that, despite its success in reducing the welfare rolls, TANF has not improved the economic situation of poor families. For families headed by working single mothers, "reductions in poverty as a result of economic growth were entirely offset by increases in poverty due to contractions in government safety net programs.[62] Others, questioning the success of TANF, attributed much of the reduction in the welfare rolls to the booming economy and record low unemployment. The chart below illustrates the close connection between unemployment and welfare levels:

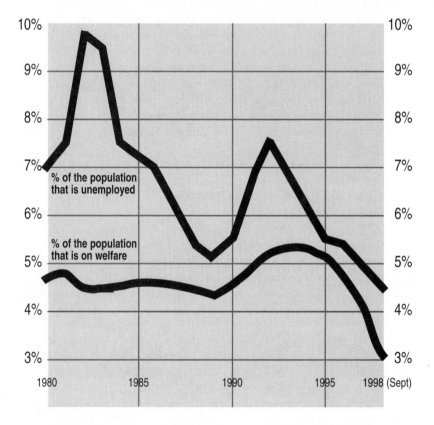

Figure 1. Comparison of Population Unemployed with Population on Welfare[63]

After six years of TANF, trends appear contradictory. In the two years after the "official" recession began in March 2001, twenty-nine states experienced TANF caseload increases, averaging 15.1 percent, seeming to confirm the tie between welfare and unemployment trends. Yet, the nationwide caseload declined by 4 percent. This decline, however, was much less then the previous four years, suggesting that the recession was a strong factor offsetting state spending

of accrued TANF surpluses and implementation of the five-year lifetime limit to reduce caseloads.[64]

Frankly, despite all the political debate over welfare, many rich
and middle-class Americans could not name five poor people,[65] much
less know their incomes, family members, habits, proclivity to work,
reasons for not working, or other essentials to forming intelligent and
fair judgments about them. Most prospering Americans have never
visited the homes or churches of poor people, and seldom had a real
conversation beyond giving instructions to servants and employees.
Nevertheless, they regularly repeat the stories, fables, rumors, and
jokes of their friends and acquaintances about the poor with scarce
regard for the truth or for the rights that low-income Americans have
for their integrity and their reputations. Many churchgoers probably
would be surprised to have the Matthew 25 parable modernized this
way: "When did we tell a joke about you on welfare, Lord?"

Ironically, when a friend is impoverished by bankruptcy, a relative
is forced onto Medicaid to cover nursing home expenses, or a child is
deserted by her husband and needs TANF and Food Stamps to feed her
two small children, the picture is different. Then, Americans somehow
disassociate this impoverished person whom they know from the mass
of others about whom they have heard only pejorative things and too
often come to believe them. The pattern is repeated in our attitudes
toward racial minorities, a greater percentage of whom are poor.

Putting it another way, our culture tells the story of and takes the
side of the rich, just like the magazines and the TV shows do. This is
not just a question of who we admire, whose hairdos we fashion our
own after, or which designer's name is on our clothes. It is not even
measured in prison or sentencing statistics, as shocking as those may
be. But, at the baseline, in its hard economic realities, our society takes
the side of the rich. The U.S. bishops gave us the overview in their pastoral on economic justice, beginning first with a discussion on wealth:

> Important to our discussion of poverty in America is an
> understanding of the degree of economic inequality in our
> nation. Our economy is marked by a very uneven distribu-
> tion of wealth and income. For example, it is estimated
> that 28 percent of the total net wealth is held by the rich-
> est 2 percent of families in the United States. The top ten
> percent holds 57 percent of the net wealth. If homes and
> other real estate are excluded, the concentration of own-
> ership of "financial wealth" is even more glaring. In 1983,
> 54 percent of the total net financial assets were held by 2

percent of all families, those whose annual income is over $125,000. Eighty-six percent of these assets were held by the top ten percent of all families.

Then the bishops immediately added to the picture by laying out the basic distribution of income in the United States:

> Although disparities in the distribution of income are less extreme, they are still striking. In 1984 the bottom 20 percent of American families received only 4.7 percent of the total income in the nation and the bottom 40 percent received only 15.7 percent, the lowest share on record in U.S. history. In contrast, the top one-fifth received 42.9 percent of the total income, the highest share since 1948. These figures are only partial and very imperfect measures of the inequality in our society. However, they do suggest that the degree of inequality is quite large. In comparison with other industrialized nations, the United States is among the more unequal in terms of income distribution. Moreover, the gap between rich and poor in our nation has increased during the last decade.[66]

When evaluating these facts in terms of the moral norms of Catholic social teaching, the bishops concluded, "In view of these norms, we find the disparities of income and wealth in the United States to be unacceptable. Justice requires that all members of our society work for economic, political, and social reforms that will decrease these inequities."[67]

Ten years earlier, Nobel Prize-winning economist Paul A. Samuelson of MIT, while approving the utility of some superiority of income to reflect harder work and special needs, nevertheless concluded about the inequality then in America: "But looking at the matter in the abstract, some reduction in the degree of unnecessary inequality will be regarded as a desirable goal by most ethical, religious and philosophical value systems."[68] The inequality Professor Samuelson was describing and that bemoaned by the bishops has worsened, not improved, to the twenty-first century.

Many of us Americans quite naturally think of ourselves and our economic system as better and fairer than other industrialized nations. Our intuitive sense is that the near-fulfillment of the American dream is enjoyed by most of us. When we look closely at total net worth and income distribution, however, we find we are among the most unequal nations and that *the gap between rich and poor in our nation has increased during the last two decades.* First, as to net worth, *Forbes* reported in 1999 that the top 1 percent of U.S. households, those with over $2.7 million, held 35.1 percent of total net worth, the top 10 percent holding more than two-thirds of the overall household net worth in America. In contrast, nearly half (46 percent) of U.S. households have a net worth below $50,000 and share a total net worth of just 3.4 percent. In addition, about a quarter of U.S. households have less than $10,000 in net worth.[69]

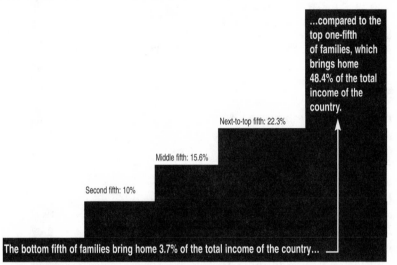

Figure 2. U.S. Family Income Distribution in 2000[70]

Figures 2 and 3 illustrate two aspects of income inequality and how it has become more severe in the past decades. Figure 2 shows the distribution of family income in the United States in 2000, divided into quintiles of U.S. families by income. Figure 3 shows how family incomes—after taxes—have changed during the period from 1979 to 1997. The income gaps both between rich and poor and between rich and the middle class widened in the eighties and nineties alike and reached their widest point on record in 1997. During this period, the average after-tax income of the richest 1 percent of Americans grew by $414,000, after adjusting for inflation; the income of those in the middle of the income spectrum grew by a modest $3,400; and the poorest 20 percent of Americans saw their income fall $100 dollars. The Congressional Budget Office anticipates that the share of income going to the top group continued to rise in 1998 and 1999. The 2001 tax reduction law promoted and signed into law by President George W. Bush no doubt exacerbated further the inequalities in U.S. income distribution as the top 1 percent received an average tax cut of more than $46,000 while the middle fifth of the population received an average reduction of $600 and the poorest fifth gaind less than $70 dollars.

These charts do not adequately reflect the cold, stark realities of life for millions of poorer Americans. Statistical inequalities in income and wealth are fleshed out in inequalities for families of real persons, especially children, in terms of neighborhood, education, access to health care, clothing, transportation, safety, nutrition, child care, and myriad other factors that middle- and upper-income America take for granted. Sister Lory Schaff, C.S.J., working in a poor community in Baton Rouge, captured the reality of the income distribution in the mid-eighties, when the bishops wrote their pastoral on economic justice, by talking about "the four dollar and sixty cent folks." If you considered total U.S. income as $100 divided by five families, she said, the poorest fifth got $4.60; the richest family got $43.70, almost ten times as much.[72] Now the poorest

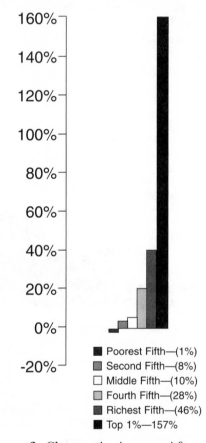

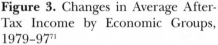

Figure 3. Changes in Average After-Tax Income by Economic Groups, 1979–97[71]

group could be called "the three dollar and seventy cent folks."

We start off in life in America radically unequal, and it is the rare individual who genuinely transcends the substantial disparities described by the bishops. While we may protest that we are the land of opportunity and cite examples of the self-made man or woman, we all know the inequalities are real and hard. Those who are better off in America not only would not trade places with America's poor, but they do not even want to drive through their neighborhoods, go to the same hospitals, or have their children play with the children of the poor or attend the same school with them. By the time Americans reach kindergarten, the inequities of poor diet, inadequate health care, single-parent households, and education in the home have effectively tracked us into two Americas.

In this context, then, it seems incongruous at best to cry foul or unfair at the Church's call to a preferential option for the poor. Unpopular, yes. Countercultural, yes. Painful, yes. Subject to the barbs of politicians and columnists, yes. But hardly unfair. Standing with the poor is the least we can do to make this a better, fairer place to live in and to live up to the noble ideals we breathed in as children with the Declaration of Independence and the Constitution, to say nothing of the Beatitudes.

There is a deeper reason for the appeal to fairness here, and it has to do with the particular need Americans have for standing with the poor at this historical moment. Not only is it not unfair to middle- and upper-income Americans, but their actual salvation requires it. The option for the *anawim* gives a preference to the poor for the sake of "the healing of the whole human family."[73] All of us, rich and poor, need this healing.

Any genuine reconciliation of the human family and the peace it will bring, however, require that what is awry be set straight, that a foundation be laid in justice. The Black bishops of the United States said this most eloquently, from the point of view of the marginalized, in their 1984 pastoral letter, *What We Have Seen and Heard:*

> The Gospel message is a message that liberates us from hate and calls us to forgiveness and reconciliation. As a people we must be deeply committed to reconciliation. This is a value coming from our Black heritage and deepened by our belief in the Gospel teaching. When in recent years, we rejected "token integration" for "self-determination," it was not to choose confrontation in place of cooperation but to insist on collaboration with mutual respect for the dignity and unique gifts of all. Reconciliation can never mean unilateral elevation and another's subordination, unilateral giving and another's constant receiving, unilateral flexibility and another's resistance. True reconciliation arises only where there

is mutually perceived equality. This is what is meant by
justice.

Without justice, any meaningful reconciliation is impossible. Justice safeguards the rights and delineates the
responsibility of all. A people must safeguard their own
cultural identity and their own cultural values. Likewise
they must respect the cultural values of others. For this
reason sincere reconciliation builds on mutual recognition
and mutual respect.[74]

Justice itself then makes demands upon all groups within this society
to honor and respect respective rights, cultures, and identities.

The particular needs of respective groups also underscore the
call to stand with the poor. The poverty of so many Americans and
hundreds of millions across the world certainly scars the have-nots
themselves. On the other side, however, rich and other nonpoor
Americans need to be healed of their anger, judgment, bigotry, and
fears. The radical inequality in our society and in the world drives the
haves behind barred gates, alarm systems, security patrols, canisters
of mace, and other indications of desperate fear for safety of person
and property. In international politics as well, it produces national
defensiveness and an increasing isolation of the United States.

Even more, however, the encounter with the poor can liberate
the haves from the slavery of the superdevelopment discussed by
Pope John Paul in his letter *Sollicitudo Rei Socialis:*

In fact there is a better understanding today that the mere
accumulation of goods and services, even for the benefit
of the majority, is not enough for the realization of human
happiness....

This superdevelopment, which consists in an excessive
availability of every kind of material goods for the benefit of certain social groups, easily makes people slaves of
"possession" and of immediate gratification, with no
other horizon than the multiplication or continual
replacement of the things already owned with others still
better. This is the so-called civilization of "consumption"
or "consumerism," which involves so much "throwing
away" and "waste." An object already owned but now
superseded by something better is discarded, with no
thought of its possible lasting value in itself nor of some
other human being who is poorer.

All of us experience firsthand the sad effects of this blind submission to pure consumerism: in the first place a crass materialism, and at the same time a radical dissatisfaction because one quickly learns—unless one is shielded from the flood of publicity and ceaseless and tempting offers of products—that the more one possesses the more one wants, while deeper aspirations remain unsatisfied and perhaps even stifled.[75]

Standing with the poor then allows the nonpoor to see things differently, both the inequalities of the world around us and our own captivity in the snares of an obsessive consumerism.

This experience also can teach us to read the scriptures in the clearer light of the *anawim* and the God who identifies personally with them.[76] When that new reading is combined with the experience of touching and tasting poverty and powerlessness, then the Christian can enter into a new depth of understanding and encounter with the Divine. Theologian Donal Dorr explains:

It is not enough to be *for* the poor; one must discover what it means to be *with* the poor. Only then can one experience what it is like to be humanly weak and powerless, but still to be powerful in the awareness that God is on one's side.[77]

The person encountering the poor experiences not only their life difficulties but one's own in trying to reach across the gulf of power, wealth, and privilege to be somehow with them. That is often a frustrating and failed experience. Even that failure, however, can help us to pass more deeply into the Holy. David Hinchen, a former director of the Jesuit Volunteer Corps: East, explains:

A genuine effort to be sensitive to the needs of those who are powerless and struggling—and a quick awareness of their own personal limits in reaching out to do something to alleviate those needs—forces the volunteer to turn to his or her God, to want to know this God and how this God relates to this world with all its needs and to him or her as one trying to reach out in concern and yet, seemingly, without power. Hence, the struggle for justice leads to a deepening of faith or, at least, to a need for it.[78]

This is no simple or pain-free matter, this journey of encountering God with the poor.

The challenge is to reach out to the poor in companionship, which literally means to break bread with them, and in compassion, which means to suffer with them. These are the essential themes of discipleship with Jesus himself.[79] Ultimately, letting go of one world and accepting the challenge of entering into another requires courage, as Dean Brackley, now teaching at the Catholic University in El Salvador, explains:

> ...what is most fundamental is the courage not to turn away from the eyes of the poor but to allow them to break our heart and shatter our world, to let them share with us how their children suffered preventable early deaths, how they spent the winter without heat, how their whole village has never seen a doctor.[80]

The appropriate religious language for this kind of heart-shattering experience is that of conversion. Repeatedly, in their pastoral letters on peace and economic justice, the U.S. bishops speak of the need for conversion on the part of Americans.

In the world of the haves, we can easily "try to buy off our spiritual emptiness, filling it up with material distractions."[81] That invariably does not work, and thus the dominating urge to acquire more and more is the hallmark of consumerism. The encounter with the poor not only does not fill up that void; it makes it more vivid:

> But confronting the material deprivation of the poor makes us painfully aware of our own spiritual poverty. This is the gift of the poor, a gift best received on their turf, and often on their terms. As Jean Vanier, founder of the L'Arche movement, puts it, "Is it not one of our problems today that we have separated ourselves from the poor and the wounded and the suffering? We have too much time to discuss and theorize, and have lost the yearning for God that comes when we are faced with the sufferings of people."[82]

What becomes vivid, though, is not that we need more things, but that we need God more. When we grasp and savor our own need for God then we can hear God's voice of invitation quietly beckoning us beneath the clamor of the world to enter into the fullness of divine love where we find out that we are infinitely valued. We discover that we and the poor are loved, without regard to our possessions, but in a communality of the goods of creation. This is the spiritual gift that comes from standing with the poor, a gift desperately needed by the nonpoor of this country and the world.

The gift is one of being converted, of becoming poor in spirit in the fullness of that term, an often painful but life-saving conversion or turning to standing with the poor and standing free of the oppression of commodities. The poor then are God's instruments for salvation, "to save all of us from the crazy madness of the world in which so many people can be starving in the midst of so much wealth."[83]

How Do We Stand with the Poor?

To understand what it means then to stand with the poor, we might start with one commentator's list of three things that it is not: not entering into some form of crude class warfare that ultimately ends in violence against the wealthy; not just a simplistic handing over to the poor by the affluent of all that they have over and above what is needed for a simple lifestyle; and not a mandate to the Church to spend no time beyond the absolute minimum in any ministry to the affluent.[84] Each of these options would seem to set up an abrupt over-against model of standing with the poor that assumes both a class struggle solution to the world's injustices and a once and for all effort to effect change.

Standing with the poor, however, while it does not begin from a stance of class struggle, clearly positions the Christian "across the line" with the poor. In the face of a society that is radically in love with the rich and powerful and that organizes many of its social and economic arrangements in their favor, the call to us then is to tell the story of and take the side of the poor. Pope John Paul II puts it this way in his 1987 encyclical letter:

> By virtue of her own evangelical duty, the Church feels called to take her stand beside the poor, to discern the justice of their requests and to help satisfy them, without losing sight of the good of groups in the context of the common good.[85]

It is popular for veterans groups and ethnic associations to say "lest we forget" regarding past wars or ethnic atrocities, so that these events will not be repeated by subsequent generations. Elie Wiesel, Nobel Peace Prize winner, put it this way at the ground breaking for a new Holocaust Memorial Museum:

> The killer killed his victims once, and there is nothing we can do about it. But if they are forgotten, they will be killed a second time, and this we can and must prevent.[86]

Our task as Christians is to say to our culture, its institutions, and peoples, "Lest we forget the poor." Doing that effectively requires that we constantly choose to move through a process of engagements with the poor and nonpoor that we might talk about in terms of the traditional see, judge, and act of Catholic thought.

Seeing Differently

Standing with the poor begins with and introduces us into a new way of seeing the world around us. This underlines the importance of personal contact with poor persons, human faces with names, families, histories, and aspirations. Many religious groups have stressed personal service to the poor for all their members;[87] church parishes often begin their social ministry in the direct assistance to the hungry, homeless, or poor; L'Arche Communities, founded by Jean Vanier, meld persons with disabilities and others in family-style living units; and ministerial formation programs often insist on internships working directly with and living among the poor.

This insistence on personal contact runs against our culture's proclivity toward the faceless poor. We can avoid them by working in an enclosed office complex, living in actual or simulated suburbia, shopping in well-policed malls, and cruising in between home, work, and social life on raised expressways in air-conditioned automobiles with tinted windows and buffering sound systems. Even if the poor were crying out to us in unison voices for bread and solidarity, we would not hear or see them unless it was filtered to us in a thirty-second spot on our television news.

Making the invisible visible, however, is our first step on the way to compassion. For some it may be the one evening a week working at the night shelter for the homeless or regular time spent as a big brother or big sister to a young person. For others it may be a year or more of full-time volunteer work among the poor. For still others it may be full-time career choices to work with the marginalized or decisions to live in poorer neighborhoods and to become, in various ways, part of their community. This is what South African Albert Nolan calls exposure. "The more we are exposed to the sufferings of the poor," he says, "the deeper and more lasting does our compassion become."[88]

Ordinarily, exposure is a personal thing; no one can do it for me. I myself have to take the step to cross the line to stand with the poor. Besides personal experience, however, our sense of exposure can be heightened by tapping into the art, music, novels, poetry, and other writings of the marginalized and poor. I think, for example, of the powerful impact on my classmates and myself in the novitiate in the early sixties, when we shared a reading of *Black Like Me*.[89] It was a unique story of a White man's experience of crossing the color line and tasting the experience of Black Americans in the fifties in the United States. Just the awareness of the unavailability of public bathrooms for Blacks in those days was an eye-opener about our society.

Exposure involves more listening than talking. Often those who enter the world of the poor are immediately moved by their sympathy to offer a long list of suggestions about what can be done to "change things around here." A fundamental strategy of community organizers suggests that listening and asking questions, lots of questions, should occur before doing anything else. This is not only the way to discover what the real problems and concerns of people are, but also is more respectful of the persons who live full time with the burden of poverty and who ultimately will have to act to change it. This listening and learning takes time and great patience for those of us with the pragmatic American approach to problems.

Empathy takes time. Empathy requires the freedom to move out of ourselves and our own matrix of institutions and into the experience of others and the matrix of formal and informal institutions that shape the lives of the poor. Empathy also takes the freedom to make the mistakes that moving from one world to another entails.[90] This freedom accepts one's own vulnerability and the reality that companionship is not a matter of one person with answers and another with questions needing answers. Empathy invites us then to see things differently.

When we come to see things differently, our new perceptions lead to new knowledge. No matter what studies we have read, how current we are in our newsmagazines or theology articles, or even our expertise in some social science, the encounter with the poor adds a whole new body of knowledge. That knowledge challenges and transforms what we have known up until that time. David W.

Marr, director of Father Lou Twomey's Institute of Human Relations in the late eighties, comments:

> The unemployed know that many Americans are pre-
> vented from participating in our social and economic life.
> The black, Hispanic, Native American and Asian members
> of our society know that racism pervades our decision-
> making processes. Women know that sexism truncates
> their own chances for fully human lives. And the poor, the
> poor know that our enfeebled efforts to change society
> have not conquered the poverty that seeks to destroy them.
> And the poor know that the scriptures condemn any sys-
> tem which blindly brutalizes the lives of millions.[91]

That new body of knowledge is transforming. It shapes the way we ourselves see, the ways in which we understand realities in the United States and around the world, and, most importantly, the way we feel about what we see and now know about the lives and realities of the poor.

Judging Differently

Seeing differently and knowing new things breeds a new consciousness, an awakening of insights into how society is organized and
what its ways of organization have to do with the day-to-day life of
poor persons. Henry Volken, former missionary and social activist in
India, uses hunger as an example of the process through which concerned people pass in their work with the poor. First, they become
involved at the level of hungry persons, and then they move on from
there to "the hunger problem":

> ...caring for the hungry puts in question one's own life and
> ways of living. Involvement in campaigns for the hungry in
> distant lands gives new eyes to discover the needy and hun-
> gry closer to home. A decisive passage takes place when one
> is helped to see, what happens in society, from the point of
> view of the marginalized. Helping them find alternative
> ways for self-help becomes more important than just charity.
> Being in solidarity with the marginalized in their struggles
> for a decent life finally leads to detect the injustice that is

embodied in the institutions, structures and policies of
one's own and all other societies.[92]

Albert Nolan calls this the second stage of spiritual growth in our
service to the poor, which begins with "the gradual discovery that
poverty is a structural problem."[93] It becomes clear that poverty is not
accidental and not the result of nature's whims. It has been created by
decisions and policies in the socio-economic-political realms, and that
"is a matter of justice and injustice."[94]

Besides arousing a variety of feelings ranging from anger to
indignation to rage, this insight provokes a critical consciousness in
the person who stands with the poor. David Marr calls it "a
hermeneutics of suspicion"[95] that demands to know how decisions
affect the poor, whether those affected were involved in the process
of decision making, and whose interests are protected and whose are
hurt. Georgetown professor Anthony J. Tambasco speaks of insights
that arise when the have-nots exercise "ideological suspicion" that
exposes predominant views, even in theology, as "subtle forms of ideologies reinforcing oppression."[96] The bishops in *Economic Justice for
All* direct us to ask of every decision, what it does to the poor, for the
poor, and what it enables the poor to do for themselves.[97] Stated simply, it is a matter of looking at the world from the point of view, not
of the haves, but the have-nots. Quite literally, this perspective is a
hermeneutic of the anawim.

What this perspective does, first, is rescue us from the indo-
lence and torpor bred by muchness. Too many Americans have let the
comfort of our own lives convince us that the present state of affairs
in this country and across the world, while perhaps frayed around the
edges, is basically benign. One of nine of our own population in
poverty and 800 million others in absolute poverty across the world,
450 million of whom are starving, is hardly benign. Viewing the world
from the vantage of the poor can save us from a plantation mentality
that maintains that "our Negroes are happy" and a political callous-
ness that proclaims that the truly needy are taken care of.

Second, this perspective sets up a critical dynamic between
those who stand with the poor and many of those who exercise political and economic power. It creates profound doubt in the minds of
those who view political decisions from the bottom up. On a subject
such as U.S. Central American policy, for example, many U.S.
churchpeople who have worked among the poor in Central America
these past decades have brought back to the larger Catholic community a radically different perspective than that propounded by the

occupants in the White House. The commitment of the church of
Latin America to the poor has placed that church and those who
stand with them here in the United States in sharp conflict with our
government and those churchpeople who are all too allied with those
in power in the region. For those who have shared in this kind of
knowledge, much of U.S. foreign policy is simply no longer credible
or even worthy of respect, much less support.

Third, this stance is transforming for the Church as well. As we
choose to be the church of the poor, comprised of the economically
poor and those who stand with them as the poor in spirit, some
would argue that we are inaugurating a new great age of the Church.
This transformation will be as radical as the alliance to Constantine
in the fourth century. The Roman alliance transformed the Church
into civic respectability, institutional status, and political power that
has continued in one cultural form or another until the present
moment. A new alliance between the Church and the *anawim,* one
which truly transforms her into the Church of the poor, would have
unforeseen ramifications for centuries to come. One sign of that
rebirth is the blood of new martyrs flowing in Latin America and
elsewhere.

Fourth, the judgments made by those who stand with the poor
are far more than visceral reactions to the injustices they see and
more than products of suspicions that they have toward structures
and ideologies of privilege and power. Presence among the poor certainly gives an urgency and a passion to the critical judgment of the
poor in spirit; but the tradition of *faithjustice* sketched out in the preceding chapters provides the framework of principles within which
concrete judgments are made. This is a combination of scripture, natural law, and reason reflecting upon human experience.

Against this background, for example, the bishops in *Economic
Justice for All* highlighted certain moral priorities affirmed by Pope
John Paul II in a 1984 address in Canada:

> The needs of the poor take priority over the desires of the
> rich; the rights of workers over the maximization of prof-
> its; the preservation of the environment over uncontrolled
> industrial expansion; production to meet social needs over
> production for military purposes.[98]

The bishops themselves enunciated certain moral priorities, as do a
number of other philosophers and theologians working out of the
tradition of Catholic social thought.[99] These can provide a reliable

foundation from which to try to articulate the judgments which arise from the experience of standing with the poor.

Fifth, principles and moral priorities do not resolve concrete cases or specify action in particular circumstances. "There will undoubtedly be disputes about the concrete applications of these priorities in our complex world," the bishops say.[100] Nevertheless, having admitted this, it seems that there are at least three resources to draw upon in resolution of such conflicts and lack of clarity at the level of applied principle. Standing with the poor is itself a touchstone for making specific judgments about political, social, and economic realities. Dean Brackley comments, for example, on concrete questions about lifestyle:

> How much we have or do not have will follow from friendships that help us joyfully appreciate how "No one is justified in keeping for their exclusive use what they do not need, when others lack necessities" (*Populorum Progressio*, 23). Our attachment to the poor will govern our "detachment" from things.[101]

Too often our debates about welfare benefits or the amount of foreign aid are done in the rarified atmosphere of legislative committee rooms or corporate meeting rooms. These meetings would be shorter and conclude with more unanimity if they were held in the homes of the poor or the favelas of the third world.

A second resource for making specific decisions is found in various communities. The lack of personal clarity can often be resolved in the context of a community that cares. The larger church community is one such community, but only one. Often, especially when in doubt, we need to tap into the common wisdom and guarantee of the guidance of the Spirit of Jesus "whenever two or more are gathered in my name...." The poor themselves are a privileged part of such groups, but so are other people of good will who stand with the poor. Such wisdom and power have been found in ecumenical coalitions formed around issues touching hunger, disarmament, housing, and many other topics of concern.

Although it may be difficult to accept, we can also be helped to make specific decisions by adopting a new standard for action that gray areas always should be resolved in favor of, not against, the poor. This is a very simple application of the meaning of standing with the poor and of a bias in favor of the poor. Too often, Christians caught in the throes of an unclear public policy decision, whether a

tax proposal or a zoning change, will side with the status quo or the
powers-that-be over proponents of social justice or advocates of the
poor. "It's just too complicated for me," they exclaim. If the question
is genuinely in dispute and cannot be resolved by doing the home-
work that justice questions deserve, the challenge of standing with
the poor is to take their side in such disputed cases.

What partly justifies this position is realizing that in almost all
cases those defending the status quo or holding office or power have
access to superior information and the ability to convey it through the
media, public relations staffs, and so on. If their case is not sufficiently convincing with all those available resources, then we can
almost assume that the opposite case would be more persuasive with
the same resources. If the question is unclear only because we do not
have the time, energy, or interest to become informed, then we
should rely on other persons who stand with the poor to guide us in
our voting and other civic actions.

Sixth, when standing with the poor begins to influence and
shape our ways of seeing and our judgments about reality, then we
find ourselves more and more deeply committed to translating our
intellectual and affective conclusions into concrete decisions and
actions. The key word is *commitment*. An unnamed Sister of St. Ann,
providing testimony about torture, described her experience working
in a shantytown in Chile:

> ...Living here forces me to look at the world and the things
> around me differently. I try to discover and to view with-
> out fear the causes of misery and injustice. This latter
> experience has led me to take concrete steps to commit
> myself more radically with the God who loves life. I have
> been led, along with some of the young people and others
> from the neighborhood, to the suffering and the pain of
> those in one of the jails of Santiago. It is a rich experience
> that has helped me and many others to appreciate what it
> means to spend oneself for an ideal, to have hope and the
> joy of being alive even in the midst of pain.
>
> Living here has also led me to make an active com-
> mitment in the defense of life, life that is so crushed and
> humiliated today in Chile. For that reason, for some time
> I have been participating in the "Sabastian Acevedo
> Movement against Torture." This movement has played a
> very important prophetic role. My participation isn't just
> a wild impulse. Rather it is the result of a discernment

> carried out with Jesus, of a desire not to be passive in face
> of the abuses and violations of Human Rights. I feel this
> participation has been very helpful in integrating faith and
> life. It is also a demand that calls me to live coherently
> what I am denouncing with every action we carry out.[102]

This commitment to action is not divorced from the arena of making new and different judgments. Rather, as we see in the story of this sister, once we make an initial commitment to action in standing with the poor, that gives rise to new experiences of the life of the poor, deeper and wider insights into the structures of society, and more refined judgments about the nature of justice and injustice. These in turn propel us to new, different, and further actions.

Acting Differently

The preferential option also means moving from personal contact, new insights, and judgments to action. On a personal level, one of the first of these is "rejecting compulsive consumption and, ordinarily, adopting the cultural resistance of a simple lifestyle, [whose] social meaning is above all the freedom to share with those in need."[103] This decision is rooted in the sense of the common destination of the goods of creation basic to faithjustice and a perception of the needs of the poor, the wasting of creation's resources, and the grossly disproportionate share of the world's goods consumed by the United States.

This choice to do something about our levels of consumption is a stance appropriate for individuals, families, religious communities, parish church communities, institutions, and governments. In the late seventies, when the United States faced a petroleum crisis that it deemed crucial to national economic well-being, stringent measures were taken by government, industry, and individuals. The entire population of the world now faces just such a critical situation, with economic, strategic, justice, and religious considerations all converging to recommend simplicity to us.

Individuals also stand with the poor in the concrete choices which they make about their own careers: to teach in inner-city or rural schools, do social work, or practice law or medicine focused on those most without resources. A wide variety of other careers, while less remunerative, serve the more direct needs of the poor. The same option is available to individual priests and religious in choices of which parish communities, schools, or hospitals they serve. Dioceses and communities of religious face similar choices in opening, maintaining, or withdrawing from various institutions.[104] A number of religious communities have made just such serious decisions in the seventies and eighties in pursuit of the option for the poor. In the United States, the most notable have been congregations of sisters.

Other serious individual actions to stand with the poor involve the commitment of volunteer time and the donation of personal resources to the needy and to worthwhile programs, agencies, and church-sponsored efforts to reach out to promote charity, justice, and peace. For example, it would seem that Independent Sector's "Give Five" program, donating five hours a week and five percent of your income, is certainly a place to start. It is one concrete form of stewardship for the poor. As for financial contributions, those with greater wealth would do well to consider Pope John Paul's guidance in his Brazil address, reflecting Jesus' own message, that those who have received more are expected to give more. In the United States, their giving surprisingly lags well behind that of other Americans.[105]

Standing with the poor demands action far beyond the private province of my own job, family, and financial resources, as critically important as these may be. The new realities that are seen and judged by standing with the poor call for new responses that address themselves to the ways in which society is organized. We begin this action by asking one question of the decisions and policies our society, over and over again: *How will this affect the poor?*

When local community decisions are being made about the school curriculum or admissions, tuition, voting, taxes, or how we spend our community development block grants, we Christians should ask, "How will this affect the poor?" When a president or a member of Congress promises new weapons or lowered taxes, we Christians should ask, "How will this affect the poor?" When our church parish decides to build a new church or school, to begin stewardship or tithing, or to raise tuition for parish programs, we Christians should ask, "How will this affect the poor?" When the city council proposes to build a new highway or overpass and certain neighborhoods will be destroyed in the process, we Christians should ask, "How will this affect the poor?" When our business decides to reorganize, to shift plants or processes, or to buy or sell assets, we Christians should ask, "How will this affect the poor?"

In this context it worthwhile to reflect again on the standard set forth by the bishops in their pastoral letter on economic justice:

> The quality of the national discussion about our economic future will affect the poor most of all, in this country and throughout the world. The life and dignity of millions of men, women and children hang in the balance. Decisions must be judged in light of what they do *for* the poor, what they do *to* the poor and what they enable the poor to do *for themselves*. The fundamental moral criterion for all economic decisions, policies and institutions is this: They must be at the service of all people, *especially the poor*.[106]

Clearly, that is our unmistakable bias. The poor of Yahweh. Our passion and concern. Lest we forget.

Undoubtedly, this will be an immensely unpopular position. Our culture has the directly opposite bias; in business, politics, arts and entertainment, fashion, criminal justice, leisure, hiring and firing, economics, and in the churches, the rich come first. Our preferential option, then, is a subversive stance whereby we cry out, over and over against the mob and against the fashion, "How will this affect the poor?" Gustavo Gutiérrez describes the experience of Dom Helder Camara in Brazil:

> For if you say, "There are poor people in the world, and we must help them," you have no problem. However, if you speak of the causes of poverty, you will immediately encounter suspicion and hostility. Dom Helder Camara, former Archbishop of Recife said, "If you speak about the poor you are a holy person; if you speak about the root causes of poverty, you are a communist."[107]

The bullets that cut down Archbishop Oscar Romero of San Salvador when he had clearly taken his stand with the poor are sad proof of Dom Helder's words. Reports in a British journal concerning the 1989 meeting of Christian base communities in Brazil, for another example, were that the opposition's current prices per head were a hundred pounds for a trade unionist, three hundred pounds for a lawyer, and six hundred for a bishop.[108]

Dean Brackley suggests that to stand with the poor means to be "free to lose status as well," to share their obscurity, insults, and the misunderstanding, injuries, and rejection at the hands of those who oppose justice.[109] The Carmelite General Congregation in 1980 warned its members of the cost of standing with the poor in similar terms:

> In making a choice for the "little ones," obviously we can-
> not remain entirely secure. This choice carries with it an
> element of risk, the risk of being misunderstood, the risk of
> losing positions we have gained, the risk of being excluded
> and of being crushed by the powerful ones of this world. It
> means that we must seriously consider making a sort of
> "martyrdom" of our lives and involving ourselves in the
> "way of the cross" of the "little ones" of this world.[110]

While we think this kind of martyrdom is reserved for the apparently
grossly unjust situations of the third world, those who stand for justice and peace in this country suffer retaliation from those in power
as well.

The exercise of such retaliatory power in U.S. society will be less
violent and more sophisticated, but real. In the Diocese of Amarillo,
Texas, for example, Bishop Leroy T. Matthiesen spoke out against the
production of nuclear weapons, a major local employer. In response,
the local United Way board in 1982 made major cuts in the requested
grant from the diocesan Catholic Charities agency.

The U.S. bishops' Catholic Campaign for Human Development
(CCHD), begun in 1969 as the Campaign for Human Development
(CHD), focuses on self-help projects, especially those that try to create new structures of empowerment for the poor or to challenge
structures of injustice. By 2001, CCHD had allocated $250 million in
grants and loans to more than four thousand local and national
organizations for community organizing and economic development.[111] This endeavor has been under frequent assault from wealthy
Catholic conservatives in this country.

In May 1989, William E. Simon mailed to all the Catholic
Knights of Malta in the United States a copy of a highly critical book
entitled *The Campaign for Human Development: Christian Charity or
Political Activism*. Simon noted in his cover letter how CCHD is "a
funding mechanism for radical left political activism in the United
States, rather than for traditional types of Catholic charities."[112] The
book sent by Simon was funded by a Capital Research Center and
authored by individuals with ties to the Reagan White House, the
Heritage Foundation, and the House Committee on Un-American
Activities.[113] More subtle than the defiant "Mater Si, Magistra No"
stance of William Buckley in the sixties, this attack on CCHD continues the consistent rejection by some conservative, wealthy, politically
powerful American Catholics of the papal and episcopal leadership
to have the Church in the twentieth century stand with the poor.

Obviously, recipients were to conclude from Simon's circulation of the book that they should apply pressure on the Church to discontinue its efforts through CCHD by threatening cutbacks on financial support. That would be a traditional exercise of economic and political power.

The anti-CCHD book prompted at least one well-timed assault on the Campaign. In the *Richmond Times-Dispatch,* on Saturday, November 18, 1989, an editorial entitled "Charity or Political Activism" attacked CCHD for funding the "political left" through its grant-making activities. The CCHD collection was to be taken up in diocesan churches at Masses that evening and the next morning, so the timing of the editorial was no accident. To their credit the diocese issued its own rejoinder and a number of pastors directly addressed the editorial from the pulpit that weekend. In his own letter to the editor on the following Wednesday, Bishop Walter F. Sullivan responded:

> In its editorial the *Times-Dispatch* attacks CHD for being faithful to its mandate—moving beyond traditional charitable activities and helping organize and empower poor people to shape their own future. All of CHD's promotional literature clearly identifies the campaign's approach as one of "a hand up, not a handout."[114]

Initial reports from the diocese later indicated that support for the 1989 campaign collection was 44 percent ahead of the previous year.[115]

Despite the political strategy of some wealthy and powerful Catholics to oppose the Church's persistent call to us to stand with the poor, the Richmond story is just one indication that many other Catholics appear to have heard the gospel's call to *faithjustice* with sympathy and support. In Seattle, for example, "officials note that contributions to the archbishop's appeal continued to increase despite Archbishop [Raymond G.] Hunthausen's public statements on peace and justice and his conflict with the Vatican."[116] Similarly, contributions to Catholic Charities USA and to local Catholic Charities agencies have continued strongly despite attacks during the past decade from those displeased with Catholic Charities USA's advocacy on behalf of low-income families.

Before leaving this point, it is important to reflect upon the process of seeing, judging, and acting differently being described by the various commentators on standing with the poor:

(1) Systemic injustices exist that create real and profound suffering for poor individuals and communities; (2) the Church as institution

or through its members stands with the poor, hearing their cry and seeing their reality; (3) when the Church or its members see and judge the reality anew from the transforming stance with the poor, that leads to the prophetic role of denouncing what is unjust in society from a faith viewpoint; (4) which then prompts criticism, accusations such as the all-time favorite "communist," retaliation, violence, and martyrdom at the hands of those who hold social, economic, and therefore political power. The result then appears strikingly similar to class conflict, with the Church standing with the poor and those in power and wealth standing against the Church and the poor. This occurs even though the Church's stance did not begin with, nor was it rooted in any traditional class analysis or ideology.

While our background, education, contacts, and other resources often prevent us, almost by definition, from being poor, standing with the poor can usher us into their experience of suffering, misjudgment, and marginalization. The conflicts imposed upon them are then imposed on anyone who dares to stand with them, often, as noted at the beginning of this chapter, with that special ferocity reserved for prophets.

Much of the discussion in this chapter has focused on the situation of poor people in the United States, the primary place where most of us can actually stand with the poor, share their joys and sufferings, and then move to an active companionship with them. Because the poor of the third world are so far removed from us, we often are less touched by their situation, even though decisions made by us individually and as a nation have a profound impact upon their lives.

Pope John Paul II has continued the reflection of the Church community on standing with the poor, but with a decided emphasis on the international dimensions of the concern, especially in his 1989 letter *Sollicitudo Rei Socialis*:

> ...the option or love of preference for the poor. This is an option or a special form of primacy in the exercise of Christian charity to which the whole tradition of the Church bears witness. It affects the life of each Christian inasmuch as he or she seeks to imitate the life of Christ, but it applies equally to our social responsibilities and hence to our manner of living, and to the logical decisions to be made concerning the ownership and use of goods.
>
> Today, furthermore, given the worldwide dimension which the social question has assumed, this love of prefer-

ence for the poor, and the decisions which it inspires in us, cannot but embrace the immense multitudes of the hungry, the needy, the homeless, those without medical care and, above all, those without hope of a better future. It is impossible not to take account of the existence of these realities. To ignore them would mean becoming like the "rich man" who pretended not to know the beggar Lazarus lying at his gate (cf. Luke 16:19–31).

Our daily life as well as our decisions in the political and economic fields must be marked by these realities....

The motivating concern for the poor—who are, in the very meaningful term, "the Lord's poor"—must be translated at all levels into concrete actions, until it decisively attains a series of necessary reforms. Each local situation will show what reforms are most urgent and how they can be achieved. But those demanded by the situation of international imbalance, as already described (above), must not be forgotten.[117]

John Paul makes it clear that standing with the poor has worldwide dimensions and yet touches our most personal decisions. It is rooted deeply in the tradition of the Church, and yet demands contemporary political and economic action.

Pope John Paul's references to the worldwide dimensions of the preferential love for the poor, decisions in the political and economic fields, and both local and international reforms also leads us naturally to the subject of the next chapter: the application of *faithjustice* to the social, economic, cultural, and political structures that weave the fabric of our national and international societies. While this chapter has touched on these matters, the option for the poor, the preferential love of the poor, standing with the poor, and the Church of the poor cannot be adequately understood or put into action without a more in-depth consideration of this structural dimension of reality.

Conclusion

Before leaving the preferential option, however, it might be good to go back over some main themes. From both the Hebrew and Christian scriptures and the current reflection of the faith community, it is clear that the poor to whom we are called with a special concern in our time are those primarily who are excluded from full membership in the community by their lack of economic resources. They are the hungry and homeless on our streets, the underclass[118] trapped in our urban ghettoes, the elderly and disabled in our Medicaid-funded nursing homes and unregulated boarding homes, the children-having-children and children-killing-children in our slums, and other groups without voice or hope in our society. And, importantly, they are the vast majority of the third world's population.

We are called to stand with them with the same love with which Christ Jesus reached out to the outcast and ostracized, to make the poor the horizon of consciousness against which we address questions of our personal lifestyle, corporate decisions, church parish goal setting, economic policy making, and the election of every political candidate today. To create and nurture that mindset, it is important that every Christian be in regular contact, not with poor people, but with tangible persons living in poverty. Work in a soup kitchen; visit a nursing home; tutor in a G.E.D. or E.S.L. program; join a prison prayer group; volunteer at the local public hospital; or whatever keeps you in contact with Christ in the poor.

But, then, always ask, "Why are these people poor?"

QUESTIONS FOR REFLECTION AND DISCUSSION

1. Write the names of five poor people whom you know on a sheet of paper and estimate their monthly income.

2. What direct experience have you had of the lives of low-income people? How have those experiences influenced your way of looking at society?

3. If God loves all people, how can there be a preferential love of the poor?

4. How would you explain the preferential love for the poor to another Christian? To someone who is not a Christian?

5. Who are "the poor" referred to in the Church's documents on social teaching? What sources would you consult to clarify this concept?

6. What are the implications of the preferential love for the poor on ourselves as individuals? Name three specific actions that result from this.

7. If we took the preferential love for the poor seriously, what would be the impact on our churches, businesses, and government?

CHAPTER FIVE

The Acid Test: Moving from Charity to Justice

> If, then, we are to be faithful to our apostolic mission, we must lead people to the fullness of Christian salvation: to the love of the Father in the first instance, and to the love of neighbor as an inseparable consequence of that love. That is the faith we preach, a faith that works through love. But since there can be no love without justice, action for justice is the acid test of our preaching of the gospel.
>
> The Jesuit General Congregation
> Rome, 1975[1]

Acadiana Neuf was the name of the primary War on Poverty agency–the Community Action Program[2]–in the heart of Acadian country in the mid-sixties. Based in Lafayette, Louisiana, it self-destructed in 1967 as I was writing a paper about it for a course in government at the University of Southwestern Louisiana. At the core of its demise was the reluctance of the dominant White majority to share power and control over substantial amounts of federal dollars and programs with those representing newer interests of poor and Black minorities.[3]

❖ ❖ ❖

After more than a decade of extremely active litigation, legal services and consumer attorneys in Georgia had pushed the provisions of the Industrial Loan Act to their literal boundaries. The act governed the kinds of loans that were at the heart of the economic system for low- and moderate-income citizens. This law, as in many states, allowed lenders to collect an extraordinary amount of "profit" by a misleading combination of interest, loan fees, credit life insurance, credit accident insurance, refinancing, and so forth.

The modest quid pro quo *for this windfall was that no lender was to "charge, collect, or contract for" any unauthorized amount. Doing so would void the loan. The courts had held that this meant that the consumer's entire debt, including principal and interest, was cancelled.*

The drafters could not have foreseen the day of federally funded legal services for the poor, when bright, aggressive, mostly young attorneys would begin to represent low-income borrowers. Legal services staff and their alumni in private practice learned to decipher the fine print in consumer contracts, calculate the financing mathematics, and analyze the ways in which just a little bit more profit had been extracted in thousands of transactions over the years.

Reading the fine print in consumer statutes, these attorneys brought to the Georgia courts a veritable wave of cases that gradually built a body of consumer law interpreting the loan act strictly. This included the interpretation of voidness indicated above. These cases did not eliminate high rates of interest and profit allowed by the statute nor did they deter poor people from borrowing frequently. They did provide strong leverage in the hands of those consumers, however, who became involved in problems with lenders or in litigation.

When these cases had begun to tilt back some small portion of the imbalances between lenders and borrowers–that is, when the cost of lending began to rise too high–loan company interests persuaded a sympathetic Georgia legislature in 1978 and the Georgia Supreme Court[4] to weaken the law's protection, raise the burden upon consumers to prove willful statutory violations by lenders, and soften the sanctions under the loan act. Lawsuits and counterclaims on behalf of consumers under the act were substantially reduced in the following years.

❖ ❖ ❖

On the national level, a similar scenario occurred during the same time period. Congress had made a pivotal decision in the sixties in its well-known Truth-in-Lending Act. Instead of instituting maximum interest rates or profit margins for lenders and credit sellers, as many consumer advocates had proposed, the drafters chose the route of requiring uniform ways of disclosing the costs and incidents of credit. The rationale was classic free-market ideology founded upon a belief that the well-informed consumer reading mandatory disclosures of comparative annual percentage rates and finance charges, for example, would shop around for the fairest and most reasonable loans and credit purchases.

In reality, except for the most sophisticated shopper, most credit consumers want to know only one thing: "What will my monthly payments be?"

What Truth-in-Lending became, however, was a powerful instrument in the hands of the consumer's attorney when consumers ran afoul of lenders and sellers or had problems with the goods they purchased. A vast and aggressive body of law soon developed, fueled in major part by staff attorneys in our nationwide network of legal services programs, including those working in Georgia. Sanctions of money damages and attorneys fees also made Truth-in-Lending litigation available through the soon active private bar.

Again, when consumer advocates had won too many battles for their clients and the cost of lending and litigating had been raised too high, creditor interests persuaded Congress in the late seventies to muzzle the disclosure requirements of the Truth-in-Lending Act and de-fang its strong sanctions. After the Truth-in-Lending Simplification and Reform Act, lawsuits on behalf of consumers under that law were far fewer. Now, no one seems much interested in the original intent of the act or the alternative solution of controlling costs of interest to consumers.

❖ ❖ ❖

The call to Catholic Community Services was from a Baton Rouge attorney working late downtown a few nights before Thanksgiving 1988. He asked where he could find night shelter for a man shivering in the doorway outside his office. I suggested one agency that he had already called. "They won't take anyone this late," he responded angrily. "I don't understand the bureaucracy. It's un-Christian."

I swallowed my defense of those on the front line of homelessness 365 days a year. Instead, I suggested another agency that might provide shelter.

"I'll pay for a hotel room, if necessary," my caller said, "it's going down to freezing tonight." But then he reiterated his anger at the first shelter and their deadline for admission. "It's not right. As a Catholic and a Christian, I can't let this man just freeze outside all night."

Having been on the city homelessness task force and the housing coalition, I was sure that our community did not have enough shelter for all our homeless. I was also aware that homelessness is only a symptom of the national problems of insufficient community-based services for those with mental and emotional problems, inadequate affordable housing, and the Reagan administration's retreat from national housing goals set back in the forties.

This awareness would have been of little consolation to my caller, since he was face to face with what had been only a statistic before his late night encounter on our cold streets. His chief and commendable concern was to meet the immediate need of a fellow human being in intolerable circumstances. It was, as he had said, a Christian response.

Having referred my late night Good Samaritan to the one place I could think of at this hour, I said goodnight. His parting remark was a delightful surprise: "If necessary, I'll take him home with me tonight."

After hanging up, I regretted not thinking faster. I should have invited this lawyer to join the homelessness task force, to see beyond one man in one doorway to the city-wide problem. Even more, he might have been able to expand his concern and his anger from the tangible homeless man to the problem of national priorities and failed commitments. His broadened Christian compassion would understand, then, that how he votes and how he spends his time and his dollars can make a big difference to the homeless.

❖ ❖ ❖

We drove on a dust-choked road around the dump outside Salvador Bahia, a picturesque city and the former colonial capital for northern Brazil. Despite the closed automobile windows, the stench was incredibly offensive even on this winter day in July 1989. We three Norte Americanos *were silenced by the reality spread out below us. Three groups scavanged the dump: pigs, vultures, and the men, women, and children whose shacks ringed the vast area. Our Brazilian Jesuit driver explained that all the people who lived here and squeezed their subsistence living from harvesting the dump had asthma from the fumes and were considered pariahs among the general population.*

As he spoke, my eyes met those of a beautiful young girl standing quietly amid children playing by the roadside. What chance did she have, I thought, for anything except a life of misery and an early death?

The second nucleus around which revolves the Church's reflection on *faithjustice* in the late twentieth century is captured in the following frequently quoted declaration of the 1971 Synod of Bishops:

> Action for justice and participation in the transformation
> of the world fully appear to us as a constitutive dimension
> of the preaching of the Gospel, or, in other words, of the
> Church's mission for the redemption of the human race
> and its liberation from every oppressive situation.[5]

Action for justice, then, constitutes part of the preaching of the gospel. Preaching of the gospel must give rise to action for justice, or it is simply not a credible Christian gospel. There are two elements here:

justice as a part, an expression, of gospel love; and action for justice as a part of our preaching.[6]

Justice, as used here and in many other contemporary Church documents on the topic, is distinct from, but related to, two earlier uses in this book. In chapter 1, we saw biblical justice, descriptive of proper relationships among the people, with a special place for the *anawim*. In chapter 3, we saw the ways in which the medieval philosophical tradition developed its concepts of justice in society and relationships. Now, we encounter a third understanding of justice, distinguished from what tradition has called charity and valued as an essential expression of gospel love. Charity, in this sense, primarily concerns person-to-person encounters; it shapes our individualized generosity to the nursing home resident or the homeless family. Justice, however, as used since the 1960s in contemporary Church teaching, focuses primarily on economic, social, cultural, and political structures.

Justice, or the lack of it, manifests itself in the ways in which societies have patterned themselves in institutions, power arrangements, systems of finance and marketing, relationships between classes, ownership of goods and technology, and the distribution of costs and benefits among groups of persons. Justice is about those arrangements, patterns, systems, and the "ways we do things here."

While charity seems focused on individuals and justice upon institutions and power arrangements, a love rooted in faith remains the underlying connector of both. More easily seen in individual charitable encounters, love is no less active or integral to the response of justice. Philip Land reminds us that love motivates all the other virtues, "exists within and motivates" them. The commitment to justice flows from the love of God and neighbor, Land writes, and that love "transforms justice from within."[7] In a memorable and powerful phrase, the Medellin bishops proclaimed, "Love is the soul of justice."[8] Conversely, justice is the framework for love in the world beyond individual encounters; it is the enfleshment of love in a highly socialized world. The Vatican declared in 1986 that there is no gap between justice and love, and "to contrast the two is to distort both love and justice."[9] In 1999, in their pastoral message *In All Things Charity*, the U.S. bishops addressed the interplay of justice and charity:

> In recent years, charity has often been perceived negatively. Those who undertake charitable activities are seen as well-meaning "do-gooders" who actually foster dependency. Those who receive charity are treated in a demeaning

manner. Even the word "charity" has been transformed by some into a derogatory term. We reject this characterization. In fact, Pope John Paul II cautioned us against a rejection of charity because of a "distorted" notion of justice: "The experience of the past and of our own time demonstrates that justice alone is not enough...if that deeper power, which is love, is not allowed to shape human life in its various dimensions."[10]

In this chapter we will see, not the diminishment of charity in the sense of individual actions done for others, but the essential complementarity of justice—addressing social systems—as developed in the past half-century to flesh out the requirements of love in the contemporary world.

In the practical order, this commitment to justice has been endorsed and taken up formally by Catholic Charities USA, the national association representing hundreds of local Catholic Charities agencies across the nation. In a sense the work of these agencies epitomizes the Church's ministry of charitable caring in this country. As far back as 1910, the then National Conference of Catholic Charities stated of itself, "It aims to become, finally, the attorney for the poor in modern society, to present their point of view and defend them unto the days when social justice may secure to them their rights."[11]

The goal of advocacy for justice was reasserted as primary to the national Charities movement and to local agencies in the movement's 1972 self-study *Humanizing and Transforming the Social Order*.[12] That goal was again reaffirmed as central to the mission of Catholic Charities in the 1986 revision of the Catholic Charities USA *Code of Ethics* as follows:

> Individually and in collaboration with others to work toward the construction of a more just social order, particularly in the development of just public social policy. This includes participating in the shaping of social legislation at the federal, state and local levels, monitoring the public budget processes to seek to assure justice to the poor and the suffering in the allocation of the nation's resources, and to study the impact of all public policy on the welfare of people, with particular reference to the protection and strengthening of the family role in society.[13]

The *Code of Ethics,* in turn, has been adopted by numerous local agencies, many of which have incorporated the advocacy for justice goal as one of the two or three primary goals of their agency.

Sister Anthony Barczykowski, director of Associated Catholic Charities of New Orleans and a nationally recognized leader in the Charities movement, wrote in 1988 that agencies would continue to exercise an active advocacy role, precisely because of its connection to the work of charitable service:

> Catholic Charities will continue to fight for changes in unjust structures and help people move toward self-sufficiency. We will continue to convene, network and organize. Each of us will continue to provide a variety of services. *It is our service role that gives us credibility in our advocacy role* as we speak out on behalf of those we are serving.[14]

The credibility given by charitable service to advocacy for justice is only one of the ways in which charity and justice, both rooted in love, are connected.

Still more recently, in 1996, Catholic Charities USA members completed a three-year planning process at the conclusion of which four strategic directions were adopted. The second direction reads, "Build an inclusive Catholic Charities which engages diverse people, organizations, and communities in transforming the structures of society that perpetuate poverty, undermine family life, and destroy communities." The transformation of the structures of society lies at the heart of the Church's call to justice in this new millennium and remains central to the self-understanding of those working for Catholic Charities. This articulation of the justice priority by Catholic Charities and other Church leadership is an important message to those Christians who, as we saw in chapter 4, attack efforts of church-people to stand with the poor. This also provides a corrective to the service-dominated responses to systemic and structural problems that have been so prominent in the United States in the eighties and nineties.

Widespread homelessness, hunger, and poverty have prompted a well-motivated surge in food pantries, night shelters, and breadlines reminiscent of the worst days of the Depression. Somehow, however, the call for voluntarism, the praise of "points of light" and "compassionate conservatism," and even the effectiveness of caring programs in a number of our communities seem to have seduced us into accepting hunger and homelessness as somehow part and parcel of

American life. Thirty years ago Americans would not have tolerated this. The justice mandate reminds us to look behind the surface outrage of homeless families sleeping in their automobiles amidst shining skyscrapers and corporate takeovers. It calls us to see the underlying horrors of overpriced housing, inequitable income distribution, and unresponsive political leadership.

Grounding the call to action for justice in the gospel also reminds us of a fundamental power struggle reflected in the scriptural presentation of the Lordship of Christ. This conflict pits God and God's anointed, on the one hand, against "the 'principalities and powers' (Eph 3:10; 6:12; Col 1:16; 2:10, 15), which is one of several designations in the New Testament for the cosmic forces seeking to enslave our humanity."[15] As we will see in this chapter, unjust social, economic, and political systems and structures in fact do conspire to rob us of our freedom, tear our human and covenant community apart, and devastate the *anawim*.

This fundamental assertion that action for justice lies at the heart of preaching the gospel, at the center of evangelization in our times, can be understood as a development from four critical insights. These insights themselves help to flesh out the fundamental thesis itself. They set the Church on a course of teaching and action that essentially brings it into conflict with those in power in the macroeconomic and political systems of the world and with many church constituents who do not or will not accept this teaching. The U.S. bishops found this in the hostile reception to their pastoral letter on *Economic Justice for All*. Their experience was mild, however, when compared to that of the nuns, priests, and other churchpeople martyred in El Salvador, or children massacred in church bombings in the Deep South in the sixties, or the assassinations of Dr. Martin Luther King Jr. and Archbishop Oscar Romero.

The First Insight Calls for Simple Observation: Look at the World around Yourselves

What you see is hundreds of millions of people starving. It is a simple fact of life. In the opening part of their pastoral letter on economic justice, after naming a complex list of positives and negatives on the U.S. economic scene, the U.S. bishops wrote this:

> *And beyond our own shores, the reality of 800 million people living in absolute poverty and 450 million malnourished or facing*

*starvation casts an ominous shadow over all these hopes and
problems at home.*[16]

Arthur Simon, president of Bread for the World, put the same reality
in terms of the children, "Every day at least 40,000 young children die
from malnutrition and disease...."[17] This initial insight needs no more
explanation than that provided by the bishops.

Beginning with this observation, the Christian observer stands
firmly in line with the frank and bold posture with which the bishops
at the Second Vatican Council opened their monumental document
on the Church in the modern world:

> The joys and the hopes, the griefs and the anxieties of the
> people of this age, especially those who are poor or in any
> way afflicted, these too are the joys and hopes, the griefs
> and the anxieties of the followers of Christ.[18]

Having looked out at the world, the followers of Christ see what all
men and women whose eyes are clear of ideology see: horrible conditions for hundreds of millions of women, men, and children. It is a
simple perversion of the original blessing, of God's vision and
Christ's dream for the human community.

The Second Insight: Reality Is Structured

Besides you and me as individual persons and the chairs we sit on and
the earth we walk on, there are what we call *social structures*[19] which
are as real as we are. These objective, historical facts come in an end-
less worldwide or street-corner variety that includes the family generally and in particular, the Boy Scouts of America, the World Bank, the
Democratic and Republican parties, checking accounts, hospitals,
schools, TV networks, and foreign trade. Social structures are as celebrated as the Super Bowl and as common but essential to survival as
stop signs.

Not only are these structures real, but in a profound number of
powerful ways they shape who we are. As we shall see in this chapter,
social structures shape our living, our loving, and our faith. In paragraph five of their pastoral on economic justice, the U.S. bishops stated
quite simply: "People shape the economy and in turn are shaped by it."[20]

Saying social structures shape our lives is not enough. We need
to try to fathom the broad and firm hold these structures have upon

our reality and our relationships. This means discerning not only how we see them, if we do, but how we are affected by them whether we see them or not. These systems, institutions, and socio-political-economic arrangements are self-projections of us as persons and are consequences of a process of interaction between individuals and their environment. Simply stated, this insight reveals that social structures interact with individuals in at least three ways: first, we as social beings structure our lives, usually for good purposes; then, these structures take on a force, power, and existence of their own, comparable to ours in many senses; and finally, we are shaped by their existence and power.

One useful way of understanding this process of interaction was developed by social psychologists Peter L. Berger and Thomas Luckmann.[21] The process they described has three stages: externalization, objectivation, and internalization. They proposed that these are actually "three dialectical moments in social reality," each of which "corresponds to an essential characteristic of the social world." In their summary form: *"Society is a human product. Society is an objective reality. Man is a social product."*[22]

The first stage of *externalization* occurs when people impose some order on our world, providing meaning and making it more useful. We establish a school, develop currency, form a club, or, in my favorite example, invent stop signs to curb automobile crashes. Because early drivers were colliding at intersections with no markers, someone decided to put up a sign that said, "STOP." This was the externalization of the desire to prevent accidents by creating some form of orderly traffic flow.

In the second, or *objectivation* stage, the product that was externalized by people is experienced as an autonomous reality which we humans now confront as an external and coercive fact. These may be a formal as the U.S. Army or IRS, or as informal as wedding customs and fraternity rush. The facticity of these realities is frequently expressed in remarks such as, "That's the way things are" or "That's the way we do things here." The lowly stop sign, for example, is multiplied into tens of millions of signs, lights, and blinkers, formidable datum for every student driver.

We might also call this second stage *personification* to imply that these structures often take on all the rights, powers, and responsibilities that people have. A classic example of this is a corporation under U.S. law. Corporations can own, buy, and sell. They can even be convicted of a crime.[23] Corporations and other institutions thus take on the characteristics of persons, become an entity, a reality. Finally, these institutions and structures remain in existence—objectivated—long after the people who founded them are dead and forgotten.

Finally, we reach the *internalization* stage where the structured reality and institutionalized patterns and processes, which resulted from objectivation, now are passed from generation to generation. This process, part of what we call socializing, makes it possible for newcomers to be taught to enter into ordered society, to live by existing ways, and thus to survive in a highly structured milieu. It is essential to civilized society. For example, we internalize how the market works, what role we have in our families, how to use forks and knives, and, yes, how to stop at stop signs even during intense conversations or family feuds.

Social structures start as our creations, and then, like us, become actors in our individual lives, our community, and across the world. They are created as expressions of values; and they later shape, not only our values, but our entire lives. Often this is for our good. But, too often, because of the imperative of institutions to protect themselves and to expand their areas of influence or resist adjusting to changing times or circumstances, they often begin to produce negative impacts in our lives. Because of the importance of this insight into social structures and the pervasiveness of their power in negatively shaping human lives, values, commitments, and the justice and injustice of our world, we should look closely at several examples.

Retirement Age: For almost all of us, whether we work in the marketplace, the Church, or the home, age sixty-five has now become a marker with far-reaching impact: RETIREMENT AGE! Internalized, it affects our self-image, the assessment of our working capacity, social stigmatizing, and even our physical health. Where did retirement age sixty-five come from anyway? FDR? HEW? OEO? Church social teaching? Gerontology? Medicine?

None of the above. It was designated by Prussia's Chancellor Bismarck in the nineteenth century as retirement age for factory workers in his newly industrialized nation, based on assessments of life expectancy (externalization). It was an idea that stuck (objectivation).

Gerontologists note that retirement often triggers what they call the cycle of aging, as clear a form of internalization as can be found. First, workers becoming nonproducers at retirement suddenly are looked down upon in a society that measures self-value by bringing home the bacon and paycheck size. This is called economic dysfunctioning. Economic dysfunctioning then triggers a social dysfunctioning. For example, when retired workers return to their former workplace they are quickly and uncomfortably shunted from employee to employee with a few questions about fishing, Winnebago trips, or the grandchildren. They just don't fit in anymore. Coworkers may even feel a kind of low-level anxiety just having them around, an anxiety that surrounds deep-seated concerns about their own aging.

Social dysfunctioning in turn can lead to the actual physical dysfunctioning that is the product of lowered self-esteem and social worth. The mind can wander; attire becomes slovenly; and personal business gets less care than before. That in turn can generate more economic dysfunctioning, and so forth. The underlying problem was described by the U.S. bishops in a letter on aging written back in 1976: "Society's negative image of the elderly reinforces their own negative self-image." Their rejection is "rejecting a part of ourselves and our connections with the human community."[24]

School Sports: As a complement to educational goals articulated by such phrases as "a sound mind in a sound body," school sports programs were begun in a variety of educational institutions (externalization). In modern times, these evolved into the interscholastic or intercollegiate sports department, often with budgets larger than, and independent of, the academic institution (objectivation). Now too rarely questioned, the school sports phenomenon can be internalized to canonize school athletes, demean the nonathletic child, and undermine the primary values of education itself (internalization). The witnesses to this are the legions of college athletes without degrees and, in some cases, who can hardly read. Along the way, the sports-media industrial complex has helped to wipe out the family Sunday dinner and even the Thanksgiving and Christmas meal. Finally, why do we pay five or ten million dollars to a person who hits, kicks, or otherwise pursues a spherical object across a grassy field when we pay our teachers, social workers, and police officers a fraction of that amount?

Prisons: Externalized as humane alternatives to bodily mutilation and places for prayerful reform, prisons have become brutal, overcrowded institutions that fail their original objectives. For example, we have basically abandoned the classic goal of rehabilitation in our jails and prisons. Now, however, the objectivated prison system has its own overwhelming needs and many allies to support it. For example, in many states it is difficult to get funding for less costly alternatives to imprisonment because of the prison jobs created in rural communities which too often lack an otherwise adequate economic base. Imprisonment so dominates our culture's response to crime that, despite immense failures and costs, prisons generate a socially acceptable "lock'em up and throw away the key" answer to complex societal problems (internalization). As a result, we now have an imprisonment rate that is six to twelve times higher than the rate of other Western countries.[25]

Advertising: Mr. Miller, the shopkeeper, wanted to let people in his community know he had a "special" this week. So he bought a little ad in the county newspaper and informed the public, using some fancy lettering provided by his wholesaler (externalization). This single example of getting the word out is only one minor example of a complex system now symbolized by Madison Avenue (objectivation). The system now is a $201 billion dollar a year business in the United States,[26] persuading, urging, and cajoling us to consume more and more and more; it is an amount of money that could feed the hungry of the world.

At the internalization stage, this advertising effects profound changes in us that go far beyond whistling the tunes from television or radio jingles. John Staudenmeier of the University of Detroit, a specialist in technology and spirituality, describes the critical paradigm shift in advertising and its impact on us as consumers:

> Beginning in 1923 with the arrival of Alfred P. Sloan as president of General Motors, the task of marketing new cars shifted from Ford's approach, stressing the economy and technical competence of an unchanging Model T, to fostering cyclic dissatisfaction with one's present car, the basis of "turnover buying." Continued expansion of the mass-production system required turnover buying for, as the recent automobile recession demonstrated, when too many owners hold on to their cars for too long, the new-car market stagnates.
>
> Sloan's marketing strategy at GM was only the most striking example of an extraordinary shift in the nature of advertising after World War I. While some areas of marketing continued to stress the older "reason why" style—effective and attractive communication of a product's virtues—the new style tried to program the consumer's emotions, creating a sense of personal inadequacy and discontent as the basis of impulse buying.[27]

The impact of advertising upon us, though, goes far beyond impulse buying.

Two frightening implications of the bombardment of advertising and its dominant themes upon American people, their values, and their commitments are described by St. Louis University philosopher and critic John Kavanaugh.[28] The first process Kavanaugh calls "personification of the commodity." Using familiar ads from prominent American magazines and television, Kavanaugh depicts the ways in which we Americans are sold products in terms that ascribe to them human characteristics and powers. The advertiser's product will "accompany us on a journey of excitement," "be our friend forever," or "fulfill our deepest longings for companionship and love." A 1990 Toyota campaign promises:

The PASSION Is Back.

An overpowering desire starts the minute you see it. It's an intense emotion you haven't felt for a car since—well, in a long time. It's called passion. And you'll feel it every time you see the all-new Toyota MRZ.

Climb inside and the cockpit-like ergonomics will cause the symptoms to accelerate. And so will you. From 0 to 60 in a heart-racing 5.96 seconds. Thanks to the twin-cam, four-cylinder, 16-valve, 200-horsepower, intercooled, turbocharged mid-engine design. Add to that superb handling and you soon realize the passion's still there. Inside you.

It's the passion you always felt for driving. And it's waiting to be rekindled. By the all-new MRZ.

Let it ignite your passion for driving all over again.

The New MRZ
"I love what you do for me."
Toyota[29]

How many of our youngsters—and not so young—are wearing the blouse, jeans, or shoes that will win them the affection and admiration of their contemporaries or convince them that they can go it alone in life! Even in the traditional love triangle, a commodity replaces the "other woman," as a woman declares in another automobile advertisement, "Tom loves me almost as much as he loves his [auto name]."

In a twist on the first dislocation of values, Kavanaugh discloses to us the second profound impact of advertising, "the commodification of the person." Moved and shaped by our commodity consciousness, we begin to treat other human beings in the same ways we use our products. Our approach is dominated by a consumerism that will "get what we can out of" a person or relationship and then discard it like an empty beer bottle or soda can. We see this consciousness most explicitly in how our society discards the elderly or the disabled worker, no longer a useful producer in the economic marketplace, or how it treats the displaced homemaker or the woman on welfare. It is there too in discarding the "inconvenient" pregnancy. This commodity consciousness also shapes too much of our attitudes toward those of the opposite sex, whether in the literal exploitation of pornography or the emotional exploitation of the one-night stand. Our most serious commitments to one another are also affected. "If this marriage doesn't work out, I'll just divorce her," can be heard from wedding rehearsals to the marriage counselor's office. Commentators also point out the phenomenon of the "trophy wife," a new model selected by the middle-aged executive to replace his worn-out and older wife (just as he would get a new car).

The underlying perversion is that both the personification of the commodity and the commodification of the person have turned the original blessing of creation on its head, snatching stewardship from our hands and subjecting us to our things. Not only are we not owners now, but we have become owned and enslaved by what we have and what we desire to have. A 1990 magazine advertisement for jewelry captures the spirit of this dislocation:

> Permanent things, that's what it is. I think you just reach a point where permanent things start becoming the most important. Where buying something like that for yourself just feels the most honestly, entirely...good. When I bought the gold earrings? That's how it felt. And now, this time, with the ring, the same thought struck me all over again. As long as there's a sun, this is going to shine.

Not commitment; not caring; not love; not fidelity. As the ad concludes, "When you really want to treat yourself, nothing makes you feel as good as Gold."[30]

A similar analysis can be done to better understand the values-and-identity-shaping-roles of such social structures as the military-industrial complex, male and female parenting, the practice of law or medicine, and the personal automobile.

Sinful Social Structures

Far from being value-free, then, social systems and institutions carry the values of their creators and impinge upon our freedom, enhancing or constraining it in a very value-laden fashion. Thus, in socializing us, these same values are reinforced or promoted in us. In families, political systems, economic and legal institutions, and even through technology, values are constantly communicated. We thus enter into the realm of good and evil, of basic morality, of grace and sin integrated into each person's identity in its public dimension.

Theologians now speak *of graced social structures* as those that promote life, enhance human dignity, encourage the development of community, and reinforce caring behavior. Such entities structure or institutionalize good in a way analogous to the good deeds of individuals. *Sinful social structures* destroy life, violate human dignity, facilitate selfishness and greed, perpetuate inequality, and fragment the human community. As such, they embody evil in the way sinful deeds do.[31]

More obvious sinful structures, the easy cases, have origins tainted with values, intentions, or activities that we call sinful. Consider, for example, child prostitution rings, criminal syndicates, and slavery. The more novel or even radical development in Church teaching on sinful social structures, however, is that even well-intentioned institutions or systems can become sinful when they produce unintended ill effects or slowly become destructive of human values or human life over time.

We tend to resist moral condemnations of institutions or structures, however, when the human actors involved are well intentioned. This is doubly true when we ourselves are deeply invested in, or derive benefit from, such structures. An attack on bank lending practices is denied because we personally know and like the bank manager. A discriminatory Church employment practice is defended because we know the bishop to be a very good man. An unfair tax plan is supported because we voted for and respect the president or the governor.

More than the threat to our friendships or associations, however, we experience the most intense internal resistance to moral judgments of social practices that comport with our deep sense of "that's the way it is." The American practice of racial segregation provides one good example. Public discussion of this novel sin was introduced into the Catholic community in a 1945 contribution to *Commonweal* by George H. Dunne entitled "The Sin of Segregation."[32]

Dunne's argument that segregation was a sin did more than unsettle many Catholics. It literally threatened our Catholic accommodation with a separate but equal civil regime, one that had been institutionalized into Catholic parishes, schools, hospitals, service organizations, and universities.

Dunne's theological opinion, however, had little effective impact on the Catholic status quo. So powerful a social structure was segregation that only a few bishops even dared to integrate their parochial school systems before 1954.[33] The U.S. bishops as a body issued their own statement on "Discrimination and the Christian Conscience" only in 1958.[34]

The moral force needed to begin a breakthrough against the wall of segregation was not primarily the churches. It was the 1954 Supreme Court decision in *Brown v. Board of Education* that unmasked the evil lurking behind the supposed even-handedness of the dual system. Simultaneously, the case and reactions to it unleashed the depth of feeling attached to segregation in the United States.[35] It also forced discussions among churchpeople of the morality of the practice and helped to sharpen the religious perception of injustice that contributed to the civil rights movement over the next fifteen years. Segregation is a prime example of the power of a sinful social structure to legitimize an evil both in law and in the deepest self-understandings of a nation. Segregation also is a good example of a point to be developed later in this chapter about the necessity of structural reactions to structural evil.

One helpful clarification in our consideration of social structures may be to introduce the concept of *mixed social structures*. The Boy Scout helping the elderly lady across the street may have a mixture of motives for his good deed: he wants to help her, but he also knows that the scoutmaster is watching. So too with our social structures, good and graced structures can continue to effect good in terms of human values and relationships. These same structures, however, may also be producing human suffering on a grand or modest scale. It is important to recognize that the capacities for such good and evil can exist side-by-side in the same social structure.

Our response to this understanding of the mixed social structure can be multifold, depending upon the mix or blend. The amount of good may be so diminished by the evil as to warrant the radical transformation or elimination of the structure. This would seem to be the case with the 1954 Brown decision. The evil may be correctable by a simple reform or reforms, a return to the clarity of purpose intended by the founders or originators of the institution.

An example here would be the needed revisions in the kinds and ways of delivering development aid to countries in extreme poverty.

Or, the evil may be incurable, but it is tolerable in terms of the great good accomplished by the system or structure. This is the argument made by those who try to defend free-market economics against any noncompetitive control or regulation. Making this last judgment credibly, however, requires freedom from the kind of investment in the system or structure that would be threatened by any change. It also suggests the following consideration of structural sin and personal responsibility.

In his 1987 encyclical letter *Sollicitudo Rei Socialis*, Pope John Paul seems at first to accept the analysis of sinful social structures laid out above. His term is the "structures of sin," but his analysis ties these structures much more acutely to the acts of individuals.

> ...it is not out of place to speak of "structures of sin" which, as I stated in my apostolic exhortation *Reconciliatio et Paenitentia,* are rooted in personal sin and thus always linked to the concrete acts of individuals who introduce these structures, consolidate them and make them difficult to remove. And thus they grow stronger, spread and become the source of other sins, and so influence people's behavior.[36]

In a footnote, the pope lays out four ways in which individuals are responsible for sinful social structures, quoting his earlier apostolic exhortation:

> Whenever the church speaks of situations of sin or when she condemns as social sins certain situations or the collective behavior of certain social groups, big or small, or even of whole nations and blocs of nations, she knows and she proclaims that such cases of social sin are the result of the accumulation and concentration of many personal sins. It is a case of (1) the very personal sins of those who cause or support evil or who exploit it; (2) of those who are in a position to avoid, eliminate or at least limit certain social evils but who fail to do so out of laziness, fear or the conspiracy of silence, through secret complicity or indifference; (3) of those who take refuge in the supposed impossibility of changing the world and (4) also of those who sidestep the effort and sacrifice required, producing

specious reasons of a higher order. The real responsibility, then, lies with individuals. A situation—or likewise an institution, a structure, society itself—is not in itself the subject of moral acts. Hence a situation cannot in itself be good or bad.[37]

Human responsibility is thus retained in John Paul's analysis of social structures. We human persons are still related to all institutions and systems as: (1) creators, supporters, or exploiters; (2) accessories through complicity or indifference; (3) accessories through fatalistic avoidance; and (4) accessories through consecration of the status quo.

Churches, of course, are the most articulate exponents of consecration of social systems or structures, both in the world around them and within the churches themselves. The list of social customs and inequities that have been baptized by church leaders is as old as the dietary laws of Israel or the slavery of St. Paul's world or the New World, and as current as the sometimes prohibition against altar girls. Churches would seem to have a special responsibility to restrain the impulse to validate customs and practices of one historical era or locale in terms of universals.

The pope's position recognizes structures of sin, which he attributes to two powerful forces: "desire for profit" and "thirst for power." Unlike other modern commentators, however, John Paul does not seem to support as much an independent existence for such structures, separated from human intentionality. This seems to derive from the stress that he and the Catholic tradition have placed upon human freedom and his desire as well that human persons not escape responsibility for the social reality around them. He is also responding to those who would rest all their hopes for a better world on changes in social, economic, and political structures without attention to personal changes as well.[38]

In the process, however, the papal position could be interpreted by some to diminish the incredible power of social structures in human life: shaping our deepest sense of ourselves and our world.[39] An accurate position would need to keep both realities in balance, recognizing "that social structures enter into a dialectical relationship with the persons establishing them, so that the structures come to have a reality of their own which becomes internalized and shapes the very humanity in which it had its basis."[40] At the same time, these social structures "are out-there-real only because they are also introjected and internalized to become part of our own subjectivity."[41] Thus they also create a sense of disorientation and even entrapment within us that can lead to cynicism, indifference, and a feeling of impotence, affecting the very human responsibility and freedom which the pope so values. The sin of the world is thus our sin, and vice versa.

One of the additional and important benefits of doing structural analysis of reality is that, as Albert Nolan writes from the South African experience, "The more we all understand the structural problem as a structural problem, the more we are able to forgive the individuals involved."[42] While Nolan writes in the context of apartheid, similar applications are appropriate when considering the structural injustices of U.S. racism, sexism in Church and society, economic inequality, and North-South international economic injustices.

This potential for such forgiveness is an important message that could be extremely liberating for members of oppressed groups or nations whose experience of structural injustice has produced not just appropriate anger and effective action, but a persistent rage manifest in extremely destructive interpersonal behaviors as well as profound personal unhappiness. This is not to deny the responsibility discussed above for those on the upside of injustice to be challenged to act effectively on behalf of justice. It is said, rather, to offer some release from one aspect of the destructiveness of injustice in the lives of the poor and marginalized.

The Third Insight Is That the Systems and the Structures Are Not Working

Not working well, if you prefer. Or they are working well for some people, a small minority of the world's peoples, and not working well for hundreds of millions of others. What does this mean? In simple form:

- we have schools that do not teach;
- prisons that do not rehabilitate;
- cities that do not work;
- governments and political parties that are unresponsive to people's real needs;
- a food and agriculture system that pays farmers not to grow while many people go hungry;
- a health care system that leaves forty-four million people out, makes some people very rich, and often is out

of focus in its approaches to human life, happiness,
health, and dying; and
- an economic system in the United States and worldwide
  that is making some people very, very rich and billions
  of other people poorer and poorer.

Not only are the macro-systems not working well, but they are creating extensive injustice, poverty, and human suffering across the world.
In addition, as we saw in chapter 3, the repeated and more insistent message of the bishops and popes in modern times is that the situation is
getting worse, not better. In fact, the social, economic, and political systems are working so badly in many areas that Church leaders, such as
the bishops gathered at Medellin, have felt compelled to speak of "institutionalized violence" as the end-product of the status quo.[43]

As the prime example, in 1989, turning to the two dominant eco-
nomic-political systems in the world, the pope himself repeatedly criticized both: "The church's social doctrine adopts a critical attitude
toward both liberal capitalism and Marxist collectivism."[44] To those
familiar with the development of the Church's social teaching over the
past one hundred years, the most recent criticism of both capitalism
and communism by the pope came as no surprise. As we saw in chapter 3, this theme had been present, with a growing clarity, for several
decades. From an approach that had first criticized communist theory
and practice and only the excesses of liberal capitalism, the modern
popes gradually turned a critical eye on both systems.

John Paul II, however, took another major step in the analysis
when he criticized, not just the two dominant systems, but their
mutual interaction and its impact upon the world's peoples. This
theme too had been present in the growing connection made in papal
and conciliar documents between war and economic well-being and
between armaments spending and domestic economic justice. John
Paul, however, sharpened the argument as follows:

> It was inevitable that by developing antagonistic systems
> and centers of power, each with its own forms of propa-
> ganda and indoctrination, the ideological opposition
> should evolve into a growing military opposition and give
> rise to two blocs of armed forces, each suspicious and fear-
> ful of the other's domination.
>
> International relations, in turn, could not fail to feel the
> effects of this "logic of blocs" and of the respective
> "spheres of influence." The tension between the two blocs

which began at the end of World War II has dominated the whole of the subsequent 40 years. Sometimes it has taken the form of "cold war," sometimes of "wars by proxy" through the manipulation of local conflicts and sometimes it has kept people's minds in suspense and anguish by the threat of an open and total war.[45]

The pope's major concern was the impact of the tension between the major blocs upon the developing nations of the Southern hemisphere:

...For as we know the tension between East and West is not in itself an opposition between two different levels of development but rather between two concepts of the development of individuals and peoples, both concepts being imperfect and in need of radical correction. This opposition is transferred to the developing countries themselves and thus helps to widen the gap already existing on the economic level between North and South and which results from the distance between the two worlds: the more-developed one and the less-developed one.[46]

The results of the impact of the East-West tension upon the nations of the South and their relations to those of the North were tragic and perverse.

After explaining the various facets of this tragedy, the pontiff concluded:

The developing countries, instead of becoming autonomous nations concerned with their own progress toward a just sharing in the goods and services meant for all, become parts of a machine, cogs on a gigantic wheel.[47]

This set of relationships resulted in continuing neo-colonialism, the diversion of development aid from its real purposes to military ends, and an "unacceptably exaggerated concern for security."

Not only was this division of the world a direct obstacle to the proper development of nations of the South, it also meant a betrayal by the superpowers of their own leadership and solidarity responsibilities in the world community.

Nations which historically, economically and politically have the possibility of playing a leadership role are prevented by

this fundamentally flawed distortion from adequately ful-
filling their duty of solidarity for the benefit of peoples
which aspire to full development.[48]

The first impact of this encyclical's analysis is its profound critique of
the East-West relationship and its widespread structural impact in the
North and the South. The secondary effect of this careful and strong
analysis is that social systems and structures such as the East-West
antagonism thus become a more integral part of the primer on the
Church's social concern.

In 1989, stunning political and economic changes swept Eastern
Europe and the Soviet Union. If anything, the tottering of European
communism manifested the abundant cost of the East-West rivalry to
the nations of the East. The cry for freedom and dignity from within
the East bloc nations underscored Pope John Paul's assessment of the
inner defects of the Marxist economic systems and the ways in which
they, like Western capitalism, make persons the objects and not the
subjects of the economy.

The seeming collapse of the Eastern bloc does not minimize the
enormous cost of the East-West conflict to this nation as well, a cost
that has continued in the aggregation of more sophisticated nuclear
weapons, the continuing and costly development of Star Wars, and
the maintenance of massive overseas military commitments despite
these changes. Moreover, we continue to suffer the bloody social costs
of economic inequity, governmental neglect, and market-driven priorities in our society. The realities of U.S. consumerism, individualism, technological drivenness, substance abuse, environmental
destruction, poverty, racism, sexism, and neo-colonialism do not sig-
nal that the seeming collapse of our Eastern rivals is unquestioning
validation for our system in the West.

Now, in fact, the growing phenomenon of globalization, driven
by unchallenged Western economics and political and cultural dominance, has magnified the intense suffering of peoples in the world
and intensified the call for an alternative and integral development—
a structural response—for the multitude of poor and oppressed peoples. Pope John Paul put it this way in 1999:

If in recent times the church's magisterium has insisted
more and more upon the need to promote the authentic
and integral development of the human person, this is in
response to the real situation of the world's peoples as well
as to an increased consciousness that not just the actions

of individuals but also structures of social, political and economic life are often inimical to human well-being.[49]

The pontiff then underscored the need for radical personal and structural changes in response to these realities:

> The imbalances entrenched in the increasing gap between those who benefit from the world's growing capacity to produce wealth and those who are left at the margin of progress call for a radical change of both mentality and structures in favor of the human person.[50]

It is abundantly clear now that the Church is aware of the profound impact of social systems, from its analysis of the two great and hostile forces of liberal capitalism and Marxist communism and now its increasingly poignant assessment of the impact of free-market economics and globalization upon the world. The awareness that systems are not working (well) extends also, as we noted earlier, to our health care delivery system, the public school system, prisons, the income tax system, our admission quotas for refugees and immigrants, the distribution of wealth and income within and between nations, our abuse of the environment, and so forth. All this is the proper and necessary concern of the Church because it affects, not just the dignity of human life, but the very existence of human life itself, as John Paul so emphasized in *Evangelium Vitae*.

The Fourth Insight Proclaims That Our Faith-Response Must Be Structural as Well as Personal

If the systems are not working, then our faith response has to be systemic and structural as well as personal. We must do justice as well as charity. It is not enough just to engage in a commendable service that reaches out to help individuals whose lives touch our own, not in the face of massive structural evil that makes these people needy. The faith of those who follow Christ must deal with social, economic, cultural, and political structures as well. We must love persons so much that we change the structures that affect their dignity. Instead of a tension between love and justice, love as the soul of justice gives the Christian passion for building a more just world.

The image I like is one of those classics myths from parochial school education, the kind of story that "Sister" either did tell us, or should have. The story is the one about the young mother whose small child is pinned under the car in the street. She hears the child screaming, runs out of the house, and with a burst of adrenaline lifts the car bumper and pulls the child clear. That's what action for justice is about: loving persons so passionately and powerfully that we change the structures that weigh them down, affect their dignity, and oppress them.

Pope Paul VI put it this way, "The rule [of love] which up to now held good for the benefit of those nearest to us must today be applied to all the needy of this world."[51] As if taking this cue from Pope Paul, the U.S. bishops specifically talk about the need to "restructure the international order along lines of greater equity and participation" and to "apply the preferential option for the poor to international economic activity."[52]

This call to respond in action directed toward systems and structures gives rise to a variety of responses. *The first step, sometimes the most painful, is to unmask the realities lurking behind the legitimized structure or institution.* When the realities of harm done to the human community are exposed, "their demise begins."[53] Exposed institutions will retain and exercise existence and power, but the possibilities of change begin with our seeing them for what they are, like the fable of the king with no clothes. The need to expose reality underscores the importance of utilizing various forms of institutional, social, and cultural analysis in understanding how society is organized and how these organizational factors shape human behavior.

Important criteria for evaluating what is seen in analysis will be the impact of social institutions upon human rights,[54] human freedom,[55] and even human life. Christians will be on the alert for the demonic "when structures and institutions implicitly claim to be ends in themselves"[56] or when they "attempt to collapse the reality of the kingdom of God into the order of the earthly world."[57] We see this clearly in exaggerated forms of nationalism that proclaim, "Our country right or wrong," or "Love it or leave it."

This unmasking is a key task for religious people and the Church precisely because of the power of institutions to cloak injustice even with religious legitimacy. It often takes the very institutional power of religion to offset powerful institutionalized injustice, as in the religious component that was at the core of the civil rights movement. Theologian Donald L. Gelpi adds to this imperative for religious people to unmask injustice by noting the ease with which religious people legitimize injustice:

> Religious people can conspire with institutional injustice
> in at least three ways. They may allow themselves and the
> rhetoric of faith to be coopted ideologically by the agents
> of oppression who seek to justify their exploitation of oth-
> ers. They may remain silent and passive before gross insti-
> tutional injustice. Or they may sacrilegiously invoke the
> divine blessing on situations of oppression.[58]

This conspiracy with institutional injustice takes a variety of com-
monplace forms in our own society today: from religious blessings on
nuclear weapons to church leaders' continued appearance at meetings of segregated organizations or as guests at segregated country
clubs.

*Specific action directed toward the unmasked injustice of institutions
includes reform of existing institutions.* Looking at the broader economic
scene in *Economic Justice for All*, for example, the U.S. bishops put it
this way:

> These perspectives constitute a call for fundamental
> reform in the international economic order. Whether the
> problem is preventing war and building peace or address-
> ing the needs of the poor, Catholic teaching emphasizes
> not only the individual conscience, but also the political,
> legal and economic structures through which policy is
> determined and issues are adjudicated.[59]

At the outset of their letter on economic justice, the bishops stress
that their recommendations on specific structural issues or actions
may be debatable and do not carry the weight of theological principles or ethical norms. They are no less emphatic, however, in calling
for structural change and reform. In doing so, they make it quite clear
that the gospel must take flesh in the social, economic, cultural, and
political structures of our times. *Faithjustice* must emerge in action to
change society's structures.

*Key social structures may also need strengthening as part of the task of
building a more just society.* One such institution is the family, assaulted
by a powerful combination of social, economic, cultural, and political
factors in U.S. and world society. Some forms of the assault are overt—
as in government-sanctioned family policies such as mandatory limitations on childbirth. Others are far more subtle, many of them
economic. Philip Land explains about one such reality:

The first is the unending shift of normal activities out of households and communities into the industrial economy. Households cook less of their food (witness the sudden growth of eating breakfast out), mend less of their clothes, do fewer small house repairs. All this and much more—taking care of children and the elderly, growing vegetables, canning foods, sick-care—were not so long ago the personalized contribution of household and community. It was not paid work. Often it was done as a matter of exchange services, or even as a gift. With industrial growth all this becomes commercialized. It now has a money tag on it. It is monetized. Writers like Ivan Illich call for the demonetization and decolonization of much of this with its restoration to home and community before it's too late.[60]

The Church and many others tend to see the more overt challenges to family life, but not to discern and respond to the more subtle and dangerous economic inroads. Significant new efforts have to be developed in the near future to strengthen family life in vital ways, without necessarily using a model of reform that only pretends to turn the clock back to when Dad went out to work and Mom stayed home to work.

Another method of responding to social injustice will be the development of new institutions and structures in societies. We often tend to think of new structures at the macro-political level in creating new governments, such as those being built across Eastern Europe or in newly decolonialized nations of the South. The Catholic tradition of subsidiarity, continued by John Paul, however, stresses the importance of "intermediate bodies (mediating structures) that pursue the common good with real autonomy and in honest collaboration with one another."[61] Included here would be unions, charitable agencies, cooperatives, small businesses, Church day-care centers, community organizations, educational centers, and a host of other traditional entities.

The call for new social structures also means developing the new forms of cooperation between and among nations of the South, which John Paul has repeatedly encouraged. In addition, in the United States, it would encompass the bishops' call for "new forms of cooperation and partnership among those whose daily work is the source of prosperity and justice of the nation."[62] Finally, it should be noted that one new structure, the Christian base community for prayer, reflection, and action, has been critically powerful in reshaping the Church in the third world. While under continuing watchfulness by Church authorities, these communities have been hailed by the same authorities as "a source of great hope for the Church" and "a treasure for the whole Church."[63]

The North American search for similar, powerful models of faith communities doing justice is reflected in small groups in some church parishes, in movements such as RENEW and Christian Life Communities, and amid groups working among the poor such as Sojourners and the Jesuit Volunteer Corps.[64] They are neither as numerous nor as transforming for the larger churches as have been the base communities of parts of South America.

Solidarity

Pope John Paul underscores the urgency of connecting action for justice to faith in a term clearly reflecting his Polish background, the duty of solidarity. Although not originating with John Paul,[65] solidarity is his term for the structural response demanded by gospel love. Solidarity involves fundamental economic and social changes.[66] In an almost shocking assertion, he says, "Solidarity is undoubtedly a Christian virtue."[67]

> Solidarity therefore must play its part in the realization of this divine plan, both on the level of individuals and on the level of national and international society. The "evil mechanisms" and "structures of sin" of which we have spoken can be overcome only through the exercise of the human and Christian solidarity to which the church calls us and which she tirelessly promotes. Only in this way can such positive energies be fully released for the benefit of development and peace.[68]

What is this solidarity that the pope speaks of?

When he answers this question, John Paul actually takes us back to the other nucleus of a stance of *faithjustice* in the late twentieth century, namely standing with the poor or the preferential option. The pope begins to tie that theme to action for justice:

> It is above all a question of interdependence, sensed as a system determining relationships in the contemporary world in its economic, cultural, political and religious elements, and accepted as a moral category. When interdependence becomes recognized in this way, the correlative

response as a moral and social attitude, as a "virtue," is solidarity. This then is not a feeling of vague compassion or
shallow distress at the misfortunes of so many people, both
near and far. On the contrary, it is a firm and persevering
determination to commit oneself to the common good,
that is to say, to the good of all and of each individual
because we are all really responsible for all.[69]

John Paul's use of solidarity for our relationships of worldwide
responsibility gives a contemporary twist to the Hebrew sense of the
web of relationships that bound the community to one another and
to Yahweh in their midst.

In the very next sentences of his 1987 encyclical, John Paul
underscores the power of sinful social structures as the reason he
gives for juxtaposing the powerful virtue of solidarity:

This determination is based on the solid conviction that
what is hindering full development is that desire for profit
and that thirst for power already mentioned. These attitudes and "structures of sin" are only conquered—presup-
posing the help of divine grace—by a diametrically
opposed attitude: a commitment to the good of one's
neighbor with the readiness, in the Gospel sense, to "lose
oneself" for the sake of the other instead of exploiting
him, and to "serve him" instead of oppressing him for
one's own advantage (cf. Matt. 10:40-42; 20:25; Mark
10:42-45; Luke 22:25-27).[70]

Solidarity then blends the themes of standing with the poor with
prophetic action for justice. Taking the *anawim*'s view of this world,
Christians are then bound to commit themselves to effective action to
change the economic, social, cultural, and political "ways of doing
things" that create and enhance injustice. In their place, those who
stand with the poor are to erect structures of justice.[71]

This solidarity takes concrete form, the pontiff says, in personal
decisions, in "decisions of government" [9]; in economic decisions
[39]; in public demonstrations by the poor themselves [39]; in sacrifice
of all forms of economic, military, or political imperialism [39]; and
in a variety of other concrete actions, both personal and structural.
Solidarity, we are told by the Vatican, will require developing new
forms of collaboration among the poor themselves, between the poor

and the rich, among and between groups of workers, and between private and public institutions.[72]

In Bolivia in 1988, John Paul preached on the virtue of solidarity and noted that it will involve "making possible democratic participation of those who are still on the fringes of society" and collaboration among Latin American states to move beyond a narrow nationalism to "create a common front" in dialogue with the industrialized countries.[73] Speaking in India in 1999, the pope set solidarity in opposition to current economic forces:

> The great moral challenge facing nations and the international community in relation to development is to have the courage of a new solidarity capable of taking imaginative and effective steps to overcome both dehumanizing underdevelopment and the "overdevelopment" that tends to reduce the person to an economic unit in an ever more oppressive consumer network.[74]

Solidarity thus remains at the heart of Catholic social teaching as the new millennium begins.

In terms of a pastoral methodology, the Canadian Catholic bishops have presented a five-step process that takes us from standing with the poor to action in solidarity with them:

> (a) to be present with and listen to the experiences of the poor, the marginalized, the oppressed in our society, (b) to develop a critical analysis of the economic, political, and social structures that cause human suffering, (c) to make judgements in the light of the Gospel principles concerning social values and priorities, (d) to stimulate creative thought and action regarding alternative models for social and economic development, and (e) to act in solidarity with popular groups in their struggles to transform society.[75]

The Canadian methodology captures the earlier discussion of seeing, judging, and acting differently. With it the bishops blend the need for action addressed to social and economic transformation of society.

"Solidarity" then has come to capture the Church's gospel-based commitment to stand with the poor and to transform the structures creating poverty. Thus, it has been invoked as a principal theme in the U.S. Catholic bishops' 1989 statement on third-world debt,[76] been connected by John Paul in 1990 to the current ecological crisis,[77] been integral to Church discussions of the negative effects of globalization in the nineties, and even provided the inspiration for a Brazilian popular song.[78] This one word has become a shorthand way of summing up the Church's *faithjustice* tradition with a late twentieth-century accent. Solidarity is "neither a handout nor a few crumbs of justice."[79]

Conclusion

There are then four foundational insights giving rise to and explaining the call of the Church to action for justice:

- the griefs and anxieties of millions of people;
- reality is structured;
- the systems and structures are not working; and
- our response must be structural as well as personal.

Even though these four insights are easily documented and readily give rise to the call to action for justice, the conclusion still remains illusive and unintelligible to many Christians.

The most common objection that these good Christians will give to the call to action for justice is this: "Jesus did not get involved with political and social structures." Our response can be equally simple and straightforward: Jesus spoke out against the most powerful and oppressive social-political institution among his people. This was not really Rome, even though Romans were the current occupation army in Israel. Rather, what oppressed the people was the power of the religious leadership and their interpretation of the law. When Jesus did confront these powers, he stood firmly in the prophetic tradition of those who had challenged the powerful institutions of their time on behalf of Yahweh's original vision and the poor whom God loved.[80]

The role of the religious leadership and the operation of the law in the time of Jesus was a religious-social structure with clear ties to the economic and political powers that dominated the nation. These structures had evolved just as certainly through Berger and Luckmann's stages of social reality as any we experience in contemporary America. The leadership's interpretation of law and righteousness was as oppressive to the people of Jesus' own time as any sinful social structure around us today. It substituted the jots and tittles of the law for the foundational sense of giftedness, stewardship, and community that was Yahweh's original blessing.[81]

Jesus repeatedly confronted them with this oppression, contrasting the leadership's interpretation of religious practice with the lived relationship of Yahweh and the chosen people which Jesus had come to set right. "Beware of the scribes....They devour the houses of widows and, as a pretext, recite lengthy prayers. They will receive a very severe condemnation" (Mark 12:38, 40). Jesus denounces them for such practices as circumventing the obligation to support aging parents by declaring property or money to be *korban,* a gift to God (Mark 7:11–13).

The leadership's interpretation of law and covenant tore down that real sense of giftedness, stewardship, and community rooted in Genesis. Law, practice, and custom had become a social structure that assaulted the truth about who the people were and how they were to be with one another in stewardship and community. And, while Jesus' denunciations so often appear focused upon the persons of the Pharisees and scribes, it was the whole fabric of their teaching, customs, and institutions against which he constantly taught *and acted.* Jesus was, in fact, "the justice of God" enfleshed against the injustice of the religious establishment.

The call to us in the late twentieth century, then, is to take all of our gifts—our minds, imaginations, arts, sciences, material and spiritual resources, and the social structures we have created—to unmask and understand better the reality of the world we live in. We are called:

> ...to cast upon our society the same critical/creative gaze which Jesus cast upon his, to acknowledge the legitimacy of extending the language of sin and grace to structures secular and sacred, and hence to let our zeal for his lordship in our lives range beyond our personal hearts to our systemic world.[82]

Seeing both the personal and structural faces of injustice, we will understand that the action response of the Christian must be both charity and justice. It is not enough to say, "Lord, Lord," or to profess, "Jesus is my personal savior." When Christians say Jesus is Lord, they claim his kingship over all the principalities and powers, all the systems and structures, and all the forms of oppression and injustice. Without action, the world will not be created in the image of the justice of Yahweh or the kingship of Christ. Without action for justice, there can be no good news.

QUESTIONS FOR REFLECTION AND DISCUSSION

1. Explain what a social structure or system is. Give three examples of your own.

2. How do social structures shape our capacity to live gospel-based lives?

3. What are the three ways in which "justice" in used in this book?

4. What is the relationship between "charity" and "justice," as used in this chapter.

5. What is solidarity? Give one personal and one structural example of living solidarity.

6. What is one justice issue that you would like to work on to promote greater solidarity?

CONCLUSION

Full Gospel

Love ought to manifest itself in deeds rather than in words.
Ignatius of Loyola, *Spiritual Exercises*

Outside on the capitol steps in downtown Atlanta, welfare mothers demonstrated to increase Aid to Families with Dependent Children. The paltry sum granted to a mother and three children in Georgia in 1978 was $141 per month, and their campaign was to raise the monthly grant to $227. Buttons worn by supporters in the Public Assistance Coalition simply proclaimed in red "$227." Inside the legislature, lawyers for the campaign worked to persuade recalcitrant lawmakers to improve benefits by a variety of economic, social, legal, and political arguments. The coordinator of the legal end of the effort commented to me that we needed both those on the street and those in the halls to get anything done. Without the inside effort, the outsiders simply produced a lot of noise, anger, and some guilt. Without the outside effort, however, there would be no receptivity to the more reasoned efforts inside.

In Miami in 1984, I attended the national conference of Catholic Charities USA, which represents over 150 local charities agencies. At the celebration of Mass one day, I was seated behind two members of the Daughters of Charity, whose congregation has a long and strong tradition of serving the very poor in this country. As Mass was ending, one of the sisters, who had spotted the "S.J." on my nametag, said to me, "My, we sure are surprised to see YOU here, Father."

In a single week at Catholic Community Services, a young man came into my office with an idea to train the unemployed for meaningful work; a

223

seventy-seven-year-old lady telephoned to suggest that the diocese needed to open a shelter for the homeless; a development consultant brought a proposal for low-cost housing for the elderly or disabled on which he had spent ten years and untold thousands of his own dollars; and a group of forty laypersons gathered for their mid-passage retreat in a year of full-time volunteer work among the poor across the South.

❖ ❖ ❖

I was on vacation at the end of my first year at Catholic Community Services when the rest and respite was broken by a telephone call from the agency, "The bishop has given our building to Mother Teresa!" It wasn't exactly our building, not yet anyway; but a diocesan planning committee had proposed assigning an unused downtown school building to our overcrowded programs and staff. We very much needed that building, and I had already drawn preliminary plans for its renovations before leaving for vacation. Mother Teresa, however, who could probably have gotten any number of other buildings in town in response to one brief request on the news, got "our building" for her sisters and their good work. As the bishop told me, "What could I do? Say no to Mother Teresa?"

I spent hundreds of hours over four subsequent years trying unsuccessfully to beg, borrow, or build adequate office space for our many staff and programs.

Happily, ten years later, I returned to Baton Rouge to participate in the ribbon-cutting ceremony at a marvelous new service center built by the diocese for programs and services of Catholic Community Services!

Understanding the history and even the contemporary contours of *faithjustice* is one thing; living it out in the twenty-first century is quite another. What ways of being and doing are building the Reign of God now? What is life giving, God being the source of all life? What is truly freeing, God being the author of all liberation? What is loving, God being the energy and bonding for all forms of loving commitment?

The answer does not lie in some cheap political gambit that highlights individuals and organizations in the voluntary sector as a means of excusing government from its responsibilities for the health and welfare of its citizens. Government leaders cannot acclaim "points of light" and "America's promise" in the private sector while casting a profound darkness over the human and social service sector in the interest of escalating defense spending or tax cuts to further enrich the wealthy. Certainly there is light to be found amid the darkness, but it is a far more complex reality than politicians would like it to be and what is really needed to build a just society often challenges the political wisdom of the day.

Seven sources of light shine forth from the discussions of the earlier chapters of this book. They provide a framework of hopefulness for those who wish to commit themselves to doing and living faithjustice in the face of political, social, and economic apathy and oppression. They also suggest the means to longevity in the struggle to stand with the poor and to build and construct the Reign of God in our own society and across the world.

Point One: Service, Advocacy, Empowerment, and a Multiplicity of Models

On the social front, the eighties and nineties have been decades of irony and contradiction. Administration and congressional leaders renowned for their lack of compassion for the poor in government action and personal commitment pressed the general populace to be people of compassion. Moreover, while the federal government has acted aggressively to eliminate all vestiges of advocacy from its social programs like VISTA, Community Action, or Legal Services, the Church community has been discovering the social mission of the Church. Harry Fagan of the National Pastoral Life Center in New York explained,

> Most of our work in parishes has proved to us that the vast majority of people enter into the social mission of the church through their initiation or connection to a specific social service.[1]

Working at the parish food bank for a few months soon raises the question about why there is hunger in a country that stores and ships surplus food and pays farmers not to plant crops. A volunteer night at the city shelter each month makes us wonder about women and children sleeping in the streets of the richest nation in the world. In a very real sense, the hungry, homeless, and poor refugees from government neglect have been messengers sent into every city and rural community: They call for social change by their sunken cheeks, shabby clothes, and shivering limbs.

Despite the social realities of the eighties and nineties, however, conservative and often wealthy individuals and organizations have

tried to persuade the newly concerned that the proper Christian
response is individual charity, not social change. Those who most
profit from the system's inequities are most blind to them and most
intensely resistant to change. In subtle and ironic ways, they have
praised charity and tried to undermine justice. The marriage of charity and justice, however, is a matter of faith, not politics, since both
flow from one love.

This blend of charity and justice has become the everyday task
of individual believers and many dioceses across the country:

> The job of connecting people's faith to the public policy
> considerations in our country has fallen squarely on the
> shoulders of the diocesan social action office. Nowhere
> else in the diocese can the lunacy of praying for the widow,
> the lame and the orphan while ignoring the legislation
> that starts or stops their needed human services be so
> clearly focused. Of course we are against bombs that incin-
> erate humans while not harming buildings, but are we as
> obviously against and involved in the politics regarding
> that line item in the defense budget? Or shocked at the
> murder of our sisters in El Salvador while not really con-
> sidering the foreign policies of our country regarding
> arms and resources to Central American governments?[2]

In the face of the temptation to divide social service and social
action, Christians who understand the gospel recognize and promote
their essential partnership.

Service to those in need is the immediate response of gospel
compassion, but it also contains the seeds of gospel justice. Not only
does it move those who see, hear, touch, and feel human suffering to
ask why, but it also proclaims to an uncaring society and its leaders
that there is no such thing as human refuse. No persons are so poor
or humiliated that their needs do not demand a response from us.
Service is advocacy; it declares loudly and clearly that persons matter.

Advocacy for gospel justice, on the other hand, must be rooted
in service, remaining connected to the persons affected by the injustices structured into the systems of our society. "Love is the soul of
justice"[3]; and action for justice is best energized, not by ideology or
even justifiable anger, but by passionate concern for the least among
us, God's privileged ones. Peter Henriot contemplated this touchstone for justice at the conclusion of seventeen years of work at the
Center of Concern:

> I've often reflected on my motivation for changing the
> world. Where do I get my passion for justice? I've come to
> realize that the primary reason to work for justice is peo-
> ple. People I know and care about, people I love. People
> whose dignity is ignored, whose rights are violated, whose
> development is stifled, whose participation is denied. It
> can't be only ideology or politics that drives me to chal-
> lenge the unjust structures of society, for that would all too
> quickly become stale and sterile. People with names and
> faces make the difference.[4]

For Henriot, persons and issues are two sides of the same realities.

In addition to service and advocacy, our Catholic social justice
tradition has highlighted the importance of empowerment of those
who are low income and vulnerable. From the base Christian communities of the Southern hemisphere to the Catholic Campaign for
Human Development in the United States, there has been a vigorous
involvement by the Church in assisting people to discover their own
gifts and capacities, their own real power—especially in concert with
one another—to become "artisans of their own destiny." In Catholic
Charities USA's major planning process of the nineties, the first of
four strategic directions called upon members to "enhance our historical commitment to quality service by making the empowerment
of those we serve, especially people who are poor and vulnerable,
central to our work."[5] A special task force commissioned to work on
the implementation of that goal defined empowerment in the context
of Catholic Charities as follows:

> Empowerment is a process of engagement that increases
> the ability of individuals, families, organizations, and com-
> munities to build mutually respectful relationships and
> bring about fundamental, positive change in the condi-
> tions affecting their daily lives.[6]

This recognition of the importance of empowerment called Catholic
Charities to move beyond the individual self-improvement of good
social casework to an emphasis on deep, abiding, fundamental
change within individuals, families, communities, and organizations,
including the helping agencies themselves.

These developments suggest also that there are a multiplicity of
ways to go about the business of *faithjustice* in our society. When I
speak to people in church meeting rooms about poverty and injustice,

they often react to the broad sweep of the world's problems and the vast numbers of the poor by asking, "What can I do?" The question reflects an underlying feeling of powerlessness before so much suffering, an easy trap for people of good will. The response, like the Reign of God that Jesus speaks of, is that of the mustard seed. We begin small, starting with the person-to-person contact with an individual or family in need.

This way of beginning may take shape in work in a soup kitchen, visits to a nursing home, an afternoon reading to an illiterate elder, or participation in a big brother or big sister program with a young person. While this sounds almost too simple to be worthwhile and certainly not world transforming, the contrary is true. Reaching out to one who is despised and discounted by society, as indicated earlier, is a radically transforming act. It can change the world; and, more importantly, it can change us in the process.

Combined with some hands-on contact with persons in need, the concerned Christian in any walk of life also can become involved in at least one social issue, one way to change the systems that create poverty and oppression. Often, the two can be connected, service and action. For example, a person volunteering at the local food pantry joins a group like Bread for the World to advocate for just food policies. But it is vitally important to stay open to the connections between "our issue" and other issues, for example, how defense spending affects domestic food programs, or family life connects to quality education.

This in no way exhausts the possibilities. In the very institutions and businesses or professions in which most of us work there are practices and policies that create justice or injustice and foster solidarity or selfishness in our world. We can easily start there, where most of our time and energies are spent. There we also have the most effective knowledge for change and often the power to be creative, no matter what our position on the organizational chart. The same is true for our own neighborhood, clubs, school, community organizations, supermarkets, and churches. We all have access to a variety of opportunities for service, advocacy, and empowerment. Imagination is our only constraint.

Above all, we ought not to limit those around us to our way of proceeding in this. There are a rich variety of ways to respond to the gospel demands for charity and justice. Too often, we can become fixated with our own commitments, our own concerns, and the specific poor whose eyes we have looked into. Peter Henriot again draws upon his experience in the pursuit of justice:

> *Avoid reductionism in any strategy of change.* Because I want
> to get things done, I tend to want to reduce a problem to
> one clear solution. But there is a great danger in any uni-
> vocal approach to working for justice. I can come to feel
> that there is only *one* way—usually *my* way—to going about
> change. For example, I can reduce the option for the poor
> to only hands-on, immediate and direct contact of living
> and working with the poor. Then only a few can exercise
> the option for the poor. I've learned that social reality is
> too complex and human creativity too unlimited to put
> the strait-jacket of a narrow reductionism on efforts to
> bring about justice.[7]

The multiplicity also comes from the variety of needs or problems
that exist, from the wealth of gifts that we each have, and even from
the kind of response most appropriate to particular persons living in
poverty. Their situation may call for meeting needs for basic necessities, educating children or adults, providing technical assistance to
individuals and communities already mobilized to work for change,
or contributing to self-empowering.

Advocacy itself can be done from inside or outside institutions:
Each has its strengths and weaknesses; and each imposes constraints
on the advocate. The outsiders are free to raise hell, demonstrate,
picket, issue studies and denunciations, and go to jail to challenge the
status quo. They are essential to change, and little of it takes place
without their gentle-or-not prodding. They make the news, and are
often the heroines and heroes whose quotations fill our posters and
prayer cards. Few of us—too few—will rise to the noteworthy status of
holy outsiders!

Insiders, though, are crucial to building the Reign of God as
well. Catholic activist Larry Ragan explains:

> The insiders? Often dull, they find it difficult to hide their
> annoyance, even anger, when they are confronted by out-
> siders. The insiders speak a different language: they know
> the tax tables, the zoning variations, the assessment equal-
> izers, the square-foot cost to educate kids. You'll find them
> on the school board, city government, on the village
> board. Ordinarily not word people, they have mastered the
> art of the platitude. Jesse Jackson is an outsider doing his
> best to become an insider. George Schultz—one's eyes

glaze over at the mention of his name—was born an insider....

The insiders resist the first answer that comes to them: they have heard it before. They are offended when they see the world's complexities reduced to slogans shouted into a microphone or preached at a town hall meeting. They are saddened when they hear someone argue that God is on his or her side, and they wonder why God doesn't speak so clearly to them....

Sometimes you've got to feel sorry for the insiders. When they win, few know of their victory. When they go wrong, their mistakes are branded as evil. Often they share the goals of the outsider but continue to say, "things aren't that simple." The insiders know, with H. L. Mencken, that every problem has a solution which is simple, obvious and wrong.

The world is filled with people who prefer to be wrong and feel good. Insiders are not always certain they are right. They are unhappy when they must resist the simplistics of popular sloganeering.

So when we tip our hats to the outsiders, as so often we must, let's not do so with so much vigor that we fail to give two cheers to the insider.[8]

The domination of structured evil is so powerful and pervasive that it calls for both outsiders and insiders to ply their trades. The one prophetically denounces evil and announces the outlines of the Reign of God, and the other works out the actual how-to in the midst of often complex structural realities. Each would find additional strength in their chosen way of proceeding if they could learn how to cooperate with one another more than usually occurs.

Point Two: Tapping into the Tradition

The second source of light for us in answering our call to faithjustice at this point in history is that we do not come to these questions as novices. Whether the question is escalating the arms race, improving Temporary Assistance to Needy Families, hiring a union-busting law firm, or designing a health-care system, our religious tradition has both principles for addressing these questions and an already developed body of thought. This is not to say that the answers are clear-cut on any question, as we learned when the U.S. bishops grappled with the nuclear arms questions in their 1983 peace pastoral or with poverty and employment in their 1986 pastoral on economic justice.

What is provided to us is a framework of Catholic social teaching, as discussed in chapter 3. Major areas in which this teaching has been developed include rights and duties of workers and management, basic economic and political rights, questions of appropriate development, and war and peace. Working on social questions in our tradition then means not having to start from scratch. The tradition must be studied carefully by those interested in advocacy for a just society, but understood as an organic and continually developing body of thought. It can enrich us personally, and can contribute to the development of approaches and solutions to a wealth of concrete problems facing our own pluralistic society and peoples across the world.

One note of importance here: Although we have developed a long and strong tradition of "rights" in Catholic social teaching, many of which seem so compatible with the political and civil rights articulated in American law and policy, the two traditions are distinct. In fact, our Catholic rights tradition is distinct from ideologies of the right and left, as moral theologian David Hollenbach explains:

> ...the foundational principle of the [Catholic rights] theory must be distinguished from an abstractly inclusive harmonization of the rights emphasized by the various competing ideologies. The fundamental value that undergirds it is neither simply the liberty of the individual person stressed in the liberal democracies nor simply the social participation and economic well-being stressed in various ways by Marxism and socialism. Rather the theory maintains that respect for freedom, the meeting of basic needs, and participation in community and social relationships are all essential aspects of the human dignity that is the foundation of all rights. The institutional protection of personal freedom is emphasized by liberal democracy. The fulfillment of human needs is stressed by the developing "basic-needs" strategies at the center of the North-South debate. And the restructuring of the social and economic order in a way that allows genuine communal participation in the corporate life of society is the program of socialist thought. Each of these ideologies links its fundamental understanding of human rights with

a particular structural obstacle to the realization of human dignity.[9]

Human dignity in the Catholic tradition, then, is understood to have these three different aspects, each of which is claimed as primary or even exclusive by different ideological groups.

Hollenbach maintains that the Catholic tradition of rights cannot be collapsed into any of these three ideological positions:

> The contemporary Catholic understanding, however, refuses to tie its notion of human dignity to only one of these three spheres of life in which persons can be either violated or protected by the structure of the social order. As John XXIII put it, "The cardinal point of this teaching is that individual persons are necessarily the foundation, cause, and end of all social institutions. We are referring to human beings, insofar as they are social by nature, and raised to an order of existence which transcends and subdues nature." Any political, economic, or social system that is to be morally legitimate must provide respect for these spheres of freedom, need, and relationship. Thus the foundational norm of human dignity does not claim to be an ideological principle of social organization but rather a principle of moral and political legitimacy.[10]

Our rationale for this foundational principle, Hollenbach argues, is twofold. Our first basis is the person's transcendence over the world of things. This is a more philosophical foundation that arguably can be understood and appropriated by others in our pluralistic society without resort to Christian faith. Our second, more explicitly Christian foundation is our belief in our creation in God's image, redemption by Jesus Christ, and call to a destiny beyond history. This was developed in part in chapters 1 and 2.

The ethical development of our tradition to specify the precise conditions necessary for protecting human dignity, especially in the past century, has given rise to two key articulations:

> The first was the indispensability of minimum economic levels for all, in the form of adequate wages and broad distribution of property. Second, in the political realm it was recognized that the freedom of the majority in a democracy or of the ruling powers in other forms of polity must

be limited by their obligation to serve the common good of the whole society. This is a principle of the limited state, a principle that places a check on all forms of state absolutism by making government accountable to the basic rights and liberties of all citizens. These two principles are respectively the bases of social/economic rights and civil/political rights.[11]

This recognition of both social/economic rights and civil/political rights has evolved in the postconciliar Church to an understanding of, and emphasis upon, the interconnection between the two sets of rights and their mutual dependency.

This is not merely a point of theological or philosophical nicety. Rather, following this dual emphasis in the concrete order has produced a stance of advocacy by the Church in the socio-economic-political realm that has "pinched both feet" in terms of the dominant political systems. For example, see Pope John Paul's discussion of both East and West in *Sollicitudo Rei Socialis*.

In our own country, contemporary Church advocacy has not matched the programs of either Democratic or Republican parties, of liberals or conservatives. John L. Carr, Director of the Department of Social Development and World Peace of the United States Catholic Conference, explains:

> The pundits and commentators can't understand leaders who are with the Moral Majority on abortion and the ACLU on capital punishment, with the political right on religious liberty in Eastern Europe and with the left on racial justice in South Africa. The bishops defend human life whether it involves innocent, unborn children, starving families in Africa, or the homeless on American streets. Those who look to the American bishops to confirm some conventional political preference will be disappointed.[12]

Catholic social teaching's unique stance simultaneously affirms economic rights of the poor, religious rights of believers, rights of women *and* the unborn, and opposition to a continuing and escalating arms race.

There is one final note about Catholic social teaching that cannot be honestly sidestepped. Those who commit themselves to *faithjustice* soon confront the painful reality that the faith community which has called them is itself often the author or protector of injustice. As we have learned in the recent church child abuse scandal, it is a rude experience and often disheartening. Like corruption in one's own family, it takes the breath away and can leave us speechless in anger or rage. As the 1971 Synod of Bishops indicated, the Church must do justice if it is to proclaim justice to the world. That was one pointed criticism against the U.S. bishops' pastoral on economic justice as well, that the bishops must get their own economic house in order before commenting on the economic realities around them.

The truth is somewhere in-between, just as we are in the space between the two comings of Christ. The Church does justice, and it does not. The Church has birthed great prophets, and it has crucified them as well. As an institution, it is capable of structuring evil into its own ways of proceeding and then defending this, in Pope John Paul's words, by "specious reasons of a higher order."[13] As a graced institution, it is capable of calling us and itself to greater love, freedom, and justice and calling us to prophetic action even within the Church.

We who hear the Church's own *faithjustice* proclamations and its call to prophetic action will often experience the suffering of those who speak prophetically over against any institution. That suffering should come as no surprise, though it invariably does. Ambiguity, complexity, and conflict have been at home in this faith community since the pages of the Acts of the Apostles when the early disciples argued and grappled with the admission of Gentiles. The unfairness of our human divisions later caused the appointment of the deacons when Greek-speaking Christian widows were not given a fair share of the community's food. And on and on....

The frailty and even venality of our faith community wars with the advocate-Spirit's guidance and inspiration on a wide range of community concerns. Sinfulness is operative in all human situations and institutions. The conclusion is not that we should be surprised by the blindness within the Church. Rather, we should be surprised and saddened if prophecy were silenced and the pattern of Jesus' own suffering were not repeated in his followers, even suffering at the hands of the Church community.

Point Three: Storytelling

President Reagan's renown as a storyteller should not go unheeded as a lesson for advocates of faithjustice. Tens of millions living in poverty, forty-plus million people without health insurance, twenty million children sleeping in the streets of Latin America—all these facts are both true and numbing. It is suffering on too grand a scale for us to comprehend.

But poverty takes on flesh and blood dimensions when we can describe Maria, a single parent whom we personally know. She was injured on a job where there was no health insurance; has children named Oscar, Carolina, and Ignatio; and now tries to live on a few hundred dollars of welfare and food stamps. Knowing Maria and her children makes socio-economic-political statistics real. Talking about her gives the lie to cultural myths about welfare deadbeats and safety nets. Telling her story becomes a way of both building the Reign of God and putting a face on Jesus found among the hungry, homeless, sick, and imprisoned.

Telling Maria's story, however, is not just about a single parent with three children deserted by an alcoholic husband unable to find work. It also highlights the structural realities of inadequate employee benefits on the job, an economic system that tolerates and even requires widespread unemployment, a defective health-care system, and insufficient family support for poor parents and children. Telling Maria's story opens the door to social analysis and advocacy, transforming poverty statistics into obvious reality.

This is why, for example, *Catholic Health World*, the newspaper of the Catholic Health Association, began a 1990 series of front-page photo essays of the health-care poor. Each edition introduced the readers to one of the tens of millions of people in America without health care: to give names and faces to statistics that seem too large to grasp. The stories and photographs were then combined into a photo exhibit for the 1990 Catholic Health Association meeting in Washington, D.C., and into a small booklet entitled, *Portraits of the Healthcare Poor*.[14]

When we come to know poor persons, people whose lives are filled with joys and sorrows, loves and hopes, and successes and failures like our own, then we are far less likely to be sanguine about political myths and vague promises. We who know them are unlikely to tolerate cultural biases against the poor or politically expedient solutions that sacrifice specific supports of the poor for some generalized economic promise (e.g., "the rising tide lifts all boats"). Storytelling, then, is one step in the promotion of *faithjustice* in a society where the poor are too often unseen, forgotten, or worse. It is a way of taking the gift of personal tutoring, nursing, counseling, or visiting with a poor child or elder and multiplying the benefit a hundredfold.

Point Four: A Spirituality of Solidarity

Repeatedly the word *conversion* has been associated with the Christian community's reflection upon social reality and our call to respond to Christ revealed in the *anawim*. We must be converted, we are told, if we are to be peacemakers, those who do justice, and artisans of a new creation. That conversion is a matter of head, heart, and hands. We must first learn to think differently about ourselves, the human community, the gift of creation, and the ways we have organized our cities, towns, and villages. Thinking differently, as discussed in chapter 4, requires us to see with new eyes, cured of cultural blindness.

We must also turn our hearts as well, freeing them from the biases of power and privilege and the forgetfulness of the cycle of Baal. Changing hearts is often the province of prayer, enriched by our personal encounter with the poor. To our traditional ways of prayer, we add contemplation of the faces of the poor. We practice looking beyond the differences and even the alienations to see persons like ourselves. We learn to look into their struggles for love, life, dignity, and community to see the God who stands with the poor and the privileged revelation of Christ.

Our conversion must be from an individualistic American emphasis on what is mine to a radical vision of social life which does not distinguish my well-being from that of others near and far or my relation to God from these same others. Archbishop Raymond Hunthausen tells us that, "This radical intimacy that binds all of us equally to God and each other is summed up in the best-known and most accessible of the passages in Scripture, when Jesus teaches us to pray to God as 'our Father,' an acknowledgement that we are brothers and sisters with a common loving parent."[15]

Living this conversion to solidarity is a matter of faith, courage, and commitment. It is a virtue, a gift, and a transforming vision of the world that is both personal and structural, both affective and active. It plunges us into the midst of the human community with our hands outstretched to the persons around us and our eyes opened to the ways that this world must be made over, recreated by our actions in the likeness of the reign of Yahweh and the year of the Lord. To do less is to fail to understand the final lesson of Jesus before his passion and death.

On that tragic night, both the servant washing of the apostles' feet and the giving of his own life in bread and wine were concluded with a command to "Do this in memory of me." It is an action mandate. Similarly, the intimate friendship of Jesus and Peter is renewed after the resurrection in the famous breakfast on the beach in John 21. There Jesus three times asks Peter, "Simon, son of John, do you love me?" Three times Peter responds that he does love Jesus. To this Jesus answers, not that he loves Peter, but, "Feed my lambs....Tend my sheep....Feed my sheep." The spirituality of solidarity ultimately concludes in action for justice, doing what we have seen the Lord do because we love.

Point Five: Critical and Competent

Doing *faithjustice* in the new millennium will require the development of a critical consciousness rooted in seeing, judging, and acting differently than our peers. As discussed in chapter 4, we are invited to begin at a different vantage point. We strain to see with the eyes of those who are denied access, not just to the power centers of society, but to decent schools, adequate health care, and safe homes and neighborhoods.

We push ourselves not to take for granted the way things are, but to ask instead, "How does it affect the poor?" This means almost requiring of public and private decisions what Peter Henriot calls a "poor impact statement" similar to the environmental impact statements required of major government projects.[16] As we have seen, this will be an unpopular stance that will invite contempt and even the rage of family, friends, and the powerful of the world.

The justice of our cause, moreover, requires that we bring to it the best of human knowledge and skills. This is a prerequisite for appropriate person-to-person ministry, as well as an essential for social change advocacy. Divinity school professor Robert Michael Franklin lays out an agenda for training and education in the context of ministry formation that could give us some pause:

> But religious leaders also must master that ensemble of skills and body of knowledge necessary for leading social change. Positing Dr. King and Malcolm X as moral exemplars, religious leaders today need to know some of what they knew. They must know intimately their religious traditions along with new knowledge from the culture, especially the social and natural sciences, technology, national and world history, and the truth claims of other religions. They must be perpetual students of human nature, and

have some competence in the arts of grassroots organizing, persuasion, debate and compromise. And they should
know how to analyze moral problems, to weigh alternative
action plans, to guide moral action by ensuring that it is
consonant with the community's theological commitments, and to justify a course of action in terms which are
intelligible in a pluralistic society. In order to become
effective, faithful interpreters of the Christian witness and
transformers of society, they must become as resourceful
in ethics as in theology.[17]

Franklin's well-conceived listing should not prevent our involvement
in the pursuit of *faithjustice*, but it should underscore the importance
of preparation and training, both before undertaking the challenge
and continuing on the job.

The breadth of the task also suggests that there are a wide range
of disciplines and skills necessary to respond to human needs and create new societies. None of us, no matter what our background or
experience, can then excuse ourselves for having nothing to contribute. We bring our own unique experience and knowledge,
together with our love for other persons. That is a firm foundation for
learning.

Point Six: A Passion for Faithjustice

Making over the world in the pattern of the Reign of God is no task
for the half-hearted. No matter what our natural demeanor, we must
beg for a passion for what is right, the same pathos of God that drove
the Hebrew prophets. When Jesus says to his disciples, "Receive the
holy Spirit," it is a Spirit who comes in the roar of the wind and the
power of fire. He promises and pours out that gift upon all of us who
are baptized in water and the Spirit of compassion and justice.

We are now heirs of that Spirit, empowered and driven by the
passion and compassion that energized and guided Jesus of
Nazareth from the banks of his Jordan baptism. His desert temptations will be ours as well. We will be seduced to use our gifts for our
own aggrandizement, to focus on our own desires and hungers to the
exclusion of others' needs, and to pile up favors and debts to make
ourselves "great" in their eyes. Our own gifts will have the fatal hook
embedded in them: to turn us from the service of others to seek

their admiration and flattery. We will be tempted from comfort to power to idolatry, powerful forces at the heart of modern societies.

The antidote is the passion of Christ. The antidote is the gift of Christ's own Spirit that now seizes us and propels us to faithful service to those in need around us and to confront injustice wherever it may arise and in whatever dress. The passion has its source in the Spirit of Jesus; but it is refined and nurtured in living contact with the *anawim* of Yahweh, in prayer that remains faithful in failure and victory, and in communities that are passion-filled and prayerful. Through these experiences, we are drawn from the caring and compassionate Galilee mission to the daring and confrontational mission at Jerusalem. It is a passion for service to the least among us and advocacy for a new world order patterned on the Reign of God.

Point Seven: Preach and Practice a "Full Gospel"

Faithjustice is "full gospel." It connects the personal journey in faith to the social obligations of neighborhoods and nations. Building on the reality of contemporary interdependence, it raises up the virtue of solidarity as a firm commitment to action for the common good that reaches across boundaries of race, religion, gender, class, and nation to embrace all women and men.

This call to action is rooted deeply in the Hebrew and Christian scriptures, in the philosophical and theological traditions that spanned two thousand years of Christian history, and in the modern reflections of the Church in the last 110 years. It has been carried in the ark of Yahweh, in the teaching of the disciples of Christ, and in the practices of charity and justice of the followers of the way across history. It is ancient, medieval, modern, and contemporary.

The full gospel only continues in our time if it is enfleshed in each of us and in the entire faith community. As Peter Henriot indicates, doing that is a matter of preaching and practice:

> I've been challenged many, many times in giving a presentation on social justice by two nagging questions, posed by myself and by others: Do I really *believe* this stuff? Do I really *live* it? Believing in the cause of justice is not difficult, but authentically living out its message is a real challenge. I don't have to be perfect. God knows I'm not! But I do need—personally and corporately—to try to be

authentic in lifestyle and policy, congruent with the message I share.[18]

Henriot is correct, as discussed earlier, that the challenge to the faith community is to live what it preaches. The message of *faithjustice* will not be accepted in an already overcommunicated world if our deeds do not reach out to meet our message. We may not be perfect in the execution, but our desires and our efforts must be consistent with what we proclaim to be our faith.

That is the present challenge: to preach and practice the full gospel revealed to us from the first pages of the scriptures. In the ceremony for the ordination of deacons, the bishop presses the scriptures into the hands of the candidate and says this:

> *Believe what you read.*
> *Preach what you believe.*
> *Practice what you preach.*

That challenge confronts all of us who profess to follow this Jesus: to believe, preach, and practice the full gospel, the good news of *faithjustice* that is so desperately needed by our world.

APPENDICES

Modern Catholic Social Thought

Some Resources

Abbott, Walter M., S.J. (ed.), *The Documents of Vatican II.* New York: Guild Press, America Press, Association Press, 1966.

Brown, Dorothy, and Elizabeth McKeown, *The Poor Belong to Us: Catholic Charities and American Welfare.* Cambridge, Mass.: Harvard University Press, 1997.

Byers, David M. (ed.), *Justice in the Marketplace: Collected Statements of the Vatican and U.S. Catholic Bishops on Economic Policy, 1891–1984.* Washington, D.C.: United States Catholic Conference, 1985.

Christiansen, Drew, S.J., and Walter Grazer (eds.), *"And God Saw That It Was Good": Catholic Theology and the Environment.* Washington, D.C.: United States Catholic Conference, 1996.

Cleary, Edward, O.P. (ed.), *Path from Puebla: Significant Documents of the Latin American Bishops since 1979.* Washington, D.C.: United States Catholic Conference, 1989.

Coston, Carol, O.P., et al., *The Catholic Social Justice Tradition.* Washington, D.C.: Network, 1989.

Curran, Charles E., *American Catholic Social Ethics.* Notre Dame, Ind.: University of Notre Dame Press, 1982.

Curran, Charles, and Richard A. McCormick, S.J. (eds.), *Readings in Moral Theology No. 5: Official Catholic Social Teaching.* New York/Mahwah, N.J.: Paulist Press, 1986.

Darring, Gerald, *A Catechism of Catholic Social Teaching.* Kansas City: Sheed & Ward, 1987.

241

Dorr, Donal, *Option for the Poor: A Hundred Years of Vatican Social Teaching.* Maryknoll, N.Y.: Orbis Books, 1983.

Gremillion, Joseph (ed.), *The Gospel of Peace and Justice: Catholic Social Teaching since Pope John.* Maryknoll, N.Y.: Orbis Books, 1975.

Haughey, John, S.J. (ed.), *The Faith That Does Justice.* New York: Paulist Press, 1977.

Henriot, Peter J., S.J., Edward P. DeBerri, S.J., and Michael J. Schultheis S.J., *Catholic Social Teaching: Our Best Kept Secret.* Maryknoll, N.Y.: Orbis Books and Washington, D.C.: the Center of Concern, 1988.

Himes, Kenneth R., O.F.M., *Responses to 101 Questions on Catholic Social Teaching.* New York/Mahwah, N.J.: Paulist Press, 2001.

Hollenbach, David, S.J., *Claims in Conflict: Retrieving and Renewing the Catholic Human Rights Tradition.* New York: Paulist Press, 1979.

In the Name of Peace: Collective Statements of the United States Catholic Bishops on War and Peace, 1919–1980. Washington, D.C.: United States Catholic Conference, 1983.

Land, Philip S., S.J., *Shaping Welfare Consensus: U.S. Bishops' Contribution.* Washington, D.C.: Center of Concern, 1988.

Land, Philip S., S.J., *Catholic Social Teaching: As I Have Lived, Loathed, and Loved It.* Chicago: Loyola University Press, 1994.

Massaro, Thomas, S.J., *Living Justice: Catholic Social Teaching in Action.* Franklin, Wis.: Sheed & Ward, 2000.

Nolan, Hugh J., and Patrick W. Carey (eds.), *Pastoral Letters and Statements of the United States Catholic Bishops (1792–1997).* Washington, D.C.: United States Catholic Conference, Vols. I–IV, 1984, Vol. V, 1989, and Vol. VI, 1998.

O'Brien, David J., and Thomas A. Shannon (eds.), *Catholic Social Thought: The Documentary Heritage.* Maryknoll, N.Y.: Orbis Books, 1995.

O'Keefe, Mark, O.S.B., *What Are They Saying About Social Sin?* New York/Mahwah, N.J.: Paulist Press, 1990.

Ulrich, Tom, *Parish Social Ministry: Strategies for Success.* Notre Dame, Ind.: Ave Maria Press, 2001.

Vatican Congregation for Catholic Education, "Guidelines for the Study and Teaching of the Church's Social Doctrine in the

Formation of Priests,", dated December 30, 1988, and released June 27, 1989, No. 17. *Origins,* Vol. 19, No. 11, August 3, 1989.

On the Web

Caritas Internationalis, at www.caritas.org, provides information on the work of Caritas agencies around the world and statements on international issues of development, justice, and peace.

The Catholic Campaign for Human Development, at www.poverty-usa.org, provides important information on poverty in America and CCHD's programs in response.

Catholic Charities USA, at www.catholiccharitiesusa.org, applies Catholic social teaching to a number of current domestic issues affecting low-income families and other vulnerable people and provides other information on the work of Catholic Charities across the nation.

Catholic Relief Services, at www.catholicrelief.org, provides valuable information and statements on the international problems of poverty, development, and peace.

Claretian Publications, at www.uscatholic.org, provides *The Busy Christian's Guide to Catholic Social Teaching* and other materials.

The Center of Concern—www.coc.org—provides a wealth of Catholic social teaching resources, as well as materials on current international and domestic social justice issues.

The Office of Social Justice of the Archdiocese of St. Paul and Minneapolis, at www.osjspm.org, provides a comprehensive bibliography on Catholic social teaching and other valuable materials, including teaching aids, as well as links to other related web sites.

The United States Conference of Catholic Bishops, at www.usccb.org, makes available a number of pastoral letters and statements of the bishops and also links to the Department of Social Development and World Peace, Migration and Refugee Services, the Pro-Life Office, and the Catholic Campaign for Human Development.

After the Pastorals: A Parish Social Ministry Inventory*

In the wake of *Economic Justice for All* (1986), *The Challenge of Peace* (1983), *Brothers and Sisters to Us* (1979), and various statements on respect for life, a parish might want to evaluate what they have already done, or consider what more they might do in response to these prophetic pastoral letters from the U.S. bishops.

The following questions are arranged in a few simple categories, with a rather primitive scoring method to help a parish take such an inventory. Obviously, no parish could or should be doing all of these activities. However, they are typical of parish efforts to address contemporary issues and problems. (You may want to do this exercise with the entire parish staff or council or a special committee responsible for the social ministry of the parish.)

Scoring

Using the scoring below, the higher your score in each section the more your parish has accomplished; the lower your score the more you might want to reexamine your response to the pastorals.

0 = No; 1 = Considering; 2 = In process, just starting; 3 = In place, but ineffective; 4 = In place, effective.

Committees and Staffing

A. Is a parish committee, organization, and/or staff member charged with direct financial assistance to the poor? ____

B. Is a parish committee and/or staff member charged with education for peace and social justice? ____

*Alfred C. Kammer, S.J., "After the Pastorals, A Parish Social Ministry Inventory" © 1988 by CHURCH Magazine, Published by National Pastoral Life Center, 299 Elizabeth St., New York, N.Y. 10012 (212) 431-7825

C. Is a parish committee and/or staff member charged with advocacy for peace and social justice? ____

D. Is there a Bread for the World or other organized advocacy effort regarding hunger in the parish? ____

E. Is there a *Pax Christi* chapter in the parish? ____

F. Do staff and/or volunteers represent the parish in local groups or civic associations working to improve the community's response to the poor and needy? ____

G. Is a parish committee and/or staff member charged with respect life programming in the parish? ____

H. Do staff and/or volunteers represent the parish in local or regional programs or with other groups working for racial justice and equality? ____

SCORE ____ (out of a possible 32)

Education and Programming

A. Does the parish plan annual programming or observances touching upon issues of war and peace, for example, peace Sunday, Central America week, Hiroshima anniversary, World Peace Day (Jan. 1)? ____

B. Does the parish plan annual programming or observances concerning workers' rights, poverty, and empowering the poor on such occasions as Labor Day, rice bowl collections (Sundays in Lent), Campaign for Human Development collection, and so on? ____

C. Does the parish promote the sign of peace at mass as "an authentic sign of our reconciliation with God, and with one another" (peace pastoral)? ____

D. Does the parish promote awareness of the needs of racial and ethnic minorities and the ways in which they contribute to the richness of the Christian community, for example, Negro and Indian mission collection, Martin Luther King celebration, Black history month (February), feast of Our Lady of Guadalupe, feast of Blessed Kateri Tekakwitha, and others? ____

E. Have copies of *Brothers and Sisters to Us, What We Have Seen and Heard, The Challenge of Peace,* and *Economic Justice for All* been made available to parishioners, at least in summary form? ____

F. If the parish has a magazine or newspaper rack in the church or parish center or offices, does it contain summaries of *The Challenge of Peace* and *Economic Justice for All* (for example, "Catholic Update" version)? ____

G. Does the parish bulletin regularly include references to *The Challenge of Peace, Economic Justice for All,* local civic facts or events, local organizations needing volunteers, social justice committee activities, peace committee activities, and diocesan activities touching upon racism, peace, and social justice? ____

H. Does the parish make peace and justice part of the regular school curriculum, the religious education program, the RCIA, and sacramental preparation programs? ____

SCORE ____ (out of a possible 32)

Budget and Finance

A. Does the parish budget allocate a specific percentage of its regular income to works of charity, emergency assistance toward the poor and needy? ____

B. Does the parish budget allocate a specific percentage of its regular income to educate and advocate for peace and social justice? ____

C. Does the parish, in lieu of or in addition to regular income, have special collections for emergency assistance for the poor, for peace and social justice, and so forth? ____

D. If the parish has a school, does the parish or school allocate a specific percentage of the budget for scholarship assistance to poorer students? ____

E. Has the parish done an assessment of wages and salaries of parish staff (and school personnel) to ensure that employees are paid a fair family wage? ____

F. Has the parish done an assessment of employee benefits to ensure that employees are receiving adequate health, retirement, and other benefits for themselves and their families? ____

G. Do the parish council, building, liturgy, or other appropriate committees each have a policy/concern that parish buildings reflect simplicity of gospel values in decor, furnishings, and overall size and style? ____

H. Are all parish buildings and facilities accessible to persons with disabilities? ____

I. If the parish has investments, does it have an ethical investor or corporate investment responsibility policy and practice? ____

SCORE ____ (out of a possible 36)

Other Considerations

A. Does the parish have an affirmative action effort to maximize participation of racial and ethnic minorities, poor parishioners, and the disabled in parish committees, staff, ministries (lectors, eucharistic ministers, and others), and parochial school student body and staff? ____

B. Has the parish made an assessment of its geographical locale to determine the demographic, social, economic, and political character of the parish; does parish planning reflect these characteristics? ____

C. Does the parish belong to Project Equality or otherwise address the question of nondiscrimination by vendors and employers with whom the parish contracts for goods and services? ____

D. Do the parish and/or school act affirmatively to buy goods and services from minority-owned businesses? ____

E. Do the parish and its school have a policy of support for unionized vendors of goods and services, or at least touch upon anti-union activities of vendors of goods or services? ____

F. Does the parish promote participation in RENEW, parish social ministry, Catholic Charities, respect life, rural life, or other such activities promoted by the diocese? ____

G. Does the parish make peace and justice a regular part of parish staff meetings, integral to the work of the whole parish staff? ____

H. Does the parish make peace and justice a regular part of the agenda of the parish council, or otherwise make it an integral part of the mission of the whole parish? ____

I. Does the parish make peace and justice a regular part of liturgical celebrations (themes, songs, homilies, offerings, announcements, prayers of the faithful, missioning of eucharistic ministers to nursing homes and prisons, and so on)? ____

J. Does the parish promote fast and abstinence, penance, and prayer on Fridays during the year as a sign of and witness to the cause of peace (peace pastoral)? ____

K. Are the peace and justice activities an integral part of the annual plan of the parish? ____

L. Are the peace and justice activities an integral part of the annual evaluation of the parish? ____

M. Does the parish choir use the hymnal of Black Masses, *Lead Me, Guide Me,* as part of its music repertoire in an effort to recognize and share the diverse cultural and spiritual heritages of the Catholic community? ____

SCORE ____ (out of a possible 52)

For Pastors: A Personal Appraisal

A. Do the rectory, automobiles, and style of life of the clergy staff reflect the simplicity of the gospel, stewardship of our natural resources, and an awareness of the poor? ____

B. Do you promote the principle of subsidiarity in the area of peace and social justice by delegating to staff and/or volunteers, by creating parish groups/committees and enabling them to act, and by affirmative responses to initiatives of parishioners directed toward peace and social justice? ____

C. Do you spend some time each week in direct contact with the poor, imprisoned, and others in need? ____

D. Do you yourself act prophetically on behalf of the poor, powerless, unborn, condemned, aged, or peace by public witness, and/or action? ____

E. Have you educated yourself on the Church's social tradition, including *Brothers and Sisters to Us, What We Have Seen and Heard, The Challenge of Peace,* and *Economic Justice for All?* ____

F. Do you personally participate in ecumenical and civic efforts to respond to the poor and needy, providing leadership to the larger church and civic communities? ____

SCORE ____ (out of a possible 24)

NOTES

Introduction

1. *Pastoral Letters and Statements of the United States Catholic Bishops,* Volumes I–VI, Hugh J. Nolan and Patrick W. Carey, eds. (Washington, D.C.: United States Conference of Catholic Bishops, 1983, 1989, 1998).

2. Communities, in the sense in which we are using the term, have a history—in an important sense they are constituted by their past—and for this reason we can speak of a real community as a "community of memory," one that does not forget its past. In order not to forget that past, a community is involved in retelling its story, its constitutive narrative, and in so doing, it offers examples of the men and women who have embodied and exemplified the meaning of the community. These stories of collective history and exemplary individuals are an important part of the tradition that is so central to a community of memory. (Robert N. Bellah, Richard Madsen, William M. Sullivan, Ann Swidler, and Steven M. Tipton, *Habits of the Heart: Individualism and Commitment in American Life* [New York: Harper and Row, 1985], p. 153)

3. *Habits,* p. 271.
4. *Habits,* p. 276.
5. *Habits,* p. 284.
6. *Habits,* p. 285.

7. The pastoral letter came shortly after the first Reagan administration's devastating cuts in human services programs and economic policies that severely damaged the economic well-being of America's poorest families. The number of Americans living below the poverty line had increased by over nine million persons, or 35 percent, in the period between 1979 and 1983. Cf., for example, Robert Greenstein and John Bickerman, *The Effect of the Administration's Budget, Tax, and Military Policies on Low Income Americans* (Center on Budget and Policy Priorities, 1983) and Robert Greenstein, *End Results: The Impact of Federal Policies Since 1980 on Low Income Americans* (Center on Budget and Policy Priorities, 1984).

8. It is no secret that the Reagan administration did its best to eviscerate any programs designed to promote advocacy or empowering of or with the poor. The principal example would be the Legal Services Corporation, which the administration tried to terminate completely in eight successive budget proposals. Similarly, the administration eliminated

advocacy themes and placements from the VISTA program and tried to eradicate any vestiges of the Community Action agencies still remaining from the War on Poverty of the 1960s.

9. The principal example of this would be the U.S. bishops' Catholic Campaign for Human Development (CCHD), a multimillion dollar self-help program for the poor that purposefully encourages and funds organizations of the poor and marginalized to promote community self-development and empowerment. CCHD and the conservative wrath it has incurred is discussed in chapter 4.

10. The work of the various denominations is represented in part by the following list of official comprehensive declarations:

"Economic Justice—Stewardship of Creation in Human Community," adopted in 1980 by the Tenth Biennial Convention of the Lutheran Church in America.

"Christian Faith and Economic Justice," a 1984 study guide approved by the General Assembly of The United Presbyterian Church, USA.

"Christian Faith and Economic Life," a 1987 study paper of the United Church of Christ.

"Economic Justice and the Christian Conscience," commended in 1987 to the Episcopal Church for study, reflection, and response by the House of Bishops.

Shorter statements on particular aspects of economic justice were issued by the United Methodist Church, the Christian Church (Disciples of Christ), the American Baptist Churches, the Union of American Hebrew Congregations, the National Jewish Community Relations Advisory Council, the Unitarian Universalist Association, and the National Council of the Churches of Christ in the U.S.A.

"Directory of Religious Statements on Justice in the Economy," in *Centerpiece,* No. 2, March 1988, Center for Ethics and Social Policy of the Graduate Theological Union, Berkeley, California.

11. John Haughey, S.J., ed., Avery Dulles, S.J., William Dych, S.J., John Donahue, S.J., John Langan, S.J., David Hollenbach, S.J., Richard Roach, S.J., and William Walsh, S.J., *The Faith That Does Justice* (New York: Paulist Press, 1977).

12. "Our Mission Today: The Service of Faith and the Promotion of Justice," No. 28, *Documents of the 32nd General Congregation of the Society of Jesus* (Washington, D.C.: The Jesuit Conference, 1975), p. 26.

13. *Habits,* p. 37.

Chapter One

1. C. J. McNaspy, S.J., *At Face Value* (New Orleans, La.: Institute of Human Relations, 1978), p. 80.

2. Robert W. Gleason, S.J., "The Immorality of Segregation," in *Thought,* Vol. 35, No. 138, Autumn, 1960, pp. 349–64.

3. Ivan Allen, Jr., *Mayor: Notes on the Sixties* (New York: Simon and Schuster, 1971), pp. 13–14 (emphasis supplied).

4. One interesting example of this is that the towns of Sodom and Gomorrah, long thought to be merely symbols of the destructiveness of sin, were in fact trading partners of the people of Ebla. Ebla site explorers also have found the name David—considered unique to the Hebrew Bible—in a list of rulers and officials of the city-state. Names similar to other biblical figures and places have also been found at Ebla.

5. Howard LaFay, "Splendor of an Unknown Empire," *National Geographic,* December 1978, Vol. 154, No. 6, pp. 731–59, at p. 744 (emphasis supplied).

6. Ibid., p. 741.

7. While initially confined to the writings of a few theologians, such as Matthew Fox, O.P., author of *Original Blessing* (Santa Fe, N.M.: Bear & Company, 1983), creation spirituality and theology recently have received far more attention from Church authorities, especially in the context of a developing concern for environmental responsibility. Pope John Paul's 1990 World Day of Peace message was entitled, "The Ecological Crisis: A Common Responsibility." In November 1991, the U.S. bishops issued their first pastoral statement on the environment entitled, "Renewing the Earth." Cf., also, *"And God Saw That It Was Good": Catholic Theology and the Environment,* edited by Drew Christiansen, S.J., and Walter Grazer (Washington, D.C.: United States Catholic Conference, 1996).

8. Anne M. Clifford, C.S.J., "Foundations for a Catholic Ecological Theology of God," in Christiansen and Grazer, op. cit., pp. 19–46, at 25.

9. John T. Pawlikowski, O.S.M., "Participation in Economic Life," in *The Bible Today,* Vol. 24, No. 6, November 1986, pp. 363–69, at 367–68.

10. Cf. Pope John Paul II, *On Human Work,* September 15, 1981, No. 4.

11. U.S. Catholic Bishops, *Economic Justice for All: Catholic Social Teaching and the U.S. Economy,* November 13, 1986, in *Origins,* November 27, 1986, Vol. 16, No. 24, pp. 409–55, no. 32.

12. The unknown God was understood and described in terms of the known man and his world. One such institution of special import is the figure of the *go'el,* the "redeemer" or "recoverer" who is so called because as next of kin he bears the solemn obligation to step in and recover any enslaved relative (or property) and to restore him to his proper position within the family. (Richard J. Sklba, "The Redeemer of Israel," in *Catholic Biblical Quarterly,* Vol. 34, No. 1, January, 1972, pp. 1–18, at 13)

13. Ibid., p. 16.

14. Anthony J. Tambasco, *Blessed Are the Peacemakers* (Mahwah, N.J.: Paulist Press, 1989), p. 11.

15. Cf. the development of the dignity of work in Pope John Paul II's 1981 encyclical letter, *On Human Work,* discussed in chapter 3.

16. Roland J. Faley, T.O.R., "Leviticus," in *The New Jerome Biblical Commentary,* Raymond E. Brown, S.S., Joseph A. Fitzmyer, S.J., and Roland E. Murphy, O.Carm., eds. (Englewood Cliffs, N.J.: Prentice Hall, 1990), pp. 61–79, at 77.

17. Pope John Paul II, *"As the Third Millennium Draws Near" ("Tertio Millennio Adveniente"),* in *Origins,* November 24, 1994, Vol. 24, No. 24, pp. 401–16, at 406, No. 12.

18. U.S. Catholic Bishops, *In All Things Charity: A Pastoral Challenge for the New Millennium,* November 1999 (Washington, D.C.: United States Catholic Conference), p. 13.

19. The Torah's definition of economic justice is that once every generation, every face-to-face community...in a society must attain equal ownership and control of the crucial means of production. If that doesn't happen once a generation, you don't have economic justice. The tradition doesn't require continuous equality from moment to moment, month to month, year to year. What it does require is that we be willing to transform the society, to start over. (Arthur Waskow, quoted by Frida Kerner Furman, "The Prophetic Tradition and Social Transformation," in *Prophetic Visions and Economic Realities,* Charles R. Strain, ed. [Grand Rapids, Mich.: William B. Eerdmans, 1989], pp. 103–14, at 111)

20. Bruce C. Birch, "You Shall Be My People," in *Sojourners,* May 1984, Vol. 13, No. 5, pp. 31–33, at 32–33.

21. The question arises how these jubilee directives (land return, resolution of debts, liberation of slaves) could have been practically carried out in any advanced state of social development. In truth, the Old Testament records no historical observance of the jubilee....Although we cannot exclude the possibility of its being observed in the early years of the land's occupation, its presence here is best explained as a social blueprint, founded on the deeply religious concepts of justice and equality, which strove to apply the simple sabbatical principle to a society that had become more economically complex. It was drawn up and added to the Holiness Code in the period after the exile. Although not realized in the letter, its spirit of appreciation for personal rights and human dignity synthesizes much of Old Testament teaching. (Roland J. Faley, T.O.R., op. cit., p. 78)

22. Article I, Section 8, Clause 4 of the United States Constitution grants to Congress the authority "to establish...uniform laws on the subject of bankruptcies throughout the United States."

23. The federal bankruptcy law allows a bankrupt debtor to keep such property as $7,500 of interest in real or personal property; $1,200 interest in a motor vehicle; $200 of household or personal items; $500 of jewelry; $750 of implements, professional books, or tools of the trade; any unmatured life

insurance; and rights to social security, veterans, disability, or unemployment benefits. 11 U.S.C. Section 522 (d).

24. ...Christians will have to raise their voice on behalf of all the poor of the world, proposing the jubilee as an appropriate time to give thought, among other things, to reducing substantially, if not canceling outright, the international debt which seriously threatens the future of many nations. (Pope John Paul II, op. cit., page 414, No. 51)

25. Cf. U.S. Catholic Bishops, *Relieving Third World Debt: A Call for Co-Responsibility, Justice, and Solidarity* (1989) and *A Jubilee Call for Debt Forgiveness* (1999).

26. John S. Kselman, S.S., and Michael L. Barre, S.S., "Psalms," in *The New Jerome Biblical Commentary,* op. cit., pp. 523–52, at 532.

27. Bruce Vawter, "Introduction to Prophetic Literature," in *The New Jerome Biblical Commentary,* op. cit., pp. 186–200, at 196.

28. Gustavo Gutiérrez, *A Theology of Liberation* (Maryknoll, N.Y.: Orbis Books, 1973), at p. 195.

29. John R. Donahue, S.J., "Biblical Perspectives on Justice," in *The Faith that Does Justice* (New York: Paulist Press, 1977), pp. 68–112, at 76.

30. Ibid., p. 69.

31. Matthew Fox, op. cit.

32. Dennis J. McCarthy, S.J., and Roland E. Murphy, O.Carm., "Hosea," in *The New Jerome Biblical Commentary,* op. cit., pp. 217–28, at 218.

33. Ibid.

34. One must understand that in much biblical thinking, both in the Old Testament and in the New Testament, history and eschatology are merged in a way that is alien to modern thought. Particular historical events that are seen as judgments of God are described in eschatological terms; the examples are too numerous for citation here, but one may mention the fall of Jerusalem in 587 BC, the fall of the Assyrian and the Babylonian kingdoms, and even minor historical events such as the fall of Edom and the fall of Tyre. (John L. McKensie, S.J., "The Gospel According to Matthew," in *The Jerome Biblical Commentary,* Raymond E. Brown, S.S., Joseph A. Fitzmyer, S.J., and Roland E. Murphy, O.Carm, eds. [Englewood Cliffs, N.J.: Prentice-Hall, 1968], pp. 62–114, at 104)

35. The monarchy served partly as a stimulus to prophecy, for with it there entered into Israelite life a new conception of the relation of Israel to Yahweh, one that had to be under constant review by prophecy. That the popular call for a king was, in a sense, a repudiation of the covenant relationship (cf. 1 Sam 8:4ff) was doubtless the preferred prophetic view in retrospect.... (Bruce Vawter, op. cit., p. 193)

36. *Economic Justice for All,* op. cit., No. 38.

37. John R. Donahue, S.J., op. cit., p. 77.
38. *Economic Justice for All,* op. cit., No. 40.

Chapter Two

1. Robert Penn Warren, *Saturday Review* 5:19 (December 1978), as quoted in *Dictionary of Contemporary Quotations,* 1981, p. 120.
2. Jerome H. Neyrey, S.J., "Jesus the Peasant: Viewing Jesus in a Cultural and Social Perspective," in *The Catholic World,* January–February, 1993, pp. 19–23, at 19–20.
3. Ibid., p. 20.
4. Ibid., p. 22.
5. Ibid., pp. 21–22.

6. In addition, both social and religious rules existed concerning what one could or could not touch. To touch something/someone considered unclean was to become unclean oneself. Lepers were, of course, unclean, as were the dead. A menstruating woman was unclean. In each case, contact with such persons demanded an elaborate ritual of purification. However, Jesus touched lepers, he touched the dead, and he was sensitive to a menstruating woman's touch....We accept that Jesus frequently touched the people he healed, but within his cultural milieu, this was truly astonishing. (Juliana Casey, I.H.M., *Food for the Journey: Theological Foundations of the Catholic Healthcare Ministry* [St. Louis, Mo.: The Catholic Health Association of the United States, 1991], p. 23)

7. Ibid., pp. 50–53.
8. *In All Things Charity,* op. cit., p. 17, citing Pope John Paul II, *On the Coming of the Third Millennium,* No. 13.

9. As the analysis of vv 18–19 will make clear, this Isaiah text is not to be found on a synagogue scroll. It is an artistic text, woven from Isa 61:1–2 and Isa 58:6, and resplendent with the colors of Luke's christology....Luke omits those elements which would spiritualize the text or narrow its focus on "true" Israel. Thus, he omits Isa 61:1c: "to heal the broken-hearted" and Isa 61:2b–3a: "(to announce) a day of vindication, to console those who mourn, to give those of Zion who mourn glory instead of ashes." He adds Isa 58:6, which...refers to releasing those who are burdened by indebtedness....Now the goal of that gift of the Spirit is underlined: it is for the benefit of those who are economically, physically, and socially unfortunate. Good news to the poor: By his modifications of Isaiah 61...Luke shows that "the poor" is not to be interpreted metaphorically as "Israel in need," the object of God's favor as the "new restoration" occurs. Luke will reinforce this message of universalism in vv 25–27. (Robert J. Karris,

O.F.M., "The Gospel According to Luke," in *The New Jerome Biblical Commentary,* op. cit., pp. 675-721, at 689-90)

10. While the New Revised Standard Version translates the Greek word *dikaiosyne* as "righteousness," it is equally translatable as "justice" or "holiness," and was used in the New Testament for both Hebrew words *mishpat* and *sedaqah,* the two main terms for justice in the Old Testament. Cf. Donahue, op. cit., ft. 3 on p. 109; John C. Haughey, S.J., "Jesus as the Justice of God," Ibid., pp. 264-90, ft. 7 on p. 290; and Michael H. Crosby, O.F.M.Cap., *Spirituality of the Beatitudes* (Maryknoll, N.Y.: Orbis Books, 1981), p. 121. Because of the popular contemporary understanding of justice in terms of courts and legalisms, righteousness in terms of self-righteousness, and holiness in terms of spiritualizing, a word like *faithjustice* may be needed even more to get at the foundational concepts here.

11. A comparison of the two versions shows that Luke has four (3 + 1) beatitudes and Matt eight (7 + 1). Probably only Luke's first three are authentic; his fourth comes from the early church; Matthew's additional beatitudes are his own expansion from the Psalms. The common source is Q, and beyond that Jesus' use of Isa 61:1-4....The original beatitudes about the "poor," the "mourners," and the "hungry" express Jesus' mission to the needy in Israel and the dawn of a new era of salvation history. All three refer to the same people. The poor, etc., are happy not because they are morally better than others but because of God's special care for them. God was conceived of as an Oriental king, and a king's duty was to protect the weak. (Benedict T. Viviano, O.P., "The Gospel According to Matthew," in *The New Jerome Biblical Commentary,* op. cit., pp. 630-74, at 640)

12. Cf. John C. Haughey, S.J., op. cit.

13. We need to be aware of the masculine imagery associated with "Kingdom" language used by Jesus and his followers. Where it can be done without awkwardness, "Reign" is substituted for "Kingdom," even though the historical usage has reflected a predominantly male royalty and understanding, even of God. Its continuing use, however, can wrongfully reinforce attitudes of male dominance and female subordination.

14. As a symbol Kingdom carries with it all the overtones of meanings it has in the Old Testament and in the intertestamental literature. As we have seen in the enthronement Psalms, Yahweh's rule and the establishment of justice are closely joined (Pss 97:1-2; 96:10). In the apocalyptic literature the coming of the time of the Messiah will inaugurate the victory of God's justice and his mercy. By identifying the advent of God's Kingdom with his ministry and teaching, Jesus proclaims the advent of God's justice.
     ...The Kingdom is the power of God active in the world, transforming it and confronting the powers of the world. It is to

find a home among the poor (Mt. 5:3) and the persecuted (Mt.
5:4), and only with difficulty will the rich enter it (Mt.
10:23)....The Kingdom and therefore the justice of God—his
fidelity and his call to fidelity—are to be manifest in history no
less than the proclaimer of the Kingdom, Jesus, was incarnate
in history. (John R. Donahue, S.J., op. cit., pp. 86–87)

15. Cf. Matthew Fox, O.P., op. cit., pp. 122–25.

16. Celine Mangan, O.P., *Can We Still Call God "Father"?* (Wilmington,
Del.: Michael Glazier, Inc., 1984), p. 57.

17. Ibid., pp. 57–60.

18. He chose the way and the lifestyle of the storyteller, the para-
ble-maker who fashions a new creation out of the holy materials of the only creation we all share in common: the birds, the
lilies of the field, the fishes caught, the fig tree in bloom, the
sheep versus the goats, the leaven in the bread, the mustard
seeds of the world, and the rains that fall on the unjust and just
alike. (Matthew Fox, O.P., op. cit., p. 124)

19. In effect, they know what justice demanded; they simply did not
know or recognize where its demands were to be met in the
world. In the scene it is the marginal and suffering in the world
who reveal the place where the Son of Man, Lord and Judge, is,
as it were, hidden....As in the Old Testament the marginal ones
become the touchstone for the doing of justice. (John R.
Donahue, S.J., op. cit., p. 105)

20. It could also be called, the "Age of the Father," though that term is
only used for God fifteen times in the Old Testament.

21. I know of a Jesuit retreat house whose often-revised prayer booklet
has multiple prayers to Father, Son, Mary, and saints, but not one to the Holy
Spirit.

22. Celine Mangan, O.P., op. cit., p. 51.

23. If the model of father used for God, therefore, continues to be
largely paternalistic and authoritarian, there will be many today
who will reject it, not only because it is downgrading of women
but because this model breeds infantilism and the kind of submission which degrades rather than upbuilds. If, however, the
more positive aspects of parenting, which include female as well
as male attributes, are posited of God by the use of the word,
"Father" then it is still an image which can speak to the people
of our time. (Ibid., p. 16)

24. Abraham Heschel said that mercy and care reveal God's pathos.
This great Jewish philosopher wrote that pathos means God is
never neutral, never beyond good and evil: "God is partial to
justice. The divine pathos is the unity of the eternal and the
temporal, of meaning and mystery, of the metaphysical and the

historical. It is the real basis of the relation between God and humankind, of the correlation of Creator and creation, of the dialogue between the Holy One of Israel and His people." (Michael H. Crosby, O.F.M.Cap., op. cit., pp. 142–43)

25. John Cardinal O'Connor and Mayor Edward I. Koch, *His Eminence and Hizzoner: A Candid Exchange* (New York: Wm. Morrow & Co., Inc., 1989), dedication page.

Chapter Three

1. C. J. McNaspy, S.J., op. cit., p. 5.

2. *Economic Justice for All,* Nos. 347 and 349 (emphasis in original).

3. Peter J. Henriot, S.J., Edward P. DeBerri, S.J., and Michael J. Schultheis, S.J., *Catholic Social Teaching: Our Best Kept Secret* (Maryknoll, N.Y.: Orbis Books and Washington, D.C.: Center of Concern, 1988).

4. Ibid., p. 3.

5. Center literature describes itself as "an independent, interdisciplinary team engaged in social analysis, theological reflection, policy advocacy, and public education on issues of peace and justice." Ibid., p. 134. Center staff have published frequently on Catholic social teaching since its founding in 1971.

6. Ibid., p. 4.

7. Cf. discussion in Charles E. Curran, *American Catholic Social Ethics* (Notre Dame, Ind.: University of Notre Dame Press, 1982), pp. 7–8.

8. Ibid., p. 21.

9. Catholic Charities USA, "Catholic Charities: The American Experience," in *Charities USA,* Vol. 14, No. 1, January/February 1987, pp. 8–22 at 11.

10. Ibid.

11. Dorothy M. Brown and Elizabeth McKeown, *The Poor Belong to Us: Catholic Charities and American Welfare* (Cambridge, Mass.: Harvard University Press, 1997), p. 98.

12. Ibid.

13. Catholic Charities USA, op. cit., p. 12.

14. Charles E. Curran, op. cit., p. 22.

15. Catholic Charities USA, op. cit., p. 12.

16. U.S. Catholic Bishops, *In All Things Charity: A Pastoral Challenge for the New Millennium* (Washington, D.C.: United States Catholic Conference), p. 24, citing Dorothy M. Brown and Elizabeth McKeown, op. cit., pp. 5, 86.

17. Dorothy M. Brown and Elizabeth McKeown, op. cit., p. 5.

18. Catholic Charities USA, op. cit., p. 14.

19. Catholic Charities USA, *National Statistics,* available at www.catholic-charitiesusa.org, summarizing the work of U.S. agencies for the year 1999.

20. Christopher J. Kauffman, "The Leadership of Father Moulinier," in *Health Progress,* March 1990, pp. 41–48, at 41.

21. See discussion of the efforts of the majority of the American hierarchy to prevent the condemnation of the Knights of Labor in 1886–87 in Charles E. Curran, op. cit., pp. 9–10.

22. Dorothy M. Brown and Elizabeth McKeown, op. cit., pp. 70–72 and 82–85.

23. Catholic Charities USA, op. cit., p. 14.

24. John Hart, *The Spirit of the Earth* (Ramsey, N.J.: Paulist Press, 1984), p. 113.

25. Charles Curran, op. cit., pp. 131–32.

26. John A. Ryan was not only the best known Roman Catholic social ethicist in the United States in the first half of the twentieth century, but he was also the foremost "official" Catholic spokesperson for progressive social reform. Ryan's significance was enhanced by the two positions he held—professor of moral theology at The Catholic University of America in Washington, D.C. (1915-1939) and director of the Social Action Department of the National Catholic Welfare Council (N.C.W.C.), the national organization of the American Catholic Bishops, (1920-1945). (Ibid., p. 26)

27. Ibid., p. 238.

28. Cf. *Empowerment and Hope: Twenty-Five Years of Turning Lives Around* (Washington, D.C.: Campaign for Human Development, 1996).

29. Charles Curran, op. cit., p. 21, citing C. Joseph Nuesse, *The Social Thought of American Catholics 1634–1829.*

30. Ibid., p. 21.

31. Ibid., pp. 24–25.

32. As noted in the Introduction, there are now six volumes of statements on matters of church practice and public policy of the U.S. hierarchy stretching back to colonial times.

33. Peter Henriot, S.J., et al., op. cit., p. 5.

34. See Appendix:Modern Catholic Social Thought, pp. 241ff.

35. *Economic Justice for All,* No. 56.

36. Cf. William J. Walsh, S.J., and John P. Langan, S.J., "Patristic Social Consciousness—The Church and the Poor," in Haughey, op. cit., pp. 113–51.

37. Quoted as "my favorite text from the Church Fathers on wealth and poverty" by William J. Byron, S.J., in *Toward Stewardship: An Interim Ethic of Poverty, Power, and Pollution* (New York: Paulist Press, 1975), p. 35.

38. William J. Walsh, S.J., and John P. Langan, S.J., op. cit., p. 131.

39. Ibid., p. 134.

40. *Economic Justice for All,* No. 57.

41. Ibid., No. 58.

42. *Guidelines for the Study and Teaching of the Church's Social Doctrine in the Formation of Priests,* Vatican Congregation for Catholic Education, dated

December 30, 1988, and released June 27, 1989, No. 17, in *Origins,* Vol. 19, No. 11, August 3, 1989, pp. 169–92, at 175.

43. As quoted in William Byron, S.J., op. cit., p. 38.

44. *Economic Justice for All,* Nos. 69–71.

45. Ibid., No. 68.

46. *Guidelines...in the Formation of Priests,* op. cit., No. 1.

47. Ibid., No. 6.

48. Donal Dorr, *Option for the Poor: A Hundred Years of Vatican Social Teaching* (Maryknoll, N.Y.: Orbis Books, 1983), pp. 9–10, 213–17, 233–35.

49. *Guidelines...Formation of Priests,* No. 4. In No. 11, entitled "Evolution of Social Doctrine," the matter is spelled out further:

> As has already been stated, due to its character of mediation between the Gospel and the concrete reality of man and society, the social doctrine of the church needs to be continuously updated and made responsive to the new situations of the world and history. In fact, decade after decade, it has had a notable evolution.

50. Ibid.

51. Ibid.

52. Peter Henriot, S.J., et al., op. cit., p. 5.

53. *Guidelines...Formation of Priests,* op. cit., No. 7.

54. Donal Dorr, op. cit., p. 7.

55. The equation of Church with hierarchy eliminates from the Church basic competency in matters "worldly," for who will willingly attribute to hierarchs expertise in economics, politics, culture, society at large? This constriction of responsibility within the Church is accompanied by the constriction of the response of the people, within and without the Church, when the thus restricted Church, that is, the hierarchy, sees fit to pronounce upon worldly matters. (Robert Kress, "The Theological and Ecclesiological Foundation of the Social Mission of the Church," in *Charities USA,* Vol. 15, No. 5, June 1988, pp. 1–7, at 3)

56. Charles Curran, op. cit., p. 1.

57. Philip Land, S.J., "Catholic Social Teaching: 1891–1981," in *Center Focus,* Issue 43, May, 1981, pp. 3–4, at 3.

58. J. Bryan Hehir, "Catholic Social Teaching as a Framework," unpublished address to Province Days, New Orleans Province of the Society of Jesus, at Spring Hill College, Mobile, Alabama, June 2, 1988, p. 3.

59. T. Howland Sanks, S.J., "Liberation Theology and the Social Gospel: Variations on a Theme," in *Theological Studies,* Vol. 41, No. 4, December 1980, pp. 668–82, at 674.

60. Ibid., p. 675.

61. Philip S. Land, S.J., *Catholic Social Teaching: As I Have Lived, Loathed, and Loved It* (Chicago: Loyola University Press, 1994), p. 105.

62. The numbers appearing in brackets in the sections discussing the specific documents correspond to the paragraph numbers in the document.

63. This brief overview of the work of the Fribourg Union is essential for a full understanding not only of its child *Rerum Novarum* but also of the directions Catholic social thought has taken since. The Fribourg Union laid down certain parameters for commitment to social reform that have survived more or less intact through much of this century. They include: (1) no absolute rejection of private property; (2) no support for class struggle; (3) no formal endorsement of capitalism, a system which in many ways undercuts the organic model of society inherited from medieval thought; (4) a preferential option for the rights of workers; and (5) firm support of unionization based on a fresh interpretation of the classical organic model. (John T. Pawlikowski, O.S.M., "Introduction to *Rerum Novarum,*" in Byers, op. cit., p. 12)

64. Charles Curran, op. cit., pp 8–9.
65. Donal Dorr, op. cit., p. 11.
66. Ibid., p. 12.

67. It ensured that social issues could no longer be treated as marginal or secondary to the mission of the Church, or as an "optional extra." This applied not merely in the sphere of official teaching but also in practical commitment. *Rerum Novarum* gave great encouragement to those of the clergy and laity who had been working for years to get the Catholic Church more involved in social issues; and it had the long-term effect of greatly increasing the numbers of such committed activists. So, if one judges in terms of the effects over a considerable period of years, it is correct to say with Vidler that the encyclical "had a truly epoch-making effect in driving home the idea that Catholics must have a social conscience." (Ibid., pp. 12–13)

68. *Quadragesimo Anno* means literally: "in the fortieth year."
69. Donal Dorr, op. cit., p. 68.
70. Ibid.

71. Edward J. Ryle, "The Principle of Subsidiarity," in *Charities USA,* Vol. 14, No. 8, November 1987, pp. 10–13, at 10. It is not uncommon for popes, bishops, and councils or synods to engage theologians and other specialists to develop drafts of documents subsequently issued as the official position of the ecclesiastical leader or body. Analogously, the Justices of the U.S. Supreme Court, committees and members of Congress, and the U.S. President all use staff specialists to develop drafts of documents, statements, and speeches.

72. Proponents of the 1996 so-called welfare reform legislation simplistically argued that subsidiarity meant that the program should be moved from the federal to the state level, without a more rigorous analysis of the effectiveness of the various levels of government in the social welfare field.

73. *Economic Justice for All,* No. 100.

74. Philip S. Land, S.J., *Shaping Welfare Consensus: U.S. Bishops' Contribution* (Washington, D.C.: Center of Concern, 1988), pp. 174–77, quoting and responding to Andrew Greeley.

75. Ibid., p. 20.

76. Pope Pius XII, *Christmas Message*, 1944, quoted in Ibid., p. 244.

77. Donal Dorr, op. cit., p. 83.

78. Radio address of June 1, 1941, commemorating the fiftieth anniversary of *Rerum Novarum*, quoted in Donal Dorr, Ibid., footnote 34.

79. Donal Dorr, op. cit., p. 97.

80. Whatever about the myth of independence for the individual, the reality was that before long there emerged an obvious need for new and different forms of social institutions and restraints....There had to be new social systems to look after security, welfare, public health, education, economic development, etc. And as society became more concentrated in urban areas, less centred on small community units, these needs expanded. No wonder then that Pope John felt it was pointless and wrong to resist the expansion of such social institutions. Rather they should be intelligently planned and controlled. The aim should be to retain as much as possible of the values of personal freedom while protecting the common welfare....Precisely because they are needed to prevent the exploitation of the weak by the strong, they are experienced by the powerful as unwarranted limits to their freedom. And one of the most powerful weapons used to resist these restraints is the invocation of the myths of the defence of the 'traditional values' of personal initiative and freedom, and old-fashioned rugged independence. (Ibid., p. 105)

81. John T. Pawlikowski, O.S.M., "Introduction to *Mater et Magistra* and *Pacem in Terris*," in Byers, op. cit., pp. 110–13, at 111.

82. Donal Dorr, op. cit., pp. 112–13.

83. According to H. D. Kreilkamp, President Kennedy thanked Pope John for Vatican intervention, including a key radio message to the world's leaders on October 25, 1962, within an hour of which Soviet ships moved out of the interdicted zone. Khrushchev also acknowledged Pope John's assistance. These events apparently inspired John to develop his encyclical letter. Cf. "Pope John XXIII's Vision of Peace," in *Social Justice Review*, Vol. 80, Nos. 9–10, September/October 1989, pp. 138–42.

84. While it is true that human rights had been defended in previous documents, they had never received such a systemic and thorough treatment. The encyclical was heralded, not for its continuity, but as a breakthrough. (Philip S. Land, S.J., *Catholic Social Teaching*, op. cit., p. 106)

85. Cf. Philip S. Land, *Shaping Welfare Consensus*, op. cit., pp. 136–38 and 178–82.

86. John T. Pawlikowski, O.S.M., "Introduction to Christmas Messages," in Byers, op. cit., pp. 91–93, at 92.

87. *Guidelines...Formation of Priests,* op. cit., No. 24.

88. Peter Henriot, S.J., et al., op. cit., p. 17.

89. The most distinctive note sounded in the text, many already agree, is that of the Church putting itself consciously at the service of the family of man. It may well be that in generations to come men will read this as a highly significant step toward a rethinking of conventional ecclesiological images... (Donald R. Campion, S.J., "The Church Today," in *The Documents of Vatican II* [New York: Guild Press, America Press, Association Press, 1966], Walter M. Abbott, S.J., ed., pp. 183–98, at 185)

90. It was the dynamic of the council that made the decisive move toward a total ecclesiology that includes both the Church looking to the Church and the Church looking to the World. That's the distinctive shift. Look at *Gaudium et Spes* as both an event in itself and a process. I would argue with [Fr. Karl] Rahner that *Gaudium et Spes* is perhaps the single most significant document of Vatican II, a document for which they had no plan, a document which was called a "Pastoral Constitution." But try and think about what has happened in the life of the Church in Latin America, in South Africa, in East Asia, in the United States, and in Europe and you get the social edge of ministry. I argue you can't explain that in random fashion. The background is *Gaudium et Spes* and the theological reflection that has flowed from it. That's the ecclesiological foundation [for social ministry]. (J. Bryan Hehir, op. cit., p. 4)

91. Cf. Donal Dorr, op. cit., pp. 139–40.

92. Pope John Paul II, *Sollicitudo Rei Socialis,* No. 9.

93. *Octogesima Adveniens* means "eightieth anniversary."

94. At the local level, it can be seen ever more clearly that in societies in which little or no political and social action ameliorates the lot of the mass of the people and liberates them sufficiently to take a full part in their own development, no amount of economic growth will lead to satisfactory modernization. On the contrary, it will tend to pile up the riches and consumption of the few and leave a growing mass of "marginal men" at the base of society for whom even the most elementary of human needs and decencies—job, home, school, diet, health,—will be almost completely lacking. (Maurice Cardinal Roy, "Message on the Occasion of the Launching of the Second Development Decade" to U Thant, U.N. Secretary General, November 19, 1970, No. 12. Quoted in Joseph Gremillion [ed.], *The Gospel of Peace and Justice: Catholic Social Teaching since Pope John* [Maryknoll, N.Y.: Orbis Books, 1975], p. 479)

95. Bishop Ricardo Ramirez, C.S.B., "Medellin and Puebla from a U.S. Perspective," in *Path from Puebla* (Washington, D.C.: United States Catholic Conference, 1989), pp. 10–21, at 12.

96. Cf. Donal Dorr, op. cit., pp. 163–64.

97. *Guidelines...Formation of Priests*, op. cit., No. 27.

98. Ibid., No. 63.

99. Ibid.

100. Ibid., quoting *Gaudium et Spes*, No. 43. Such a divorce between faith and daily life also ignores the practical political implications of such a posture, namely that those who espouse this separation impliedly endorse the existing political system and its effects in people's lives.

101. The distinction between lay and clergy roles might be termed strategic because the bases upon which the distinction is made are not entirely clear. If it is by baptism that the laity are charged with responsibility for the secular world, the clergy are likewise baptized. If the distinction is based upon the prophetic preaching responsibility of the clergy, the laity too, baptized as prophet, priest, and king, are charged to be prophetic and often are more so. If the distinction is based upon the ordination of the clergy, meaning formal office in the institutional Church, such that they should not also exercise civil office and civil power (Canon 285, Section 3), then broader ramifications follow. To consistently rule out the exercise of civil (i.e., political) power by the clergy in the social teaching would suggest that clergy also not exercise civil power on the boards of economically powerful institutions such as banks, corporations, universities, and even the nonprofit corporations that are widely utilized in church ministries.

102. *Guidelines...Formation of Priests*, op. cit., No. 43.

103. The distinction between political and partisan, of course, may be more notional than real once issues become identified popularly with either political parties or officeholders. An example worth reflecting on has occurred in the case of the debate over abortion in the United States. Here, there have occurred a number of separate, but related, apparent overlaps of the political with the partisan, including: (1) the ease and frequency with which single-issue political advocacy by churchpeople has been manipulated by political parties or figures; (2) the likelihood of single-issue political advocacy being read by the public to be identified with particular parties or politicians, whether intentional or not; (3) the media's inability to distinguish the political from the partisan and the electronic media's soundbite approach being incapable of reporting complexity; and (4) the resistance to, and criticism of, pro-life civil disobedience as inappropriate political action violating church-state separation.

However one might try to maintain the political-partisan distinction in the above situations, the genius of the consistent life ethic proposed by Cardinal Joseph Bernardin in an address at Fordham University on December 6, 1983, was that it was not easily identified with either large political party in the United States. It could be used to press both parties for more attention to the full spectrum of life issues. In the sense discussed above, it seems political without being partisan.

The same is true of the statement "Faithful Citizenship: Civic Responsibility for a New Millennium," issued in September 1999, by the Administrative Board of the U.S. Catholic Conference. In that statement, the bishops recommended that a full spectrum of family and social issues should be considered in assessing the suitability of candidates for public office and party platforms. It too defied attempts to make it a partisan endorsement of any party or candidate.

104. The bishops later renamed it as the Catholic Campaign for Human Development.

105. Donal Dorr, op. cit., p. 190.

106. Paul in these eleven paragraphs uses the word *liberation* as if he had invented it. His uses of it are owing to a singular conversion, which I can testify to from personal experience. In my eight years of half-time work for the Pontifical Commission on Justice and Peace I had a number of occasions to introduce into documents I was preparing for the commission the word *liberation*. But in every such document that underwent scrutiny by the secretary of state, that word was stricken out. (Philip S. Land, S.J., *Catholic Social Teaching*, op. cit., p. 108)

107. Cf. comprehensive and insightful discussion of liberation in Donal Dorr, op. cit., pp. 193–201.

108. *Justice in the World*, No. 16.

109. A social structure can then be meaningfully said to be sinful. It can be sinful in its source: a social structure emerges as people act out a decision which is biased, narrow and destructive. It can be sinful in its consequences: others confronted with a situation so structured are provoked to react defensively and so to reinforce the destructive characteristics of the situation. Still other people, lacking the power to react defensively, will experience sharp limitations on their effective scope of freedom and hence will experience the structures as offensive to their human dignity. (Patrick Kerans, *Sinful Social Structures* [New York: Paulist Press, 1974], p. 79)

110. His two earlier encyclical letters, *Redeemer of Humankind (Redemptor Hominis*, 1979) and *Rich in Mercy (Dives Misericordiae*, 1980) provide important foundational insights into both his philosophy and theology and a deeper grasp of the social implications of the gospel.

111. *Guidelines...Formation of Priests*, op. cit., No. 26.

112. Philip Land, S.J., "Pope John Paul on Human Labor," in *Center Focus*, Issue 46, December 1981, pp. 3–4, at 3.

113. J. Bryan Hehir, "Overview of the Pastoral," in *The Peace Pastoral: Renewing Perspectives, Reordering Priorities* (Washington, D.C.: Proceedings of

the National Committee of the Campaign for Human Development, October 28–30, 1983), pp. 1–10.

114. Ibid., p. 8.

115. Five years later, in June 1988, the bishops issued "Building Peace: A Pastoral Reflection on the Response to *The Challenge of Peace*," accompanied by a report on policy developments during the period 1983–88. In the pastoral reflection, the bishops reiterated their position on deterrence and called for "urgent and more persistent efforts to move more decisively toward effective arms control and mutual disarmament…" [11].

116. While the bishops were largely addressing the question of major nuclear and other wars, they opened up the implications of this nonviolent resistance: "These principles apply as well to all forms of violence, including insurgency, counterinsurgency, 'destabilization' and the like." In so doing they may have laid the foundation for developing a more adequate model for active confrontation by the oppressed in society with powerful and widespread social, economic, political, and cultural injustices which have even been termed "institutionalized violence." In providing this approach, the bishops supply a more complete response to those—like Donal Dorr—who have searched the tradition of Catholic social teaching for an adequate treatment of resistance and confrontation and found some few signs in such developing concepts as "solidarity." Cf. Donal Dorr, op. cit., pp. 246–51 and earlier.

117. The fourth chapter in the final document evolved from what was initially a section of the Part on Policy Applications in draft one of the *Pastoral Letter on Economic Justice.*

118. John Langan's criticism that the chapter "has virtually nothing to offer by way of specific recommendations" is probably too harsh and may reflect the second draft more than the final. His observation that "the principles which it proposes could lead to a radical restructuring of the American economy and society or to a series of collaborative reforms" seems more accurate, if the principles were implemented. Cf. John Langan, S.J., "The American Context of the Bishops' Letter," in *The Deeper Meaning of Economic Life* (Washington, D.C.: Georgetown University Press, 1986), R. Bruce Douglass, ed., pp. 1–19, at 14.

119. Philip Land argues that the chapter emphasizes the decision-making dimension of the tradition of subsidiarity. Philip Land, S.J., *Shaping Welfare Consensus,* op. cit., pp. 177–78.

120. Though dated December 30, 1987, the letter was actually released February 19, 1988.

121. J. Bryan Hehir, "East, West Stonewall the Southern Agenda," in the *Los Angeles Times,* Monday, March 14, 1988, Part II.

122 J. Bryan Hehir, "'Interdependence' in *Sollicitudo Rei Socialis,*" in *Woodstock Report,* No. 15, June 1988, pp. 9–10.

123. Edward B. Arroyo, S.J., "Solidarity: A Moral Imperative for an Interdependent World," *Blueprint for Social Justice,* Volume 42, No. 1, September 1988, pp. 1–7, at 5.

124. The title literally means "The Hundredth Year."

125. Socialism's flaws included atheistic anthropology, class struggle, and state control of productive means [13–15].

126. The pope also affirmed charity and solidarity [49], proper evangelization [50], grievance resolution [51–52], social human nature [54], the need for Western economic reforms [56], credible Christian action [57], and promotion of international justice [58].

127. Much of the third world would be included by the pope in these regions dominated by foreign companies and "ruthless" capitalism.

128. Illegitimate ownership is that which does not serve useful work, and illegitimate profits are those not related to expansion of work and the wealth of society [35, 43].

129. Pope John Paul II, *Tertio Millennio Adveniente,* November 10, 1994, in *Origins,* Vol. 25, No. 24, November 24, 1994, pp.401–16.

130. Pope John Paul II, *Incarnationis Mysterium* (Vatican City: Vatican Press, 1998).

131. Pope John Paul II, *Evangelium Vitae,* March 25, 1995 in *Origins,* Vol. 24, No. 42, April 6, 1995, pp. 689–730.

132. Pope John Paul II, *Ecclesia in America* (Vatican City: Vatican Press, 1999).

133. The closing statement of the 1997 Synod included the following declaration:

> Indeed, of all the concerns of God's people that have resounded in the hall of this special synod for America, the cry of the poor has been heard with a special attention. Not a single Episcopal conference in America has failed to speak clearly and with deep emotion about the quest for justice for our brothers and sisters whose lives and human dignity are challenged by poverty and want. These concerns have their origins not only in the personal sinfulness of individuals but also in "the structures of sin" to which personal sin can give rise and which in turn reinforce personal sin and widen its impact. (Special Assembly for America of the Synod of Bishops, *Message to America,* December 12, 1997, in *Origins,* Vol. 27, No. 28, January 1, 1998, pp. 461–66)

134. Pope John Paul II and Interdicasterial Commission, *Catechism of the Catholic Church* (New York/Mahwah, N.J.: Paulist Press, 1994).

135. See, also, paragraphs 1924 to 1927 summarizing the common good.

136. Pope John Paul II, *Ecclesia in America,* op. cit., No. 54.

137. William J. Byron, S.J., "Ten Building Blocks of Catholic Social Teaching," in *America,* Vol. 179, No. 13, October 31, 1998, pp. 9–12.

138. Thomas Massaro, S.J., *Living Justice: Catholic Social Teaching in Action* (Franklin, Wis.: Sheed & Ward, 2000), pp. 113–167.

139. U.S. Catholic Bishops, *A Century of Social Teaching: A Common Heritage, A Continuing Challenge* (Washington, D.C.: United States Catholic Conference, 1991).

140. U.S. Catholic Bishops, *Sharing Catholic Social Teaching: Challenges and Directions* (Washington, D.C.: United States Catholic Conference, 1998).

141. Edward B. Arroyo, S.J., op. cit., p. 7.

142. Pope John Paul II, *Centesimus Annus,* op. cit., No. 35.

143. Ibid., No. 42.

144. Richard John Neuhaus, "The Pope Affirms the 'New Capitalism,'" *Wall Street Journal,* editorial page, May 2, 1991. Neuhaus even violated the Vatican's press embargo in order to give his own spin to the encyclical before other commentators could report on the encyclical.

145. Michael Novak in "The Pope, Liberty, and Capitalism: Essays on *Centesimus Annus,*" *National Review,* Special Supplement, p. S-12.

146. Cindy Wooden, "Marxism Worsened Problems of Working Class, Pope Says at Audience," *Catholic News Service,* May 1, 1991.

147. Pope John Paul II, "What Social Teaching Is and Is Not," in *Origins,* Vol. 23, No. 15, September 1993, pp. 256–58, at 257.

148. Pope John Paul II, *Centesimus Annus,* op. cit., No. 43.

149. Ibid., No. 32.

150. Ibid., No. 33.

151. Peter Henriot, S.J., et al., op. cit., p. 17.

152. Pope John Paul II, *Centesimus Annus,* op. cit., No. 43.

153. On the chart, encyclical or apostolic letters of the popes are presented in one type size, with the line lengthening if there is more than one letter from that pope. The conciliar documents are presented in a larger type face, with the most important, *Gaudium et Spes,* having the longest line.

154. See, for example, U.S. Catholic Bishops, *Renewing the Earth: An Invitation to Reflection and Action on Environment in Light of Catholic Social Teaching* (November 14, 1991) and *Global Climate Change: A Plea for Dialogue, Prudence, the Common Good* (June 15, 2001); The Dominican Episcopal Conference, *Pastoral Letter on the Relationship of Human Beings to Nature* (January 21, 1987); The Catholic Bishops of the Philippines, *What Is Happening to Our Beautiful Land?* (January 29, 1988); Indiana Catholic Conference, *Care for the Earth* (February 2000); Catholic Bishops of the Boston Province, *And God Saw That It Was Good* (October 4, 2000); and Twelve U.S. and Canadian Bishops, *The Columbia River Watershed: Caring for Creation and the Common Good* (February 22, 2001).

155. Thomas Massaro, S.J., "The Future of Catholic Social Teaching," in *Blueprint for Social Justice,* Volume LIV, No. 5, January 2001, pp. 1–7, at 6.

156. Cardinal Joseph Bernardin, "The Bishops and Their Conference," in *Origins,* Vol. 20, No. 9, July 19, 1990, pp. 146–48, at 147.

157. Rembert G. Weakland, "'Economic Justice' for All 10 Years Later," in *America,* Vol. 176, No. 9, March 22, 1997, pp. 8–22.

158. John P. Langan, S.J., "Issues in Catholic Social Thought," in *Origins,* Vol. 30, No. 3, June 1, 2000, pp. 45–8.

159. Ibid., p. 48.

160. Rembert G. Weakland, op. cit., p. 16.

Chapter Four

1. Harper Lee, *To Kill a Mockingbird* (Philadelphia: Lippincott & Co., 1960), p. 294.

2. Though the precise expression cannot be found in the documents of the 1968 Medellin Conference, there is no doubt that—as the Latin American Bishops stated 10 years later at Puebla—it *adopted a clear and prophetic option expressing preference for and solidarity with the poor* (Puebla 1134). (Henry Volken, S.J., "Preferential Option for the Poor," in *Promotio Justitiae*, No. 29, January 1984, pp. 11–26, at 15)

3. For those in favour of the term its main value is that it expresses succinctly and uncompromisingly the practical implication for the Church of committing itself firmly to the promotion of social justice. (Donal Dorr, op. cit., p. 209)

4. Ibid.

5. But no one could ignore the basic, authentic, *halakhic* demands to take the poor more seriously than any other segment of society, to unite with their needs and their demands....As Hermann Cohen always insisted, we see that neighbor whom we must love as ourselves pre-eminently in the poor. God has more than a preferential option for the poor....What is beyond debate is the straightforward law that obligates us to reduce inequities at our own expense, to do nothing that widens the gap between rich and poor. This is no mere "preferential option for the poor"; it is plain identification with them. (Arnold Jacob Wolf, "The Bishops and the Poor: A Jewish Critique," in *Strain*, op. cit., pp. 99–100)

6. Quoted by Gustavo Gutiérrez, "The Church of the Poor," in *The Month*, July 1989, pp. 263–67, at 264.

7. ...the pope, in a whole series of addresses in 1984–85, was rather chagrined that he could have given the impression of not believing in the preferential option for the poor, or of not believing in it very strongly. To a group of cardinals in Rome, Dec. 21, 1984, he protested:

    This option which is emphasized today with particular force by the episcopacy of Latin America, I have confirmed repeatedly....I gladly seize this occasion to repeat that engagement with the poor constitutes a dominant motif of my pastoral activity, a concern which is daily and ceaselessly part of my service of the people of God. I have made and I do make this option. I identify myself with it. I feel it could not be otherwise, since it is the eternal message of the Gospel. This is the option Christ made, the option made by the apostles, the option of the Church throughout its two thousand years of history. (Jean-Yves

Calvez, S.J., "The Preferential Option for the Poor: Where Does It Come for Us?" in *Studies in the Spirituality of Jesuits,* Vol. 21, No. 2, March 1989, pp. 21–35, at 23)

8. Ibid., p. 18, citing a 1980 address of Pope John Paul to the dwellers in the Favela of Vidigal in Rio de Janeiro.

9. Pope John Paul II, *Ecclesia in Asia,* November 6, 1999, No. 34, in *Origins,* Vol. 29, No. 23, November 18, 1999, pp. 357–84, at 376.

10. For an in-depth discussion of the beatitudes see Michael Crosby, O.F.M.Cap., *Spirituality of the Beatitudes* (Maryknoll, N.Y.: Orbis Books, 1981).

11. Donal Dorr, op. cit., p. 227.

12. Cf. Jean-Yves Calvez, S.J., op. cit., p. 24.

13. Perhaps Pope John Paul's "not exclusive" may also be helpful to resolving this resistance.

14. Some Church people use this kind of language to justify the work they are doing. They see themselves as helping the spiritually poor when they educate the children of the rich or provide medical services for the wealthy. This, they argue, is just as important for the Church as service of those who are materially poor. The effect of this use of language is to deprive the notion of an 'option for the poor' of any effective meaning, since everybody can be seen as poor in some respect. (Donal Dorr, op. cit., p. 241)

15. Any of us could easily become one of the "new poor" in America by the combination of ill health or injury, rising health care costs, decline of family or religious community assets, and so forth.

16. *Economic Justice for All,* No. 38.

17. See, for example, discussion of "release to those in prison" (Luke 4:18) in Robert F. Karris, O.F.M., "The Gospel According to Luke," in *The New Jerome Biblical Commentary,* op. cit., pp. 675–721, at 690.

18. *Economic Justice for All,* No. 49.

19. Thomas E. Clarke, S.J., "Option for the Poor: A Reflection," in *America,* Vol. 158, No. 4, January 30, 1988, pp. 95–99, at 96.

20. Ibid., p. 97.

21. The average U.S. poverty lines in 1997 were: $8,813 for one person, $10,743 for two persons, $12,802 for three people, $16,400 for four people, and $19,380 for five people, based on a complex formula revolving around the cost of food. In 1997, by this formula, 35,574,000 Americans lived in poverty. (Source: Richard Saul Wurman, op. cit., section on "Poverty by Characteristic.") Many social scientists believe that the formula is now woefully outdated. According to the Catholic Campaign for Human Development, a 2000 poll by Lake, Snell, Perry, and Associates indicated that most Americans believe it takes at least $35,000 annually for a family of four to make ends meet, more than 200 percent of the current poverty threshold. See www.usccb.org/cchd/povertyusa, December 12, 2001.

22. William Byron, S.J., *Towards Stewardship,* op. cit., pp. 23–24.

23. Richard Saul Wurman, op. cit., section on "Poverty by Characteristic."

24. Women's earnings have increased as a percentage of men's from 69 percent in 1986 to 75 percent in the late nineties. Ibid., section on "The Economy."

25. In 1983, less than half of women raising children alone had been awarded child support, and of those only half received the full amount to which they were entitled. Even fewer women (14 percent) are awarded alimony, and many older women are left in poverty after a lifetime of homemaking and child rearing. (*Economic Justice for All*, No. 180)

26. Richard Saul Wurman, op. cit., section on "Aging & Retirement."

27. Joni Seager and Ann Olson, *Women in the World: An International Atlas* (New York: Simon and Schuster/Touchstone Books, 1986), p. 101.

28. *Economic Justice for All*, No. 176.

29. Kathryn Porter and Wendell Primus, *Changes Since 1995 in the Safety Net's Impact on Child Poverty* (Washington, D.C.: Center on Budget and Policy Priorities, 1999), p. 25.

30. *Economic Justice for All*, No. 177.

31. Children's Defense Fund, *Every Day in America* (Washington, D.C.: Children's Defense Fund, April 2001), www.childrensdefense.org, December 14, 2001, pp. 1–2.

32. Pontifical Justice and Peace Commission, "The Church and the Housing Problem," dated December 27, 1987. and released February 2, 1988, in *Origins*, Vol. 17, No. 35, February 11, 1988, pp. 602–5, at 603.

33. An estimated 3 million Americans are homeless today. The crisis of homelessness continues to grow in every community of our nation—urban, suburban and rural. Experts say that the number of homeless may increase six-fold in the next 15 years. While many factors have contributed to this crisis, the lack of affordable housing is the most common and universal. During the last eight years, Federal support for housing has been all but eliminated. Since 1981, budget authority for all Federal housing assistance programs has been cut 77 percent—from $32 billion to less than $8 billion per year....At the start of Reagan's first term, the U.S. spent $7 on defense for every $1 spent on housing. Today the ratio is $44 to $1. (*Jesuit Social Ministries Newsletter*, Vol. 2, No. 3, Summer 1989, p. 7)

34. U.S. Department of Housing and Urban Development, *Waiting in Vain: An Update on America's Rental Housing Crisis*, March, 1999, p. 6.

35. Ibid., p. 8.

36. Andrew Cuomo, Secretary of U.S. Department of Housing and Urban Development, Transmittal Letter to the Congress introducing *Rental Housing Assistance–The Worsening Crisis* (Washington, D.C.: U.S. Department of Housing and Urban Development, 2000), March 2000.

37. Richard Saul Wurman, op. cit., section on "Homelessness."

38. United Nations High Commissioner for Refugees, January 1, 2001, statistics, reported on UNHCR website under "Publications," www.unhcr, December 16, 2001.

39. A Resolution of the U.S. Conference of Catholic Bishops, "Renewing U.S. Leadership in Refugee Protection," June 20, 2001.

40. "The Church and the Housing Problem," op. cit., p. 603.

41. U.S. Department of Housing and Urban Development, *What We Know about Mortgage Lending Discrimination,* September 1999.

42. *Washington Post,* "GU Study Finds Disparity in Heart Care," February 25, 1999, pp. A1, A13.

43. *Washington Post,* "Insurer Tied Race to Rates for Years," June 23, 2000, pp. A12–13.

44. *USA Today,* "Race vs. Justice," editorial, April 27, 2000, p. 16A.

45. *Washington Post,* "Study Finds Wide Disparities in Customs' Intrusive Searches," April 10, 2000, pp. A1, A18.

46. Associated Press, "Study finds Hispanics segregated within Roman Catholic church," March 1, 2000, report posted to the Web.

47. Bishop Sean O'Malley, "Solidarity: the Antidote to Resurgent Racism," in *Origins,* Vol. 29, No. 33, February 3, 2000, at p. 532.

48. "Throughout the Bible material poverty is a misfortune and a cause of sadness." *Economic Justice for All,* No. 49.

49. As preachers of the Gospel, we must be really convinced that an option for the poor is the option of the very God we are proclaiming. The poor cry out. God hears their cry and vindicates them (cf. Ex. 22, 21–23). To call the poor "blessed" (as in the Magnificat and the Beatitudes) is to announce to them the hope of a Messiah who came for them in the first place and lived among them, sharing their condition so that he could set them free. (From the Dominican General Chapter in Rome, 1983, par. 15, quoted in Volken, op. cit., p. 23)

50. John Sweeney, S.J., Review of Victorio Araya's *God of the Poor: The Mystery of God in Latin American Liberation Theology,* in *Pacifica,* Vol. 2, No. 2, June 1989, pp. 229–31, at 231.

51. Gustavo Gutiérrez, op. cit., p. 266.

52. Pope John Paul II, Address to the 150 bishops of Latin America, Rio de Janeiro, July 2, 1980, quoted in Volken, op. cit., p. 17.

53. Robert J. Karris, O.F.M., "The Gospel According to Luke," in *The New Jerome Biblical Commentary,* op. cit., p. 710.

54. *Washington Post,* "As If It Weren't Bad Enough Being Poor," February 7, 1999, p. B5, reported on the recent book by University of Michigan social policy professor John Tropman and his just-published book, *Does America Hate the Poor? The Other American Dilemma.* In its story, the *Post* reported Tropman's conclusions, including his observation that negative attitudes toward the poor result in punitive policies and "quick fixes" instead of

addressing the root causes of poverty. Yet, Tropman concedes, Americans do not withhold basic material support of the poor.

55. Ibid.

56. Isaac Shapiro and Robert Greenstein, *Holes in the Safety Net* (Washington, D.C.: Center on Budget and Policy Priorities, 1988), p. 11.

57. Ibid., p. 9.

58. Ibid., pp. 6–9. And, Committee on Ways and Means, U.S. House of Representatives, *Overview of Entitlement Programs,* June 5, 1990, p. 555.

59. *Economic Justice for All,* No. 193.

60. Eileen P. Sweeney, *Recent Studies Indicate That Many Parents Who Are Current or Former Welfare Recipients Have Disabilities or Other Medical Conditions* (Washington, D.C.: Center on Budget and Policy Priorities, February 29, 2000).

61. *Economic Justice for All,* No. 194.

62. Kathryn H. Porter and Allen Dupree, *Poverty Trends for Families Headed by Working Single Mothers: 1993 to 1999* (Washington, D.C.: Center on Budget and Policy Priorities, August, 2001), p. iii.

63. Richard Saul Wurman, op. cit., section on "Welfare."

64. Cf. "Welfare Caseloads in 27 States Decline in First Quarter of 2003," *Center for Law and Social Policy,* July 18, 2003, for trends for 6 years of TANF. Caseload decline under TANF measured: 20.1% in FY98, 16.9% in FY 99, 14.6% in FY00, 6.9% in FY01, 2.2% in FY02, and 1.9% in FY03, the last two being the recession years....For time limits, see where 7 of the 8 states reaching a time limit for the first time in the first half of 2002 also reported a caseload decline between April and June 2002. All eight states reaching time limits in the third quarter of 2002 also reported caseload declines between April and June 2002. Cf. "TANF Caseloads Declined in Most States in the Second Quarter, but Most States Saw Increases over the Last Year," *Center for Law and Social Policy,* October 1, 2002.

65. I sometimes ask groups with whom I speak to write the names of five poor persons on a sheet of paper. Many cannot. Those who can seldom know much about the family life, church attendance, income, or other basics about these poor people. A recent survey by the Catholic Campaign for Human Development (CCHD) indicates that 41 percent of the general public currently knows someone living in poverty, men more than women (46 to 36 percent) and older Americans least likely to do so. Source: Market Research Bureau LLC on the website for CCHD at www.povertyusa.org, December 12, 2001.

66. *Economic Justice for All,* Nos. 183 and 184.

67. *Economic Justice for All,* No. 185. I believe the bishops were more to the point and more true to the tradition of *faithjustice* in the wording of this section in the first draft of the pastoral letter, where they said:

> However, gross inequalities are *morally unjustifiable,* particularly when millions lack even the basic necessities of life. In our judgment, the distribution of income and wealth in the United States is so inequitable that it violates this minimum standard of distributive justice. (No. 202, emphasis supplied)

68. Paul A. Samuelson, *Newsweek,* December 17, 1973, p. 84, quoted in Byron, op. cit., pp. 79–80.

69. Peter Brimelow, "Who's Got the Bucks," in *Forbes,* July 5, 1999, at p. 88.

70. Pie chart created from figures in Richard Saul Wurman, op. cit., section on "The Economy," using data from the Council of Economic Advisors.

71. Source: "Pathbreaking CBO Study Shows Dramatic Increases in Both 1980s and 1990s in Income Gaps Between the Very Wealthy and Other Americans," *Center for Budget and Policy Priorities,* Washington, D.C., May 31, 2001.

72. Sister Lory Schaff, C.S.J., speaking to the members of Leadership Greater Baton Rouge, December 12, 1988, Earl K. Long Hospital Conference Room, Baton Rouge, Louisiana.

73. The Jesuit thirty-third General Congregation, Rome, 1983, Document No. 1, No. 48.

74. *What We Have Seen and Heard,* A Pastoral Letter on Evangelization from the Black Bishops of the United States, September 9, 1984 (St. Anthony Messenger Press Edition, 1984), pp. 6–7.

75. Pope John Paul II, *Sollicitudo Rei Socialis,* op. cit., No. 28.

76. The civil rights and women's movements in the United States, and liberation theology and the base Christian communities of the third world have taught us that the oppressed read the bible with different eyes. The scriptures are filtered through their own experiences of oppression. The story of the exodus and the prophetic books of the Hebrew testament carry a profound promise of justice, and a call to faithfulness and empowerment for today's oppressed. Likewise, the gospels' emphasis on Christ's identification with the marginalized of his day is good news indeed for the poor today. The result for the nonpoor is a tremendous potential to experience "mission in reverse": to uncover more fully the truth of the bible and the ways of God through our friends' experience of oppression. (Patrick G. Coy, "Spirituality and Solidarity with the Poor," in *Fellowship,* Vol. 54, No. 1–2, January/February 1988, pp. 13–14, at 14)

77. Donal Dorr, op. cit., pp. 135–36.

78. David Hinchen, S.J., "Solidarity with Poor Challenges Formation," in *National Jesuit News,* January 1988, p. 5.

79. Scholars of the *Spiritual Exercises* of St. Ignatius Loyola tell us that the grace of the Second Week of the Exercises, which focuses on the mysteries of the life of Christ, is one of *companionship.* The grace of the Third Week of the Exercises, spent in contemplation of the passion and death of Christ, is *compassion.*

80. Dean Brackley, S.J., "Downward Mobility: Social Implications of St. Ignatius's Two Standards," in *Studies in the Spirituality of Jesuits,* Vol. 20, No. 1, January 1988, p. 38.

81. Patrick G. Coy, op. cit., p. 13.

82. Ibid.

83. Albert Nolan, O.P., "Spiritual Growth and the Option for the Poor," in *Church*, Vol. 1, No. 1, Spring 1985, pp. 45–48, at 47.

84. W. G. Smith, S.J., "The Church's Concern for Society—XIII," in *Social Survey*, Vol. 33, No. 3, May, 1989, pp. 112–16, at 113–14.

85. Pope John Paul II, *Sollicitudo Rei Socialis*, No. 39.

86. Elie Wiesel, quoted by Colman McCarthy, "Wiesel and the Ways of Remembrance," in *The Washington Post*, October 26, 1986, p. G-2.

87. St. Vincent de Paul Societies stress the personal contact and home visit to the needy, not primarily to verify needs, but for the personal growth in holiness of their own members.

88. Albert Nolan, O.P., op. cit., p. 45.

89. John Howard Griffin, *Black Like Me* (Boston: Houghton Mifflin, 1961).

90. Phil Boroughs, S.J., tells this story on himself and the awkwardness of moving into a small Black parish on Chicago's south side:

> After the liturgy, one of the men of the parish took me aside and gently but clearly told me that the phrase "you people" was considered condescending and paternalistic when spoken by a white person in the black community. Embarrassed and apologetic, I resolved to drop that phrase from my vocabulary. However, the following week, while meeting with the key leadership of the parish, I used it again. Mortified that I could be so careless, I stopped my presentation and apologized to the assembled group. In response, a few people replied that they weren't offended, and a few others said that they understood my intentions and overlooked my choice of words; but the discussion ended when one woman commented, "Look, if he wants to become sensitive to our reality, let's not stop him." ("Vulnerability and Not Competency..." in *Studies in the Spirituality of Jesuits*, Vol. 21, No. 2, March 1989, pp. 45–46, at 45)

91. David W. Marr, "Loyola Day Speech," October 13, 1988, Loyola University of New Orleans, pp. 8–9.

92. Henry Volken, S.J., "Hunger in the World—New Challenges—New Responses by the Church—Theological Pastoral Reflection," 17th Plenary Assembly of the Pontifical Council *Cor Unum in Rome*, November 1988, quoted in *Jesuit Social Ministries Newsletter*, Vol. 2, No. 1, February 1989, p. 11.

93. Albert Nolan, O.P., op. cit., p. 46.

94. Ibid.

95. David W. Marr, op. cit., p. 9. Marr, in turn, would seem to be making a particular application of the hermeneutic circle described by Juan Luis Segundo in which an "ideological suspicion" arises out of our way of experiencing reality and is applied to the whole ideological superstructure in general and in particular to theology and then to biblical interpretation. Cf. Juan Luis Segundo, S.J., *Liberation of Theology* (Maryknoll, N.Y.: Orbis Books, 1976), p. 9.

96. Anthony J. Tambasco, op. cit., p. 12.
97. *Economic Justice for All*, No. 24.
98. *Economic Justice for All*, No. 94.
99. Network's publication *The Catholic Social Justice Tradition* quotes approvingly the three moral priorities developed by David Hollenbach in his book, *Claims in Conflict:*

> (1) The needs of the poor take priority over the wants of the rich.
> (2) The freedom of the dominated takes priority over the liberty of the powerful.
> (3) The participation of the marginalized groups takes priority over the preservation of an order which excludes them.
> ([Washington, D.C.: Network Education Program, 1989], p. 3)

100. *Economic Justice for All*, No. 94.
101. Dean Brackley, S.J., op. cit., p. 34.
102. An unnamed Sister of St. Ann, "Chile: With the Young and the Tortured," Testimony No. 108, July–August 1988, in *LADOC*, Vol. IV, October 1989, p. 8.
103. Dean Brackley, S.J., op. cit., p. 30.
104. The documents of 12th General Chapter of the Divine Word Missionaries (S.V.D.) included the following:

> Our commitment to the promotion of justice should become visible in these [educational] institutions by making them places where people are educated in the gospel values of justice and charity and awakened to their Christian responsibility towards the poor and oppressed in society. This holds true for all our institutions irrespective of whether they are in the first or third world. Likewise our preferential option for the poor demands that our schools be open as far as possible to those who have no access to other institutions of learning. We should seriously consider closing down those which do not achieve these goals. ("The Promotion of Justice and Peace in Solidarity with the Poor," 1982, paragraph 1.5., quoted in *Promotio Justitiae*, No. 29, January 1984, p. 21)

105. Sadly, the giving record of the wealthy in the United States indicates that affluent Americans "give a much lower proportion of their income to charity than does the rest of the population." The conclusion was based on a study of 800 Americans whose household income exceeds $100,000. Their charitable giving of 1.5 percent of their income lagged well behind the U.S. average of 2.4 percent. Study conducted jointly by Ernst & Young, an accounting and consulting firm, and Yankelovich, Clancy, and Shulman, a market research firm, was reported in *The Chronicle of Philanthropy*, October 31, 1989, p. 16.
106. *Economic Justice for All*, No. 24, emphasis in original.
107. Gustavo Gutiérrez, "The Church of the Poor," op. cit., p. 265.
108. Margaret Hebblethwaite, "Down to Basics in Brazil," *The Tablet*, August 5, 1989, pp. 891–93, at 892.

109. Dean Brackley, S.J., op. cit., p. 35.

110. Carmelite General Congregation in Rio de Janeiro, "Called to Account by the Poor," Section 3, 1980, quoted in *Promotio Justitiae,* No. 29, January 1984, pp. 19–20.

111. Catholic Campaign for Human Development, reporting as of October 1, 2001, at www.povertyusa.org, December 16, 2001.

112. William E. Simon, letter dated May 1989, and addressed, "Dear Confrere."

113. William T. Poole and Thomas W. Pauken, *The Campaign for Human Development: Christian Charity or Political Activism* (Washington, D.C.: Capital Research Center, 1989).

114. Walter F. Sullivan, *Richmond Times-Dispatch,* November 22, 1989, p. A-10.

115. "Support for Catholic Campaign 44% ahead of Last Year's Pace," *Richmond Times-Dispatch,* December 8, 1989, p. B-2.

116. Thomas J. Reese, *Archbishop* (San Francisco: Harper & Row, 1989), p. 177.

117. Pope John Paul II, *Sollicitudo Rei Socialis,* op. cit., Nos. 42–43.

118. Cf. William J. Wilson, *The Truly Disadvantaged: The Inner City Underclass and Public Policy* (Chicago: University of Chicago Press, 1987) and Isabel V. Sawhill, "Poverty and the Underclass" in Sawhill (ed.), *Challenge to Leadership: Economic and Social Leadership for the Next Decade* (Washington, D.C.: Urban Institute Press, 1988).

Chapter Five

1. "Our Mission Today: The Service of Faith and the Promotion of Justice," No. 28, *Documents of the 32nd General Congregation of the Society of Jesus* (Washington, D.C.: The Jesuit Conference, 1975), p. 26.

2. Community Action Programs (CAP) were the largest one of the ten parts of President Johnson's War on Poverty. They were designed to be local, community-controlled groups to coordinate programs and services directed towards alleviating the problem of poverty. While initial thinking in the new Office of Economic Opportunity (OEO) was that community action was an experimental concept, OEO's first chief, Sargent Shriver, is credited with quick expansion. "Within a month of Shriver's appointment the plans called for not ten or seventy-five community-action agencies but many more; by 1967 there were more than a thousand." Nicholas Lemann, "The Unfinished War," (Part One) *The Atlantic Monthly,* Vol. 262, No. 6, December 1988, pp. 37–56, at 49. Lemann's article provides fascinating background on the personalities and players in the rise and fall of OEO.

3. In the legislation creating the War on Poverty, the phrase "maximum feasible participation" set the standard for representation of poor peo-

ple on boards of directors of CAP agencies. It also prompted its fiercest
fights and most bitter criticism:

> Today it seems obvious that community action was headed for
> political trouble. Politics then was more organized than it is
> now, but even now politicians don't like surprises. Spending
> federal money in the district of a congressman, the state of a
> senator or governor, or the city of a mayor will not automati-
> cally be popular with the official: he or she wants to know
> ahead of time who is going to get the money (preferably a
> political supporter) and to announce the grant personally, if
> possible. In return for these favors, the local official should
> become a loyal defender of the federal program.
>
> Because community action broke all these rules, it eroded
> political loyalty to the War on Poverty....
>
> The War on Poverty became embattled almost instantly....
> On January 20, 1965—not yet half a year into the existence of
> the OEO—President Johnson received a confidential letter
> from Theodore McKeldin, the mayor of Baltimore, complain-
> ing about the community-action program and adding that the
> mayors of St. Louis, Cleveland, and Philadelphia didn't like
> the agencies in their cities either. At the end of 1965 several
> Democratic mayors set up a meeting in Miami just to grouse
> about community action, and Vice President Hubert
> Humphrey, whom one would have expected to be an ally of
> the War on Poverty, had turned against community action,
> because of his role as Johnson's liaison to the mayors.
>
> The most important enemy, by far, of community action
> among the mayors was Daley, who at the time was the single
> most powerful politician not just in Chicago but also on
> Capitol Hill....To Daley, community action was the political
> equivalent of original sin. "You're putting M-O-N-E-Y in the
> hands of people who are not in my organization," he told Bill
> Moyers, "They'll use it to bring you down." (Ibid., pp. 50,
> 53–54)

The saga of OEO and community action grew and festered until dis-
mantled under President Nixon after his 1972 reelection. Daniel Patrick
Moynihan, Nixon's urban affairs advisor and a noted critic of OEO, wrote
a 1969 book attacking community action entitled *Maximum Feasible
Misunderstanding.* Cf. Lemann, "The Unfinished War" (Part Two), *The
Atlantic Monthly,* Vol. 263, No. 1, January 1989, pp. 53–68, at 65.

    4. *Southern Discount Co. v. Ector,* 246 Ga. 30 (1980).

    5. Introduction, *Justice in the World,* Synod of Bishops, Rome 1971.
This widely quoted section of the document has stirred a lively debate focus-
ing on the word "constitutive." Those not happy with the essential and central nature of justice being asserted for the Church have argued that the word
"integral" should replace "constitutive" and thus action for justice could
take a second place in the Church's evangelizing mission to more spiritual

or religious matters. Cf. Dorr, *Option for the Poor,* op. cit., pp. 187–89 and later. The statement has also been played down by those who hold that the Synods of Bishops are merely advisory to the pope. Its widespread usage however evokes a power and credence among contemporary Catholic Christians reflecting a kind of *sensus fidelium* building among both laity and clergy.

6. This emphasis is akin to that contained in liberation theology as presented by Gustavo Gutiérrez:

> Much more could be said about the theology of liberation as presented by Gutiérrez, but it should be clear by now that this is a theology directed toward *action* in the political, economic, and social spheres. Gutiérrez says in his concluding remarks: "if theological reflection does not vitalize the action of the Christian community in the world by making its commitment to charity fuller and more radical..., then this theological reflection will have been of little value," and "...all the political theologies, the theologies of hope, of revolution, and of liberation, are not worth one act of genuine solidarity with exploited social classes." (T. Howland Sanks, S.J., op. cit., p. 672)

7. Philip Land, S.J., *Shaping Welfare Consensus,* op. cit., p. 144.

8. Medellin Documents, Section 2.14.

9. Congregation for the Doctrine of the Faith, "Instruction on Christian Freedom and Liberation," No. 57, March 22, 1986 (Washington, D.C.: U.S. Catholic Conference), p. 33.

10. U.S. Catholic Bishops, *In All Things Charity: A Pastoral Challenge for the New Millennium* (Washington, D.C.: United States Catholic Conference, 1999), p. 17, quoting Pope John Paul II from *Dives in Misericordia,* No. 12.

11. *Toward a Renewed Catholic Charities Movement,* Final Report, A Study of the National Conference of Catholic Charities (Washington, D.C.: National Conference of Catholic Charities, 1972), p. 32.

12. Ibid., p. 13.

13. Catholic Charities, USA, *A Code of Ethics* (Washington, D.C.: Catholic Charities, USA, 1983, 1987), p. 14.

14. Sister Anthony Barczykowski, D.C., "Reflecting on Catholic Charities in the 1990s: The Role of Service," in *Charities USA,* December 1988, Vol. 15, No. 9, p. 8–9, at 9.

15. Thomas E. Clarke, S.J. (ed.), *Above Every Name: The Lordship of Christ and Social Systems* (Ramsey, N.J.: Paulist Press, 1980), p. 2.

16. *Economic Justice for All,* No. 4 (emphasis in original).

17. Arthur Simon, "Greed Keeps Third World Hungry," *Baton Rouge Morning Advocate,* Friday, March 11, 1988, p. 9B.

18. *The Pastoral Constitution on the Church in the Modern World,* No. 1.

19. I am using "social structures" and "social systems" without the precision of any one school of social science or the disagreements between schools. As was true for the authors of *Above Every Name,* "The reader will find that the term 'social system' is often used without being sharply distin-

guished from terms like 'structure' or 'institution.'" Ibid., p. 5. Systems will tend to have broader applications to combinations of arrangements, institutions, and patterned ways of doing things, while structures and institutions will tend to be more particular or localized. The several examples used in this chapter will suggest more content to the meaning and, especially, the operation of these systems and structures in human living.

20. *Economic Justice for All*, No. 5.

21. Peter L. Berger and Thomas Luckmann, *The Social Construction of Reality* (Garden City, N.Y.: Doubleday & Co., 1966, Anchor Books Edition, 1967), pp. 47–62.

22. Ibid., p. 61 (emphasis in original).

23. See, for example, *Granite Construction Co. v. The Superior Court of Fresno County*, 149 Cal. App. 3d 465, 197 Cal. Rptr. 3, 45 ALR 4th 1011. In this case, the Court of Appeals denied the corporation's challenge to its indictment for manslaughter following the accidental deaths of seven workers at a power plant under construction by the defendant. In summary,

> The court held that corporations may be prosecuted for manslaughter since provisions of the state's penal code defined person to include a corporation as well as a natural person, and since under provisions of the penal code any person was capable of committing crimes except children, idiots, and those lacking mens rea through mistake of fact, etc. (*Case and Comment*, July–August 1986, p. 59)

24. U.S. Catholic Bishops, "Society and the Aged: Toward Reconciliation," May 5, 1976, in Hugh J. Nolan, op. cit., Vol. IV, Nos. 4–5, pp. 138–45, at 138.

25. U.S. Catholic Bishops, "Responsibility, Rehabilitation, and Restoration: A Catholic Perspective on Crime and Criminal Justice," November 15, 2000, in *Origins*, Vol. 30, No. 25, November 30, 2000, pp. 389–404, at 393.

26. Richard Saul Wurman, op. cit., section on "Advertising."

27. John Staudenmeier, S.J., "U.S. Technology and Adult Commitment," *Studies in the Spirituality of Jesuits*, Vol. 19, No. 1, January, 1987, p. 14.

28. Cf. John Francis Kavanaugh, S.J., *Following Christ in a Consumer Society* (Maryknoll, N.Y.: Orbis Books, 1981) for the underlying themes discussed here. In Kavanaugh's popular but unpublished slide presentation on advertising in America the themes are further developed with numerous examples.

29. © 1990 Toyota Motor Sales, USA

30. © 1989 World Gold Council

31. Wesley Theological Seminary professor of biblical theology Joseph Weber describes this reality in these terms:

> The demonic is not an abstract force that can be separated from human existence or from the social and political structures of the world. The demonic forces exist in and through structures.

They enter human existence in such a way as to be inherent in human existence. (Joseph Weber, "Christ's Victory over the Powers," in *Above Every Name*, op. cit., pp. 67–82, at 69)

Weber argues that, while a variety of names are used for the demonic forces—principalities, lords, gods, angels, demons, spirits, elements, Satan, and the devil—the terminology all expresses the power of Satan.

32. George H. Dunne, S.J., "The Sin of Segregation," *Commonweal,* Vol. 42, No. 23, September 21, 1945, pp. 542–45. As Dunne himself tells the story, the article itself barely got through his two brother Jesuit censors, and only because it was the "less rigorous form of censorship which I had devised with consent of the provincial." Cf. George H. Dunne, S.J., *King's Pawn: The Memoirs of George H. Dunne, S.J.* (Chicago: Loyola University Press, 1990), p. 130.

33. Archbishop Joseph E. Ritter desegregated St. Louis diocesan schools in 1947, as did Bishop Vincent S. Waters in Raleigh, North Carolina, in 1953 against strong Catholic and non-Catholic opposition. John Tracy Ellis, *American Catholicism* (Chicago: The University of Chicago Press, Second Edition, Revised, 1956, 1969), p. 148.

34. Cf. Hugh J. Nolan, op. cit., Vol. II, pp. 201–6.

35. The "Impeach Earl Warren" billboards of the 1960s epitomized the anti-Supreme Court feeling that focused on the then Chief Justice the hostility that many conservative Americans had toward the court's decisions on race and a wide range of other social issues.

36. *Sollicitudo Rei Socialis,* No. 36.

37. Ibid., footnote 65, quoting *Reconciliatio et Paenitentia,* AAS 77 (1985), p. 217 (numbers inserted in text).

38. Nor can one localize evil principally or uniquely in bad social, political or economic "structures" as though all other evils came from them so that the creation of the "new man" would depend on the establishment of different economic and socio-political structures. (*Instruction on Certain Aspects of the "Theology of Liberation,"* Sacred Congregation for the Doctrine of the Faith, August 6, 1984 [Washington, D.C.: United States Catholic Conference, Publication No. 935], p. 12)

39. Those who would so constrain the pope's position in *Sollicitudo* would need to consider the almost simultaneous release of, "What Have You Done to Your Homeless Brother? The Church and the Housing Problem," and the following section of that document:

In light of what has been previously stated, it is evident that this injustice is clearly a structural injustice, caused and perpetuated by personal injustices. It is likewise, however, an autonomous and independent phenomenon, with its own interior, unjust and disordered dynamism. (Pontifical Justice and Peace Commission, dated December 27, 1987, and released February

2, 1988, in *Origins,* Vol. 17, No. 35, February 11, 1988, pp. 602–5, at 605)

40. Anthony J. Tambasco, op. cit., p. 123, citing Joseph Weber's discussion of the demonic in social structures in Weber, op. cit., pp. 66–72.

41. Roger Haight, S.J., "Foundational Issues in Jesuit Spirituality," in *Studies in the Spirituality of Jesuits,* Vol. 19, No. 4, September 1987, p. 27.

42. Albert Nolan, O.P., op. cit., p. 46.

43. He [the Christian] recognizes that in many instances Latin America finds itself faced with a situation of injustice that can be called institutionalized violence, when, because of a structural deficiency of industry and agriculture, of national and international economy, of cultural and political life, "whole towns lack necessities, live in such dependence as hinders all initiative and responsibility as well as every possibility for cultural promotion and participation in social and political life," thus violating fundamental rights. (Second General Conference of Latin American Bishops, *The Church in the Present-Day Transformation of Latin America in the Light of the Council* [Washington, D.C.: United States Catholic Conference, 1973], Section 2.16, p. 61)

44. *Sollicitudo Rei Socialis,* No. 21.

45. Ibid., No. 20.

46. Ibid., No. 21.

47. Ibid., No. 22.

48. Ibid., No. 23.

49. Pope John Paul II, *Ecclesia in Asia,* November 6, 1999, No. 32, in *Origins,* Vol. 29, No. 23, pp. 357–84, at 375.

50. Ibid.

51. *Populorum Progressio,* No. 49.

52. *Economic Justice for All,* No. 291.

53. Anthony J. Tambasco, op. cit., p. 125.

54. "The Pontiff's theology demands that concern for human rights be the primary concern of all human institutions." James A. Donahue, "The Social Theology of John Paul II and His Understanding of Social Institutions," in *Social Thought,* Vol. 13, No. 2/3, Spring–Summer 1987, pp. 20–33, at 26.

55. "Indeed a liberation which does not take into account the personal freedom of those who fight for it is condemned in advance to defeat." *Instruction on Christian Freedom and Liberation,* op. cit., No. 31, p. 18.

56. Joseph Weber, op. cit., p. 78.

57. James A. Donahue, op. cit., p. 26.

58. Donald L. Gelpi, "The Converting Jesuit," in *Studies in the Spirituality of Jesuits,* Vol. 18, No. 1, January 1986, p. 28.

59. *Economic Justice for All,* No. 259.

60. Philip Land, S.J., "The Earth Is the Lord's," in *Above Every Name,* op. cit., p. 229.

61. James A. Donahue, op. cit., p. 25.

62. *Economic Justice for All,* No. 296.

63. *Instruction on Christian Freedom and Liberation,* op. cit., No. 69, p. 41.

64. Cf. James E. Hug, S.J., *Tracing the Spirit: Communities, Social Action, and Theological Reflection* (New York: Paulist Press, 1983).

65. Solidarity, of course, is not new in the thinking of John Paul II. His 1981 ON HUMAN WORK used the word frequently enough to cause comment about his explicit support for he Polish workers' movement. But the theme if not always the word is also not new in the previous social teaching of the Church. John XXIII in his 1963 PEACE ON EARTH spoke of the "active solidarity" which benefits relations between states, promoting the "common good of the entire human family" (#98). (Peter J. Henriot, S.J., "The Politics of Solidarity: John Paul II's Analysis and Response," in *Promotio Justitiae,* No. 39, October 1988, pp. 3–7, at 6)

66. The principle of social solidarity suggests that alleviating poverty will require fundamental changes in social and economic structures that perpetuate glaring inequalities and cut off millions of citizens from full participation in the economic and social life of the nation. The process of change should be one that draws together all citizens, whatever their economic status, into one community. (*Economic Justice for All,* No. 187)

67. *Sollicitudo Rei Socialis,* No. 40.

68. Ibid.

69. Ibid., No. 38.

70. Ibid.

71. Those who do not appreciate the difference between personal and structural injustice miss the crucial point about an option for the poor. They think of it in purely interpersonal terms as a rejection of wealthy *people;* they fail to realise that it has to do above all with *structures;* it is primarily an attempt to develop a society that is structurally just. (Donal Dorr, *Spirituality and Justice* [Maryknoll, N.Y.: Orbis Books, 1984], p. 78)

72. *Instruction on Christian Freedom and Liberation,* op. cit., No. 89, p. 53.

73. Edward B. Arroyo, S.J., op. cit., p. 6.

74. *Ecclesia in Asia,* No. 32.

75. Gregory Baum, *Compassion and Solidarity* (New York: Paulist Press, 1990), p. 58. This is Baum's slightly edited version of the Canadian bishops' text.

76. United States Catholic Conference Administrative Board, "Relieving Third World Debt: A Call to Co-responsibility, Justice and

Solidarity," September 27, 1989, in *Origins,* Vol. 19, No. 19, October 12, 1989, pp. 305-14.

77. "The ecological crisis reveals the *urgent moral need for a new solidarity,* especially in relations between the developing nations and those that are highly industrialized." Pope John Paul II, "Peace with God the Creator, Peace with All of Creation," January 1, 1990 World Day of Peace Message, No. 10 (emphasis in original).

78. The words to the Brazilian song "Solidarity," by Claudio Fontana, were distributed in six languages at the February 1989 Solidarity conference in Washington, D.C., sponsored by the Department of Social Development and World Peace of the U.S. Catholic Conference, the Roundtable, the Catholic Rural Life Conference, and the Campaign for Human Development. The first verse of the English version, slightly edited, follows:

> There is a word
> That everyone has to shout
> A strangled cry
> And we must fight to free it
> A word easy to say
> So easy to burst out
> Say it and a change
> Will come about
> Solidarity.
> —Gravadora COMEP, Sao Paulo, Brazil

79. "They have a right to effective help, which is neither a handout nor a few crumbs of justice, so that they may have access to the development that their dignity as human beings and as children of God merits." Pope John Paul II to peasant farmers in Culican, Oaxaca, Mexico, on January 29, 1979, quoted in Robert J. Vitillo, "Recent Papal Teachings on Rural Development," in *Charities USA,* Vol. 14, No. 4, May 1987, pp. 7–11 at 10.

> 80. ...The function of prophecy was to form the conscience of a people, not to dictate its politics. It did not necessarily desire the coming of the monarchy, but it assured that its coming would be in accordance with Yahweh's will. (194)
>
> Against the backdrop of Israelite history, prophetic social doctrine fits into its proper place and is not out of proportion. The prophets themselves could only have been puzzled by the designation "social." They were only insisting on the social virtues inherent in the doctrines of election and covenant, virtues which had been flagrantly violated in an Israel that had largely abandoned its ancient ideals, assimilating itself to Gentile ways. In presuming a social character to the religion of Yahweh, the prophets were proposing nothing new but recalling a known, although much ignored, morality. (196) (Bruce Vawter, C.M., "Introduction to Prophetic Literature," in *The New Jerome Biblical Commentary,* op. cit., pp. 186–200 at 194 and 196)

81. Paul's understanding of the Law profoundly illustrates how the demonic can pervert God's intention for his creation. The Law was given by God as an order serving life. It was good and holy. Now, however, it has been perverted by the power of sin. What was intended to serve life, has become a means of death and a curse (Rom 7:1–3; Gal 3:13). Structures of creation which were intended by God to serve life are used by the demonic forces to bring death. (Joseph Weber, op. cit., p. 70)

82. Thomas Clarke, S.J. (ed.), *Above Every Name,* op. cit., p. 302.

Conclusion

1. Harry Fagan, "Ten Points for Effective Diocesan Social Action Offices," in *Origins,* Vol. 12, No. 42, March 31, 1983, pp. 672–76, at 674.

2. Ibid., p. 675.

3. Medellin documents, Section 2.14.

4. Peter J. Henriot, S.J., "Lessons of Seventeen Years...," in *Center Focus,* Issue 88, January 1989, p. 6.

5. *Vision 2000* (Alexandria, Va.: Catholic Charities USA, 1997), p. 9.

6. "A Catholic Charities Framework for Empowerment," *Catholic Charities USA,* 1998, p. 2.

7. Henriot, op. cit., p. 6.

8. Larry Ragan, *The Ragan Report,* January 9, 1989, quoted in "100 Years" in *Initiatives,* October 1989, No. 35 (National Center for the Laity).

9. David Hollenbach, S.J., *Justice, Peace, & Human Rights* (New York: The Crossroad Publishing Co., 1988), p. 95.

10. Ibid.

11. Ibid., p. 97.

12. John L. Carr, "The Bishops and Politics," in *Church,* Vol. 5, No. 2, Summer 1989, p. 51.

13. Pope John Paul II, *Sollicitudo Rei Socialis,* footnote 65.

14. Suzy Farren (ed.), *Portraits of the Healthcare Poor* (St. Louis: Catholic Health Association, 1990).

15. Archbishop Raymond Hunthausen, "To Discover an Ethic That is Social," address to the 1988 Mansfield Conference, Missoula, Montana, May 23, 1988, in *Origins,* Vol. 18, No. 5, June 16, 1988, pp. 72–75, at 73.

16. Peter J. Henriot, S.J., *Opting for the Poor: A Challenge for North Americans* (Washington, D.C.: Center of Concern, 1990), p. 28.

17. Robert Michael Franklin, "The Case for Social Ethics: Lessons from the Civil Rights Movement," in *Theological Education,* Vol. 26, No. 1, Autumn 1989, pp. 43–61, at 54.

18. Peter Henriot, "Lessons of Seventeen Years...," op. cit., p. 6.

INDEX